Computer Peripherals

Third edition

Barry M Cook
Lecturer
Keele University

and

Neil H White
Lecturer
Keele University

Edward Arnold
A member of the Hodder Headline Group
LONDON NEW YORK SYDNEY AUCKLAND

Edward Arnold is a division of Hodder Headline PLC
338 Euston Road, London NW1 3BH

© 1995 B M Cook and N H White

First published in the United Kingdom 1980
Second edition 1987
Third edition 1995

1 3 5 6 4 2
95 97 99 98 96

British Library Cataloguing in Publication Data
A catalogue record for this book is available from the British Library

Library of Congress Cataloging-in-Publication Data
Available on request

Typeset by the authors
Printed and bound in the United Kingdom by
J W Arrowsmith Ltd, Bristol

NAin UD
BK 6 WKD

Computer Peripherals *old ed i/s*

**Books are to be returned on or before
the last date below.**

Dedications

B. M. Cook

To my loving and much loved wife, Elaine.

N. H. White

To Lidia

▸ Contents ◂

► Preface to the First Edition ◄

Anyone coming into contact with computers, even if only superficially, cannot fail to become aware of the importance of peripherals. Developments in peripheral devices have been many and varied in recent years and a wide range of devices with differing capabilities is now manufactured.

However, the current interest in this topic is not generally reflected in the many books on computers. Most of these books devote no more than a chapter to peripheral devices and are unable therefore to describe more than a few of them.

This book attempts to meet the need for a wide-ranging and straightforward account of how present-day peripheral devices work and what they are capable of doing. Emphasis is placed on the underlying principles of operation of the devices, rather than on providing a product description of manufacturers' wares. The aim is to include all the main types of peripheral device which may be encountered.

To maintain the relevance of the material, and keep the page count within reasonable limits, devices that are still at the development stage and not yet fully available are not included. One or two exceptions to this have been made where it can be foreseen, with some confidence, that a device is to be marketed in the near future.

No special academic or technical background is required of the reader, although some interest in, and knowledge of, basic computer operation is assumed. Also, familiarity with simple concepts and ideas of electronics would be helpful in some parts of the book.

This text should be of value to students studying engineering and computer technology at polytechnics, technical colleges and universities, especially when used in conjunction with one of the many books on computers. This book will also be of interest to those dealing with computers, in and out of the computing industry, who would like an account of the subject which is informative but not over-technical.

The first chapter discusses the role of peripherals and is followed by a chapter which presents the ways that peripherals connect to a computer and how information and data are passed between them.

Chapters 3–9 deal with the various peripheral devices, mechanisms and techniques under major headings and form the main part of the book. These chapters need not be read in order, and the reader can safely turn first to those chapters of greatest interest.

The final chapter, on data communications, which can be considered as an extension of Chapter 2, gives an account of the communication equipment and techniques used when peripherals, perhaps large in number, are remote from the processor.

The writing of this book has been an enlightening experience, and a co-operative venture for its authors, neither of whom would claim to have made the larger contribution.

DHH and ABW

► Preface to the Second Edition ◄

Encouraged by the success of the first edition we have extensively revised the text both to broaden the coverage in some areas (for example, transducers are now dealt with) and to describe the many new and important devices that are now available.

Changes have occurred among all types of peripheral devices: in display devices large panel displays are now common, some of which use the new super-twist liquid crystal display technology; low cost laser printers now enable desk top publishing to be done; small computers with high quality graphics now display 'icons' and 'windows' under the control of a 'mouse'; for backing stores, Winchester disc technology has resulted in devices with the virtues of low cost, high storage capacity, and small size. Other developments have occurred with voice input and output systems, badge readers, 'smart cards', optical storage, etc.

The interconnection of computers and peripheral devices using data communication has also seen significant changes; both wide area and local area networking are now prevalent.

We have endeavoured to include all these significant developments in this second edition.

DHH and ABW

► Preface to the Third Edition ◄

Since Barry Wilkinson and David Horrocks wrote the first edition in 1980 advances in computer technology have resulted in associated advances in peripheral equipment. An extensively revised second edition was published in 1987. Since then the pace of change has increased. The widespread use of computers in offices and homes has driven the development of new peripherals; and seen the demise of others.

Sections of the previous editions covered devices that are not now in everyday use; these sections have been deleted. This has made room for new or extended descriptions of current peripherals.

We have also taken this opportunity to re-organize material, for example by grouping it by underlying principle; topics may not be in the same numbered chapter as in previous editions. Some of the text has been copied from the original editions but most has been either extensively rewritten or written from scratch for this edition.

As in previous editions, no special academic or technical background is required of the reader. Some elementary electronics knowledge will enable some sections to be understood in more detail, but it is not essential.

This text should be of use to those interested in computers and wanting to know more about what goes on behind the scenes as well as anyone studying engineering and computer technology at universities and colleges.

The first chapter discusses the role of peripherals and is followed by a chapter describing the ways that peripherals connect to the computer and how data are passed between them.

Chapters 3 and 4 concern, respectively, output and input devices for human–computer communication – the most commonly used peripherals. Chapter 5 describes bulk storage devices based on disk and tape formats. Analogue input and output is the province of Chapter 6 and Chapter 7 deals with those devices not easily classified into any of the earlier headings.

Finally, Chapter 8 covers the now much more important area of data communications. In a sense this is an extension to Chapter 2 but the new field of data networks is so broad as to warrant a chapter to itself.

We have considerably enhanced the index so that casual readers will be able to find sections of interest without necessarily reading the whole book. The meanings of many abbreviations may also be discovered from the index.

Even in the time it has taken to prepare this edition new technologies have emerged and been incorporated. Without doubt there will be advances over the next few years and some of the present material will date. We had to draw the line somewhere or we would be constantly writing and never publishing. If there is a significant change between now and the time you read the book, we apologise.

BMC and NHW

► Acknowledgements ◄

Information for this book was sought from many places. We would like to acknowledge their help and give them our thanks. In particular we wish to acknowledge the patient assistance of Professor WA Ainsworth and Professor D Budgen, the Information office of British Telecom Research Labs, the QIC Drive Standards Inc, Division UK, and the Usenet community.

Table of Abbreviations used for Numerical Measures

The abbreviations used when quoting numerical information are shown below. Other abbreviations are explained in the text and can also be found in the index.

Note that, in computing circles, and when referring to *bytes*, the unit of 1024 (2^{10}) is used instead of 1000.

b	Bit - a binary digit with value 0 or 1
B	Byte - a group of 8 bits
k	1000 - but 1024 when the quantity is bytes
M	1 000 000 - but 1024 × 1024 (1 048 576) for bytes
G	1 000 000 000 - but 1024 M for bytes
bps	bits per second - communications speed measurement
Hz	Hertz frequency - cycles a second
v	Electrical voltage
I	Electrical current

1

The Role of Computer Peripherals

▶ 1.1 Introduction

A simple digital computer system comprises a central processing unit (CPU) with an attached memory and some peripheral devices. The CPU performs arithmetic and logic operations and controls the operation of the entire system. For some tasks, the CPU controls the activity completely but for others it merely initiates a sequence of events which are controlled elsewhere, such as in a peripheral device.

A typical arrangement is shown in Figure 1.1. The peripheral devices permit communication of information and storage of information. They normally communicate through the CPU as shown but some peripherals can transfer information between themselves and the memory, bypassing the CPU by means of a system called *direct memory access (DMA)*. The number and types of peripheral devices depend on the main applications for which the computer system is intended. A small personal computer may only have a few devices such as a keyboard, screen, disk storage and a printer. A large commercial system may have many devices attached and many instances of one device.

In many situations, several computer systems may be linked together and share their resources. Such a network would also be called a computer system.

Typically over 80% of the cost of a computer system is due to the peripheral devices. This book is concerned with the construction, operation and control of these peripheral devices or, as they are more commonly called, peripherals.

This chapter introduces examples of many different applications of computing and of typical computer systems that are used to satisfy them.

▶ 1.2 A Historical Perspective

Computer systems have a relatively short history – the first working computers did not appear until the late 1940s – but during the short period since, the advances made have been remarkable. More remarkable still is

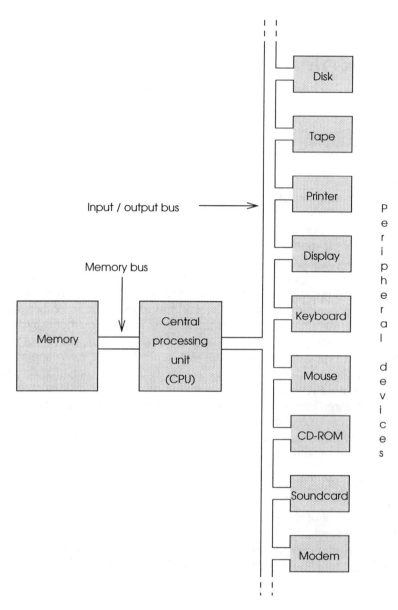

Figure 1.1 *Typical computer system*

that this pace of change is not abating. In the 1950s and 1960s there were few computer systems, they occupied rooms the size of small warehouses and cost billions of pounds, taking inflation into account. Today there are millions of computer systems sitting on desks and even in people's pockets. They are much more powerful and cost hundreds of pounds.

The creation of computing was inspired by Charles Babbage whose design in around 1835 for an *Analytical Engine* showed a machine whose operation is organized in much the same manner as today's computers. The technology did not exist to build fully such a machine and it was not until the 1930s and 1940s, due largely to the Second World War, that any serious backing was given to computing. This resulted in, amongst others, the American *ENIAC* and British *COLOSSUS* computing systems. Neither can be described as a true computer by today's definition and, in particular, could not store their own programs and needed constant manual intervention.

In 1948 the first stored program ran on a machine in Manchester University. This machine had too small a memory to do much more than the simplest tasks, but within a few years computers were being produced in both the UK and the USA. In the 1950s it was firmly believed that world demand for computers would be small – in single figures. By the 1970s, however, most large companies, government and research institutions had their own computer systems.

Such installations were physically large and usually consisted of one CPU. They could only be used by one person at a time. Programmers would prepare their programs, usually on punched cards, and wait for their turn. The results from this would be printed and then studied later. The peripherals common to such systems were the *card punch* and *line printer.* Storage would be provided by low capacity disks and by magnetic tape.

Very soon *multi-access* computer systems became common, where many people could use the system simultaneously and, more importantly, interactively. These early systems were usually called *mainframe* systems due to their size and power, to differentiate them from the smaller and cheaper *minicomputers* which were emerging at the time. Both these systems allowed more access to computer facilities. Users would interact with the computer using a *teletype,* which is little more than a typewriter with a bidirectional communications link. Later the teletype was replaced by the *visual display unit (VDU).*

In the late 1970s and early 1980s the next major development was the computer integrated onto one silicon chip and, with it, the birth of the *microprocessor.* The microprocessor permitted far more access to computing facilities and home computers became a real possibility. (Some believed that they would be a passing phase and that the dominance of the mainframe and minicomputer would continue.)

The situation today is that the microprocessor has advanced so much in power, capacity and speed that its diminutive name is no longer used. It has dominated computing and, by connecting many systems together, can satisfy most computing needs. Computers are commonplace in the home and almost every organisation.

The increase in computer networks has also been a major influence and the *information superhighway,* involving computers all around the world in almost instant contact with each other, has revolutionized many aspects of

society. A major use of these computers is passing information for of all
sorts of purposes, around global networks, of which the *Internet* is probably the best known.

▶ 1.3 Computers in the Office

Many office tasks can be performed by or assisted by computers. Prepara-
tion of letters and documents is routinely achieved using computer word-
processors or more sophisticated desk top publishing packages. Analysis
of numerical information can be accomplished using a spreadsheet package in which any small change can be explored by changing the input in
order to see its effect on the more global analysis. The spreadsheet can also
be used in conjunction with a database and both can be used to produce
graphical representations such as piecharts which are then incorporated in
the document produced by the wordprocessor.

In all but the smallest offices there will be several workstations accessing computer facilities. Information needs to be shared around the office
and a practical solution is to use several computers linked together in a
local network. In this type of situation it is common to include one or
more larger systems in the network, whose principal task is to serve the
workstations by giving them shared access to storage and printing devices.

In addition to using computers to perform tasks associated with the
office's business, computers perform the routine internal tasks such as handling the staff records and payroll and producing financial reports for audit
and taxation purposes.

A large organization may have several offices which, while being geographically separate, are connected by networking their computer systems
together in order to share resources and information between all offices.
Such a network is called a *wide area network (WAN)* to distinguish it from
the *local area network (LAN)* contained within one office.

▶ 1.4 Computers in the Supermarket

Modern supermarket companies rely heavily on computers. Each branch
in a region is likely to be serviced by a regional warehouse, and stock control and ordering is automated. The supermarkets' computer systems can
automatically keep track of each item of stock and, with accumulated
knowledge of shopping trends, can provide 'advice' on how to order
replacements from the warehouse, so that the supermarket neither runs out
of a particular item nor maintains more stock than necessary.

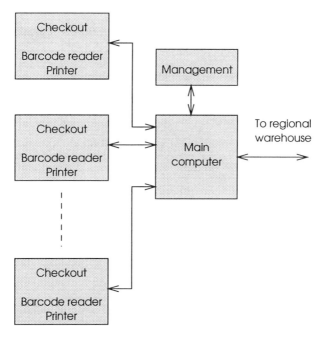

Figure 1.2 *A typical computer system for supermarket control*

Such a system is illustrated in Figure 1.2. Each checkout point contains a link to the central computer system. As each item is sold it is identified automatically, usually by reading a barcode. With this system the price of each item is held centrally and thus it is easy to change items' prices instantly. This type of system can also implement special offers such as *three for the price of two*. This allows the computer system to both produce an invoice with a list of items involved in each transaction and also to update its list of total stock held.

The supermarket management can produce daily and weekly graphs of sales performance for analysis. With the aid of this information the system can be adjusted to decide more satisfactorily when more stock should be ordered or when a particular item should be cancelled.

▶ 1.5 Monitoring and Control

Computers can be used to monitor aspects of an environment and to take certain actions when particular events occur. One example is patient monitoring in a hospital. A typical system used for this purpose is shown in Figure 1.3.

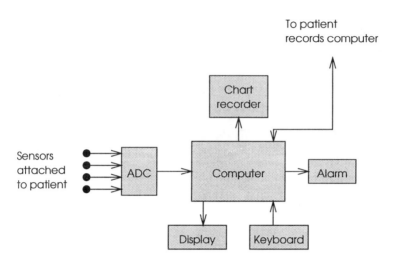

Figure 1.3 *Patient monitor computer system*

Sensors are placed on the patient to monitor parameters such as ECG (electrocardiograph) readings, blood pressure and temperature. If any parameter or combination of parameters move out of a certain range then an alarm is sounded. These measurements are also continuously displayed on a screen so that small fluctuations can be observed at any time. The sensors produce voltages which can be input to the computer system through an *analogue-to-digital converter (ADC)* as described in Chapter 6. One computer may be responsible for monitoring several patients. There may also be a link to a central system which holds the patients' records.

Another instance of monitoring and control is in the process-control industry. This industry is involved in the production of materials such as steel, paper, oil, cement and chemicals. Direct control by a computer system means that pneumatic valves and switches are operated automatically when the need arises. Certain factors such as temperature and pressure are read and, as with the patient monitor, converted by an ADC prior to input.

▶ 1.6 Computer Aided Design (CAD)

Computer aided design (CAD) involves the use of a computer in the design of engineering products such as cars, bridges and electronic circuits.

The main peripheral device associated with this is the graphical display which shows diagrams. These diagrams can be input by moving a positional cursor which is constantly displayed on the screen.

While a product is being designed, simulations can be performed on it even though it only exists as a computer representation. This can reveal problems before the more expensive construction phase is entered. In addition, the product could be displayed in formats that would be difficult to reproduce in reality. For example, a computer generated display can depict a cut-away view which reveals the internal components of the design. The peripherals used in this process include almost all of those described in Chapter 3 and Chapter 4.

▶ 1.7 Computers in the Home

Computers in the home are very commonplace nowadays. A small home computer may include peripherals such as disks, a printer, mouse, keyboard and screen. Other popular attachments include a modem for communications, a soundcard for entertainment and a CD-ROM which gives access online to large quantities of reference information.

Home computers are mainly used for education, home finance, personal organisation and games. They are also beginning to be used to control aspects of the house itself. The computer system can read from remote sensors and switches in order to control such things as lighting, heating and a music centre.

Computers also exist in the home in less obvious places, controlling washing machines, for example.

▶ 1.8 Laptops

In addition to the home or business computer, laptop computers are convenient ways to extend the use of computers as they are completely portable. Because they run on battery power, the computer and its peripherals are designed to be small and to require as little power as possible. These factors make them more expensive than their larger mains-powered counterparts.

In addition to allowing computer access almost anywhere, laptop computers often incorporate a communication port that can be used to link up to another fixed computer and exchange information. In this way, some tasks which are normally performed on the user's main computer system may be carried out on the laptop while travelling to and from a meeting, for example, and then the results can be deposited on the main system later.

▶ 1.9 Notebooks

Portable computers such as the laptops just described are convenient but are still too large to be carried around as a matter of course. The notebook computer is small enough to fit in a briefcase. Some will fit in a pocket. They are useful for keeping diary information and performing simple tasks such as using spreadsheets or databases. The diary section can be set up to sound an alarm in advance of noted important appointments. Like the laptop they are battery powered and use specially designed components that require little power.

2

Peripheral/Computer Connections

▶ ## 2.1 Introduction

Modern computers perform operations (instructions) very much faster than most peripherals can generate or accept data. Programs and data are moved between memory and the *central processing unit (CPU)* at such a speed that it would be inappropriate to connect peripherals directly to the CPU. So, some form of *peripheral adaptor* is required to convert between the fast internal communications and the (relatively) slow external devices.

2.1.1 A Model for the Basic Computer

Figure 2.1 shows the main components of a computer (within the shaded area) and its peripheral connections. Computer instructions are taken from memory and executed (carried out) in the CPU, typically involving requests for data from memory and sending results back to memory.

Usually, part of the computer's memory consists of unchangeable or *read only memory (ROM)* so that a program is available when the machine is first switched on. This program then reads other programs into normal, *random access memory (RAM),* a process known as *bootstrapping* or *booting.*

Special instructions are often available for accessing the peripheral interfaces although, on some processors, the peripheral interface is made to act as though it were a part of normal memory so that standard instructions can be used.

2.1.2 Data Highways

Data (including programs) are moved around the computer on a set of wires forming a data highway or, more commonly, a *bus.* The bus is divided into three distinct groups of wires for carrying data, address and control signals.

Data lines contain the information or program instructions required by the CPU. The speed of operation of a computer depends on the rate at which data can be made available and a good way to improve speed is to add more data lines to transfer more data at a time. Small systems use an

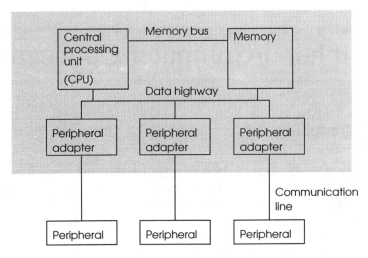

Figure 2.1 *Components of a digital computer*

8-bit data bus because this is low cost, but it is also relatively slow. Processors such as the 8086 have a 16-bit bus and the 80386 a 32-bit bus. Where there is a great demand for performance, for example in CAD workstations a 64-bit bus may be used.

Address information is carried on the address bus. The number of lines available for this determines the maximum amount of physical memory that can be distinguished (addressed). If there are n lines then 2^n locations can be addressed. Small systems may have only 16 address lines, giving access to $2^{16} = 65\,536$ locations. The original IBM personal computer (PC) used an 8086 processor having 20 address lines, giving it access to $2^{20} = 1\,048\,576$ locations; each location holds one byte of data so this allows up to 1 megabyte of memory to be used. When the IBM PC was designed this seemed a lot of memory, but it is now considered rather restricting. Later processor developments extended the number of address lines, 24 lines (16 megabytes) was common for a while but most machines now allow 32 lines which provides for a relatively future-proof 4000 megabytes of addressable memory.

Control signals are required to maintain an orderly flow of data along the highway and include lines to indicate whether to read or write data during a transfer, how much data to transfer, timing signals, status lines, etc. One important line often included is used to indicate whether a transfer is to memory or to a peripheral adaptor.

Figure 2.2 shows the data highway in more detail, along with the registers in the peripheral adaptor connected directly to the busses. It is necessary to distinguish between adaptors used for different peripherals and so the address lines are compared with a value that is allocated to that adaptor

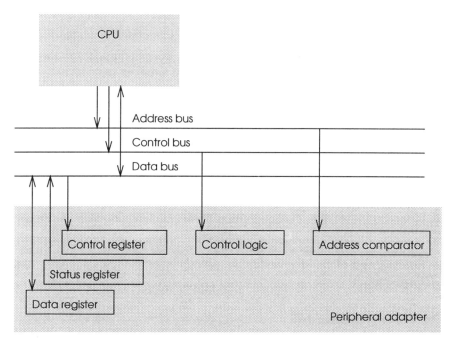

Figure 2.2 *Connection of peripheral adapter to highway*

(often set with switches or jumpers). An adaptor may recognize a single address or a small group of addresses (an adaptor for an IBM PC typically recognizes a group of 16 addresses). If the address on the bus matches that of the adapter then the control lines are interpreted by the control logic to perform the required function, typically to read from or write to a register connected to the data bus.

Regardless of the function of the adapter there are a number of standard registers. The *control register* usually has values written to it to control the operation of the adaptor. The *status register* can be read by the CPU to determine the status of the device (e.g. whether it is ready for use, busy, switched on/off etc.). Each piece of information stored in the control and status registers usually needs only a single bit and several such bits are stored in each register, each bit is often known as a *flag* (by analogy with a real flag that can be raised or lowered to communicate at a distance). The *data register* is used to hold, temporarily, a value to be transferred to or from the peripheral so that it is not necessary to synchronize the computer with the peripheral.

Modern adapters are often highly complex and may contain a powerful computer themselves! This complexity removes mundane work from the main computer, removing load from it and improving overall performance, often quite considerably.

▶ 2.2 Computer Input/Output Operations

Various methods may be used to control the peripheral adaptor and pass data to and from the attached peripheral. The simplest method is to use a program which waits for the peripheral to be ready with data (or ready to receive data) and then explicitly transfers the data. This results in the processor sitting idle waiting for the device for significant periods, especially when slow peripherals are involved. This idle time could have been used for more useful work. Allowing the peripheral to signal its readiness by *interrupting* the processor, releases the processor from idly waiting but still requires action from the CPU for each datum to be transferred. Block data movement, typically under the control of a *direct memory access (DMA)* controller, reduces the processor involvement to a single action at the end of a complete sequence of transfers and is the most efficient method.

Since the operations of sending and receiving data are usually closely associated, and often very similar we usually refer to these as *input/output (I/O)* operations.

2.2.1 Programmed I/O

In this case all transfers between the CPU and the peripheral adapter are completely under program control. The instruction set for the CPU typically contains instructions such as:
• input data to the CPU from the peripheral
• output data from the CPU to the peripheral
• set individual bits in the peripheral adapter's control register
• test individual bits in the peripheral adapter's status register.

Output of a data item is usually straightforward. The CPU addresses the adapter and tests the status register. If the relevant bit in the register shows that the peripheral is *ready* (it is ready if it has finished handling the previous piece of data), then the CPU puts the data into the interface unit transmit data register. This will automatically set a flag to indicate that data is available for the peripheral. If the peripheral is not ready, the program must wait and try again.

Similarly, the status of an input device may be tested and data taken from the input data register if it is available (ready), or the program must try again later if it is not.

When a number of peripherals may be active at the same time it is necessary to test each one for readiness. The technique of testing a number of peripherals in turn is known as *software polling*. Often special *service routines* known as *device handlers* are provided for this purpose. The asynchronous nature of peripheral operations often requires device drivers to be complex programs.

Processor instructions for communicating with peripherals are often given obvious mnemonics such as "IN" and "OUT". The 80x86 instruction shown in Figure 2.3(a) indicates that the value held in the CPU register AL is to be sent to the peripheral whose address is given by the value associated with the identifier "DATA". The input instruction shown in Figure 2.3(b) similarly takes the address of the peripheral from "STATUS" and reads a value into the CPU register AL.

OUT   DATA,AL

(a)

IN   AL,STATUS

(b)

Figure 2.3 *80x86 instructions: (a) output; (b) input*

A more complete example is shown in Figure 2.4 which sends a character via an Intel 8251 interface circuit. The 8251 contains a status register whose least significant two bits indicate the readiness of the transmit and receive sections of the device. The program first reads the status register and tests the appropriate bit, if the device is not ready it repeats the test until it is. When ready a datum is sent and the program proceeds.

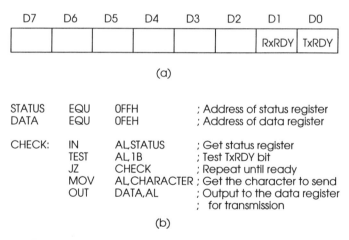

(a)

STATUS	EQU	OFFH	; Address of status register
DATA	EQU	OFEH	; Address of data register
CHECK:	IN	AL,STATUS	; Get status register
	TEST	AL,1B	; Test TxRDY bit
	JZ	CHECK	; Repeat until ready
	MOV	AL,CHARACTER	; Get the character to send
	OUT	DATA,AL	; Output to the data register
			; for transmission

(b)

Figure 2.4 *Transmitting a character via an 8251; (a) schematic view of the status register; (b) program used*

Some processors do not employ special I/O instructions but require the registers of the peripheral adapter to be addressed as though they were just another segment of memory (as already noted in Section 2.1.1). In this case normal read and write instructions are used and the method is known as *memory mapped I/O*.

2.2.2 *Interrupts*

Interrupts improve on programmed I/O by not requiring the program to sit idle while waiting for a peripheral to become ready. This allows more effective use of the processor, including running programs at the same time as I/O is being performed.

When a peripheral is able to transfer data, it sets its *ready flag* in its status register and also asserts a control line connected to the CPU. This control line is interpreted by the CPU as an *interrupt request (IREQ)*. As soon as it is able (often at the end of the current instruction) the CPU then stops what it is doing, stores enough information to be able to resume later and starts executing an *interrupt routine*. This routine deals with the device and then uses the information stored at the beginning of the interrupt to return the CPU to executing the interrupted program – without that program being aware of what has taken place. Figure 2.5 shows the simplest of connections for implementing an interrupt.

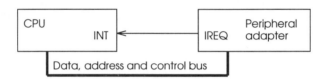

Figure 2.5 *Interrupt connection*

Many devices may be able to interrupt and, if there are several interrupt lines or some other method of distinguishing which device caused the interrupt, an appropriate *interrupt service routine* may be selected. Usually there is a list of addresses for the interrupt routines and one is chosen by using the interrupt identifier as an index into a table. This table is often known as a *vector* and this method is therefore known as a *vectored interrupt*.

Whenever a peripheral is ready to transfer data it is necessary to service its interrupt within a reasonable time or else subsequent data may be lost. Faster peripherals require faster servicing. If two (or more) peripherals are ready at the same time it is better to service the faster one first since the slow one can be made to wait a little while.

Multiple interrupt requests can be resolved by using a *priority interrupt* scheme, in which a hardware *priority encoder* arbitrates between requests and sends a single value – that represents the highest priority device – to the CPU. The interrupt request is formed by performing a logical OR of the peripheral's IREQ lines (see Figure 2.6).

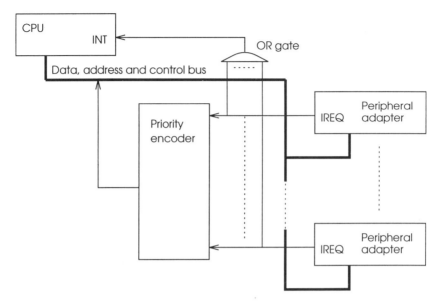

Figure 2.6 *Priority interrupts using a priority encoder*

Interrupt requests are assumed to remain asserted until reset by instructions in the service routine but this is not the most efficient technique. Until a request is de-asserted it is not possible for another request to be seen. This may result in data from a fast peripheral being lost while a service routine is getting around to clearing a low priority interrupt. It would be better if the request could be cleared quickly after the request is noticed. To assist in this most computers have a signal generated by the CPU that is returned to the peripheral as soon as the interrupt is detected, known as the *interrupt acknowledge (IACK)* signal. This clears the interrupt request from that device and allows other devices to use the interrupt line. At its simplest this may be used with one device as shown in Figure 2.7.

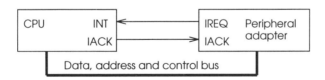

Figure 2.7 *Interrupts with acknowledge*

Using an interrupt acknowledge enables the construction of a simpler priority interrupt scheme. The CPU is able to determine priority not from the interrupt request but by which device the acknowledge is sent to. Figure 2.8 shows the IACK signal being sent down the line of peripherals in *daisy chain* fashion. All the interrupt request lines are OR'ed together, typically with circuitry that allows them simply to be connected together – known as *wired OR*. The CPU IACK is connected directly to the highest priority device so that if more than one request has been made the highest priority device sees it first. If that device has not made a request it passes the IACK along to the next device. This continues down to the lowest priority device which will receive an acknowledge only if no other device has made a request. The only problem with this is that the chain must be kept intact when peripheral adaptors are not inserted, usually by the insertion of a dummy circuit board which simply links the IACK input and output pins.

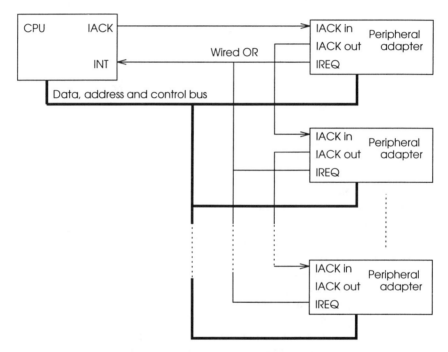

Figure 2.8 *Priority interrupts using a daisy chain*

In order to ensure a fast response to a high priority interrupt it is possible to allow interrupts to interrupt interrupts! This *nested interrupt* behaviour means that a high priority device can always rely on its service routine being run quickly, even if a lower priority device is having its interrupt serviced. Figure 2.9 shows a sequence of interrupts. Device C interrupts the main program and its service routine runs to completion, returning to the main program. Device B similarly interrupts the main program but is, in turn, interrupted by a higher priority device, A. Execution of the service routine for A is nested within that for B. When the service routine for device A completes the CPU returns to performing the service routine for B and when that completes the main program continues.

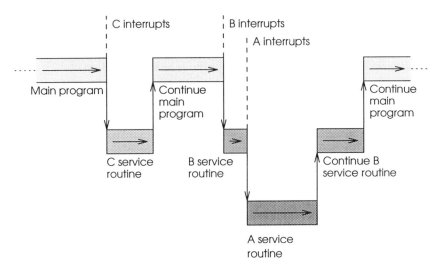

Figure 2.9 *Nested interrupts*

2.2.3 Block Data Transfer and Direct Memory Access

Certain processors have instructions for moving blocks of data which may be used for I/O also in what is known as a *block data transfer.* Since it is known that register contents need not be saved (as they would be for an interrupt) data can be moved faster than programmed or interrupt driven I/O. The CPU has to synchronize its block move with the peripheral and is unable to perform any other function while the block move is in progress. Thus it is only suited to fast transfers where the CPU and peripheral speeds are reasonably well matched. It is not commonly used.

Better still is to avoid using the CPU completely for I/O transfers. The immediate function of the CPU is to transfer data between the peripheral and memory for further processing. This involves generating the correct addresses for the peripheral adaptor and memory and driving the bus control lines to effect a transfer. For this the CPU executes one or more instructions but it is possible to add hardware to implement these functions instead. Use of such hardware is known as *direct memory access (DMA).* When a peripheral indicates that it is ready for a transfer (probably via its interrupt line) the DMA unit gains control of the bus, places appropriate address and control signals on it to make the transfer and then releases the bus. This action of taking over the bus for a period and executing a memory access cycle instead of the CPU doing so is known as *cycle stealing.*

Since there is very little overhead in a DMA transfer, apart from setting up the hardware beforehand, it is possible to use this method for very high speed peripherals. Alternatively, it is possible to view DMA as a method that has very little impact on the processor's speed, since the CPU does nothing for the transfer while it is in progress and only loses occasional bus cycles.

▶ 2.3 Terms

Depending upon the degree of parallelism involved in the communication between devices and the CPU, we can classify systems as belonging to one of three classes:

- *Full-duplex (FDX)* systems permit simultaneous transmission to and from a peripheral.
- *Half-duplex (HDX)* allows data transfer in either direction but in only one direction at a time. This requires the direction of transmission on the connecting line to be reversed as required but allows faster transmission in each direction. It is used where the flow of data is one-sided, for example for the transmission of *facsimile (FAX)* images.
- *Simplex* describes uni-directional transmission, such as that from a computer to a printer.

▶ 2.4 Character Codes

Data passing between the computer and a peripheral comprise groups of bits. On many occasions these data represent letters of the alphabet and other characters used in connection with keyboard devices, printers, etc., and agreed coding schemes are used.

Groups of bits were used to code printed characters for use in telegraphy long before the modern computer was developed. Over the years many different coding schemes have been used as new data terminals and transmission practices have evolved. The maximum size of the data set is determined by the number of bits in each character. For example, a 7-bit coding scheme allows 2^7, that is 128, different characters to be defined. The characters in such a code fit into one of the following groups: numeric (0 to 9), alphabetic (upper and lower case), special characters (punctuation marks, brackets, etc.), or control characters (used to control data flow, etc.).

The two most widely used codes are the *Extended Binary Coded Decimal Interchange Code (EBCDIC)* and the *American Standard Code for Information Interchange (ASCII)*.

2.4.1 ASCII

The 7-bit ASCII code was originally proposed by the *American National Standards Institute (ANSI)* and was developed by the *international organisation for standardization (ISO)* and the *Comité Consultatif International Téléphonique et Télégraphique (CCITT)* into the *international alphabet No. 5 (IA5),* as is shown in Table 2.1.

Table 2.1 *ASCII codes*

				b6→	0	0	0	0	1	1	1	1
				b5→	0	0	1	1	0	0	1	1
				b4→	0	1	0	1	0	1	0	1
b3	b2	b1	b0									
0	0	0	0		NUL	DLE	Sp	0	@	P	`	p
0	0	0	1		SOH	DC1	!	1	A	Q	a	q
0	0	1	0		STX	DC2	"	2	B	R	b	r
0	0	1	1		ETX	DC3	#	3	C	S	c	s
0	1	0	0		EOT	DC4	$	4	D	T	d	t
0	1	0	1		ENQ	NAK	%	5	E	U	e	u
0	1	1	0		ACK	SYN	&	6	F	V	f	v
0	1	1	1		BEL	ETB	'	7	G	W	g	w
1	0	0	0		BS	CAN	(	8	H	X	h	x
1	0	0	1		HT	EM	)	9	I	Y	i	y
1	0	1	0		LF	SUB	*	:	J	Z	j	z
1	0	1	1		VT	ESC	+	;	K	[	k	{
1	1	0	0		FF	FS	,	<	L	\	l		
1	1	0	1		CR	GS	-	=	M	]	m	}
1	1	1	0		SO	RS	.	>	N	^	n	~
1	1	1	1		SI	US	/	?	O	_	o	DEL

Eight bits are usually transmitted, the eighth being used as a *parity bit* to check for possible errors during transmission of a character. The additional bit is set so that the total number of 1's in the data word is either an even number, *even parity,* or an odd number, *odd parity.* Examples are shown in Table 2.2. If the parity of the received data is not as expected it is known that the data has become corrupted in transmission. Correct parity indicates that the data are correct or that there were 2, 4, or any other even number of errors. Thus, parity checking is only useful if single bit errors are expected; multiple errors may not be detected.

Table 2.2 *Parity bits for error checking*

Data	Odd parity added	Even parity added
1001011	10010111	10010110
0010101	00101010	00101011

Additional characters, for example graphics and accented letters, beyond those defined in *IA5* are sometimes required. The eighth bit is often used for this purpose (although it was originally intended that it should be achieved by other means) and parity, if it is required, becomes a ninth bit.

2.4.2 EBCDIC

Eight-bit EBCDIC is used primarily by large IBM computers and compatible equipment (note: IBM Personal Computers use ASCII). Table 2.3 shows a version of the code.

▶ 2.5 Parallel Interface

2.5.1 General Purpose

Simple parallel interfaces can be provided very easily. Virtually all that is required is an extension of the computer's internal bus to include the necessary buffers and registers. Such a scheme is shown in Figure 2.10. An address comparator is used to determine when the interface is being accessed and a signal indicating a match is combined with either a read or write signal to operate the buffer or register, respectively. A register is used on output so that data presented is available after the instruction to write the value, in fact it is retained until it is altered in a subsequent write. The buffer is required to ensure that input data correctly drives the internal bus when a read operation takes place. The number of bits input or output simultaneously will be the same as that of the internal data bus, that is 8-, 16-, 32- or even 64-bits. Industrial controllers often use such a simple scheme.

Other features are sometimes required. On output it may be useful to provide a signal when new data is written in order to indicate to a peripheral that a transfer has taken place (otherwise it could not tell whether there had been no change or the same data value had been written again). Input may benefit from using a register to capture transient data.

Table 2.3 *EBCDIC codes*

					b7b6b5: 000	001	010	011	100	101	110	111
b4	**b3**	**b2**	**b1**	**b0**								
0	0	0	0	0	NUL		SP					
0	0	0	0	1					a		A	
0	0	0	1	0					b	s	B	S
0	0	0	1	1					c	t	C	T
0	0	1	0	0					d	u	D	U
0	0	1	0	1	HT	LF			e	v	E	V
0	0	1	1	0		EOB			f	w	F	W
0	0	1	1	1	DEL				g	x	G	X
0	1	0	0	0					h	y	H	Y
0	1	0	0	1					i	z	I	Z
0	1	0	1	0				|				
0	1	0	1	1			.	,				
0	1	1	0	0			<	%				
0	1	1	0	1			(	_				
0	1	1	1	0			+	>				
0	1	1	1	1				?				
1	0	0	0	0			&					0
1	0	0	0	1					j		J	1
1	0	0	1	0					k		K	2
1	0	0	1	1					l		L	3
1	0	1	0	0					m		M	4
1	0	1	0	1	NL				n		N	5
1	0	1	1	0					o		O	6
1	0	1	1	1					p		P	7
1	1	0	0	0					q		Q	8
1	1	0	0	1					r		R	9
1	1	0	1	0			!	:				
1	1	0	1	1			$	#				
1	1	1	0	0			.	@				
1	1	1	0	1			)	'				
1	1	1	1	0			;	=				
1	1	1	1	1				"				

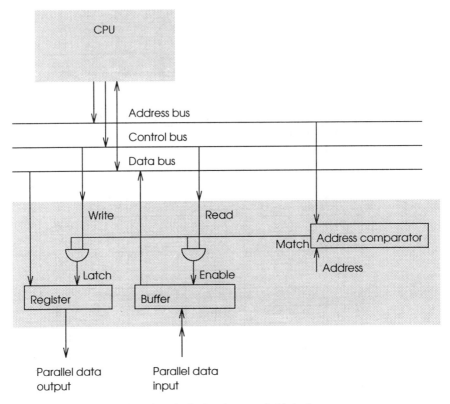

Figure 2.10 *A simple parallel interface*

2.5.2 *Centronics*

Used mainly for connecting printers to computers, this interface provides relatively high-speed operation, at up to about 70 000 bytes per second. All eight bits containing the output character are transmitted in parallel along twisted pair lines, together with control signals. The pin numbers for the major signals are shown in Table 2.4.

A *handshaking* scheme is used to control the flow of data, and is illustrated in Figure 2.11. The sequence of events is:
(i)   Wait until the peripheral is not busy.
(ii) Place data on the data lines and allow time for the signal levels to settle, at least 500 ns.
(iii) Take the strobe line low for at least 500 ns; this will result in the peripheral changing to the 'busy' state. 500 ns after the end of this pulse data may be removed from the data lines.
(iv) When the peripheral has dealt with the data it will set the

Table 2.4 *Centronics pins and signals*

Signal pin	Return pin	Signal	Direction	Description
1	19	Strobe	Out	Indicate valid data
2	20	Data1	Out	Data
3	21	Data2	Out	Data
4	22	Data3	Out	Data
5	23	Data4	Out	Data
6	24	Data5	Out	Data
7	25	Data6	Out	Data
8	26	Data7	Out	Data
9	27	Data8	Out	Data
10	28	Acknlg	In	Indicate data received
11	29	Busy	In	Indicate device busy
12	30		In	Error signal
16		0V		Logic 0V
17		Chassis		Isolated from logic 0V

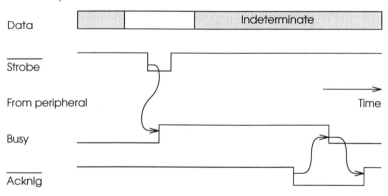

Figure 2.11 *Centronics data transfer sequence*

acknowledge (acknlg) line low to indicate this, and will also clear its 'busy' state ready for the next cycle.

2.5.3 *IEEE488*

Defined by the *Institute of Electrical and Electronic Engineers (IEEE)* the *Digital interface for programmable instrumentation* is standard number 488, otherwise known as *IEEE488*. It is also known as the *Hewlett-*

Packard Interface Bus (HPIB). It has been widely accepted for computer controlled instruments such as data-loggers, signal generators, digital meters, oscilloscopes and other measuring devices. The general scheme is shown in Figure 2.12. Up to fifteen devices may be connected to the bus. A device may be a *listener,* a *talker,* or both; one of the devices (usually the computer) must be able to control as well as talk and listen. A very large number of instruments which can be plugged onto the IEEE488 bus are now available from different manufacturers.

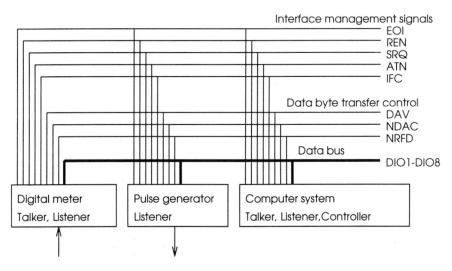

Figure 2.12 *IEEE488 instrumentation interface*

Connection is by a 16-line bus contained in a screened cable and using defined 24-way connectors. A connector socket is fitted to each instrument and the cable has both a plug and a socket at each end to permit daisy-chaining. The cable length is limited to 2 metres per instrument, up to 20 metres in total. The signals are electrically the same as those produced by gates from the TTL logic family. The connector contact and signal designations are shown in Table 2.5. Eight data lines, DIO1 to DIO8, carry address, program data, measurements and status bytes in parallel form under the control of LAV, NRFD and NDAC. The remaining lines are for general interface management.

2.5.4 SCSI

The *small computer system interface (SCSI)* is rather a misnomer since it is widely used on computers that are far from small! It is used to connect computers to disk drives and other peripherals, generally those needing a high data rate, but the attraction of this standard is such that many slow

Table 2.5 *IEEE standard 488 bus*

Signal pin	Return pin	Signal	Description
1		DIO1	Data I/O line
2		DIO2	Data I/O line
3		DIO3	Data I/O line
4		DIO4	Data I/O line
5		EOI	End or Identity
6	18	DAV	Data valid
7	19	NRFD	Not ready for data
8	20	NDAC	Not data accepted
9	21	IFC	Interface clear
10	22	SRQ	Service request
11	23	ATN	Attention
12		SHIELD	Cable screen
13		DIO5	Data I/O line
14		DIO6	Data I/O line
15		DIO7	Data I/O line
16		DIO8	Data I/O line
17		REN	Remote enable
24			Logic ground

devices also conform to it.

Only eight devices can be supported on the SCSI bus but each device can have eight *logical units* and each logical unit can have 256 *logical sub-units* – a very large total number of possible devices. Each device can be an *initiator,* a device that issues commands, a *target,* a device that performs commands, or both. To be useful a SCSI bus must have at least one initiator and one target but it can have multiple initiators and/or targets. Thus devices can be shared between computers merely by connecting them all to the same bus, see Figure 2.13.

Data is transferred over an 8-bit bidirectional bus according to the signals on associated control lines. Optionally, there is a parity line which can be used to check for errors in transmission. The data and control lines may be implemented using one wire each together with a common ground in *single-ended SCSI,* or with a pair of wires for each line in *differential SCSI.* The single-ended version is intended for short (less than 6 metres) runs within a single cabinet, whilst the differential version is specified to 25 metres and may be used between cabinets.

Because there may be multiple initiators the protocol for using the bus begins with an *arbitration phase* during which it gains control. A *selection phase* follows in which the target is addressed and then an *information transfer phase* is used to actually send data. At the end of a transfer the bus is released and waits in the *bus free phase* for another transaction.

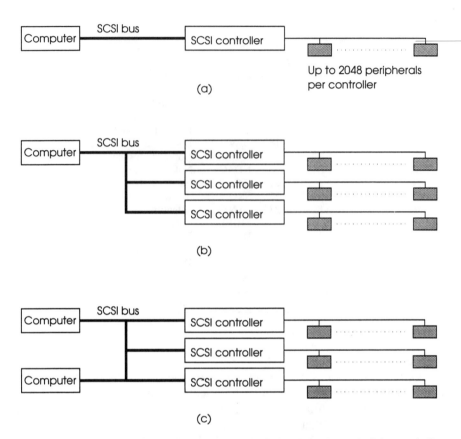

Figure 2.13 *Possible SCSI systems: (a) one initiator, one target; (b) one initiator, multiple targets; (c) multiple initiators, multiple targets*

It is not necessary for one initiator to hog the bus, and commands may be set up for execution and the bus then freed for use by another initiator. When the target is ready to respond to the given command it can re-establish contact with the initiator by using the *reselection phase*. It is quite possible that several commands will be received before the first is completed and devices can queue requests. An advantage of queueing is that devices such as disk drives can select commands out of sequence, in order to optimize the response time.

Several extensions to the original SCSI standard have been made, including:
- *SCSI-2* which makes more of the features mandatory, including a minimum command set, to permit more interchangeability between manufacturers.
- *Fast SCSI* dramatically increases the synchronous transfer rate from 4 MB/s to 10 MB/s but requires differential mode cabling.

- *Wide SCSI* increases the size of the data path from 8 bits to 16 bits or even 32 bits, thus increasing the throughput. It requires a second cable called the *B-cable* to add the extra wires; the original cable is retained as the *A-cable*. When wide and fast options are used together the data transfer rate is 40 MB/s.

▶ 2.6 Serial Interface

2.6.1 Principles

Transmission of the bits of a data word takes place sequentially, one bit after another, along a single wire.

Single wire transmission is cheaper to provide than parallel communication but at the cost of lower speed. In some instances, such as transmission by telephone line, parallel transmission is not a practical option.

Data is moved in parallel within a computer and so a *parallel-to-serial convertor* is needed in the interface unit. The simplest convertor is a shift register, as shown in Figure 2.14. For transmission, the parallel data word is loaded into the shift register. A pulse on the clock input causes the data to be shifted one place to the left and the first bit is output. For an *n*-bit data word a burst of *n* clock pulses will output the word in serial form.

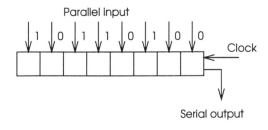

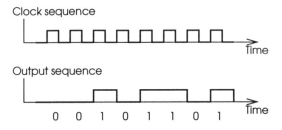

Figure 2.14 *Parallel-to-serial conversion using a shift register*

Reception of the serial data is performed by another shift register, in a *serial-to-parallel convertor,* see Figure 2.15. A sequence of *n* clock pulses causes the input to propagate along the shift register until it is all available in parallel. Note that the first bit to arrive is shifted all the way through the shift register and appears at the right-hand end. The clock in the receiver must operate with the same timings as that at the transmitter; this need for *synchronization* adds complication to the overall scheme.

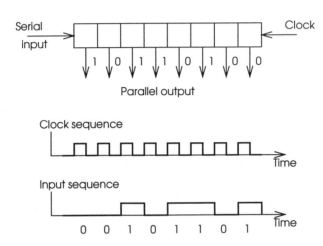

Figure 2.15 *Serial-to-parallel conversion using a shift register*

2.6.2 Asynchronous

For asynchronous transmission, characters are transmitted in the format shown in Figure 2.16. Between characters the line is in the idle state which is the *mark* or '1' condition. This comes from telecommunications practice and is convenient because a break in the line results in a lack of signal that can be easily detected.

The first bit of the character, the *start bit,* is in the *space* or '0' condition. The '1' to '0' transition is used to start the receiver clock and indicates that a character is arriving. The first bit of the data could not be used as a start bit because on those occasions that it was a '1' it would be indistinguishable from the idle condition.

For the data part of the character, five, six, seven or eight bits are transmitted with the least significant bit first. Following the data bits there may be a parity bit to allow transmission errors to be detected.

Finally the line returns to the idle state for 1, 1½ or 2 *stop bits* which allow the receiver to settle ready for the next character. Because of this format, this is also known as *stop-start* transmission.

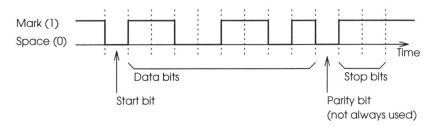

Figure 2.16 *Asynchronous character format*

Irregular intervals may occur between characters in this format, that is the sender and receiver are not synchronized at the character level and hence this is known as an *asynchronous* format. (Of course, the sender and receiver must be synchronized at the bit level for correct data transfer; it is the function of the *start bit* to establish this temporary synchronism.)

Within a character the bit timings must be regular so that the receiver clock, once started, can accurately sample the line for data. There are a number of standard bit rates. Lower rates were used for electro-mechanical peripherals, for example 45.5, 50, 75 and 110 bits/second but are now rarely found to be available. Standard rates in current use include 150, 300, 600, 1200, 2400, 4800, 9600, 19 200 (sometimes called '19k2') and 38 400 (or '38k4') bits/second; higher rates are sometimes found. The default rate for devices such as printers is usually 1200, 2400 or 4800 bits/second.

Transmission rates are sometimes expressed in *bauds* and *transmission rate* is synonymous with *baud rate.* The baud is a communication engi-neering unit which expresses *modulation rate* and is the reciprocal of the shortest signalling element. One baud is one signalling element per second but a signalling element does not always represent one bit and hence 1 baud is not necessarily 1 bit/second. For example, if a signalling element can have one of four possible voltage levels, say, 0, 1, 2, or 3 V then each level can represent a pair of data bits, say, 00, 01, 10 and 11, and 1200 baud would convey 2400 bits/second. Such a multi-level signalling scheme is at the heart of modern *modems* which achieve data rates of around 20 000 bits/second over telephone lines allowing a signalling rate of only a few thousand baud.

2.6.3 *Synchronous*

Synchronous data transmission is achieved by supplying a clock signal as well as a data signal. Transmission may be along a pair of lines, one for data and the other for the clock, or, with a suitable modulation scheme, the clock may be merged with the data stream onto a single line and recovered at the receiver.

This scheme has two major advantages over the asynchronous format. First, no time is wasted on non-data bits (the *start bit* and *stop bit,* for example) which increases the utilization of the line. Second, less margin of error is required to ensure correct recovery of data which significantly increases the acceptable transmission speed.

Data are sent continuously and there is no *start bit* to indicate where a character begins, so this must be achieved by using special sequences of data known as *protocols*. One such protocol is the widely used *HDLC* (high-level data-Link control) format whose basic structure is shown in Figure 2.17.

01111110	1 byte	1 or 2 bytes	Variable length	2 bytes	01111110

Opening   Address Control   Information   Check   Closing   Time
flag   flag

Figure 2.17 *HDLC synchronous format*

Character synchronization is achieved by identifying a special pattern of bits (01111110) known as a *flag*. This pattern is unique and can never occur in the data stream except as a flag. The unique characteristic of the flag is that it contains a sequence of six consecutive 1's, it is only necessary to ensure that data does not generate this pattern. Data to be transmitted is checked for five consecutive 1's and if found a 0 is inserted after them, a technique known as *bit stuffing*. An example is shown in Figure 2.18. At the receiver a 0 following five consecutive 1's is simply discarded to re-create the original data stream.

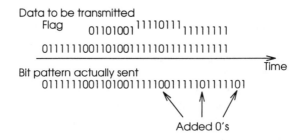

Figure 2.18 *Example of bit stuffing*

2.6.4 The RS232/V24 Standard

Probably the most widely used standard, RS232, has undergone a number of revisions and the current version is now known as EIA-232D; that is it comes from the Electrical Industries Association (EIA), is standard number 232, revision D. Its use ensures that equipment from different manufacturers can be interconnected and operate correctly. The European equivalent, V24, is very similar but does not define which pins to use in a connector, instead, it describes circuit numbers. Born in the early days of telephone line data communication using *modems* it includes features, such as the secondary channel, that are now very rarely used. A list of the connections and V24 circuit numbers is given in Table 2.6 and the pin connections shown in Figure 2.19. This also shows how a subset of these signals is used on a 9-pin connector, a form that is increasingly found on physically small computers, where a 25-pin connector is unattractive.

Table 2.6 *RS232/V24 signal and pin allocation*

Pin	V24 circuit	Abbreviation	Direction DTE:DCE	Description
1	101	PGnd	=	Protective earth
2	103	Tx	→	Transmitted data
3	104	Rx	←	Received data
4	105	RTS	→	Request to send
5	106	CTS	←	Clear to send
6	107	DSR	←	Data set ready
7	102	Gnd	=	Signal earth
8	109	RLSD	←	Received line signal detect
9				Unassigned
10				Unassigned
11	126			Unassigned
12	122	RLSD2	←	Secondary RLSD
13	121	CTS2	←	Secondary CTS
14	118	Tx2	→	Secondary Tx
15	114	TSET	←	Transmitter signal element timing
16	119	Rx2	←	Secondary Rx
17	115	RSET	←	Received signal element timing
18				Unassigned
19	120	RTS2	→	Secondary RTS
20	108	DTR	→	Data terminal ready
21		SQD	←	Signal quality detector
22	125	RI	←	Ring indicator
23	111	DSRS	←	Data signalling-rate selector
24		XTxCk	→	External transmitter clock
25				Unassigned

Communication is assumed to be between *data terminal equipment (DTE)* and *data communication equipment (DCE)*. A DTE can be a computer or a peripheral and a DCE is a, possibly non-existent, device such as a *modem.* Figure 2.20 shows the arrangement used to connect a computer to a peripheral. The DTE to DCE connection is by a 25-way cable and 25-way 'D' type connectors (so called because of their shape). It should

PGnd	1		14	Tx2
Tx	2		15	TxCk
Rx	3		16	Rx2
RTS	4		17	RxCk
CTS	5		18	NC
DSR	6		19	RTS2
Gnd	7		20	DTR
RLSD	8		21	SQD
NC	9		22	RI
NC	10		23	DSRS
NC	11		24	XTxCk
RLSD2	12		25	NC
CTS2	13			

25-pin connector

DCD	1		6	DSR
RX	2		7	RTS
TX	3		8	CTS
DTR	4		9	RI
Gnd	5			

9-pin connector

Figure 2.19 *D-type connector pin assignments*

be noted that the DTE, computer or peripheral, has a male connector while the DCE has a female connector. If we bear in mind that modems are used over the telephone network then the need for signals such as 'Ring Indicator' and 'Received Line Signal Detect' becomes apparent.

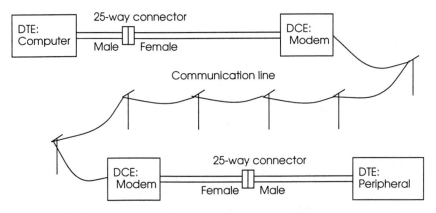

Figure 2.20 *Connecting a computer to a peripheral*

A slight problem arises if there is no need for a modem, as is the case when the computer and peripheral are close to each other. We have two devices which expect to talk to modems and exchange control information as well as data. A cable with two female connectors is required with lines suitably cross-connected to permit correct operation. Such a cable is known as a *null-modem* and a suitable configuration shown in Figure 2.21. Lines 2 and 3 (Tx and Rx) are crossed so that data sent by one device is received by the other; 4 and 5 (RTS and CTS) are locally connected to allow transmission. The connection from line 6 to 20 (DSR to DTR) allows the sending device to determine if the receiving device is ready to accept data; this provides a *handshake* mechanism to prevent data being lost in the event that data is generated faster than it can be accepted (for example, where a computer is driving a printer). Sometimes the connections shown as dashed lines are also made; this is rarely necessary but some devices may require it.

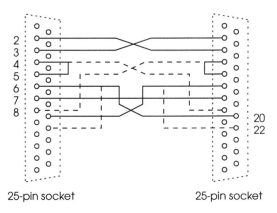

25-pin socket   25-pin socket

Figure 2.21 *The null-modem cable*

Fast peripherals, or those that can use data handshaking, can dispense with the hardware handshake lines and need only connect earth and data lines. This is commonly known as the *3-wire interface* and is popular because it is very much easier to install than the full 25 wires in the standard. If such a scheme is to be used with a computer expecting full hardware handshaking then those lines must be driven so as to indicate permanent readiness of the peripheral, see Figure 2.22.

Data handshaking uses the control codes designated DC1 and DC3 to control the flow of data. DC3 or XOFF (available on a keyboard as Control-S) indicates an inability to accept data thus stopping its transmission and DC1 or XON (Control-Q) indicates readiness for more data. Not surprisingly this is known as *DC1/DC3* or *XON/XOFF* handshaking.

2.6.5 The EIA-562 Standard

Given the trend to lower power computers with lower supply voltages in portable equipment it is not surprising that a new serial standard has been developed. *EIA-562* is an improved version of *EIA-232* and is compatible in that *EIA-562* and *EIA-232* devices can be interconnected.

Minimum output levels are ±3.7 V rather than ±5 V which allows the levels to be reached more quickly, increasing the maximum speed from 20 k to 64 k bits/s as well as reducing power consumption by over 40%.

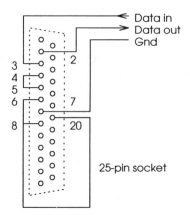

Figure 2.22 *Defeating hardware handshaking*

The receiver sensitivity is unchanged at ±3 V which reduces the noise margins to only 0.7 V; this is adequate for the fairly short (a few metres) connections that are most commonly found.

▶ 2.7 Line Drivers

2.7.1 Transmission Speed and Line Length

Data are transmitted via a transmission line. The line may be quite short or very long, less than a metre for connections to local devices to hundreds or thousands of metres for communication to another room or building. The maximum data rate that can be reliably utilized depends on the line length with the relationship being as illustrated by Figure 2.23.

For short lines the maximum rate is determined almost entirely by the characteristics of the line driver circuit. Long lines limit the rate as a consequence of their physical characteristics, such as the resistance of the wire used. There is a smooth transition between these extremes. A better (usually more expensive) transmission line gives a better speed/length point.

Reliable transmission can only be achieved if the waveform at the receiver is a reasonably faithful reproduction of that at the transmitter. A longer line increases the time taken to change voltage levels and may also reduce the voltage levels reached. Figure 2.24 illustrates this effect. Eventually it becomes impossible to distinguish between levels, and data cannot be recovered. Even before this time the signal may be unusable because noise signals on top of a small wanted signal can look like valid levels and produce corrupt data.

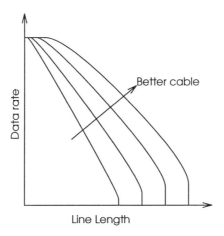

Figure 2.23 *Maximum data rate versus line length*

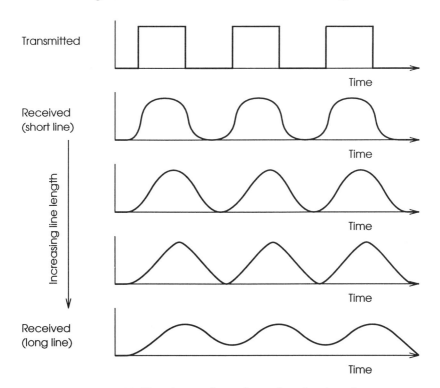

Figure 2.24 *Signal waveforms for various line lengths*

Compromise is necessary between line length, speed of transmission and cost. Some of the techniques used are described in the following sections.

2.7.2 *Single-ended Transmission*

As can be seen from Figure 2.25 the term *single-ended* is used because the line is connected at a single point on the driver and receiver at each end of the line.

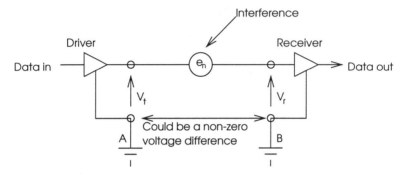

Figure 2.25 *Single-ended line driver and receiver*

Direct connection of a driver and receiver is the simplest scheme. Typically the drivers and receivers are standard logic gates. For Transistor-Transistor Logic (TTL) gates the voltage levels they produce and respond to are shown in Figure 2.26. To ensure that the receiving end does not misinterpret the driver output sent down the line it is necessary that $V_{oh} > V_{ih}$ and $V_{ol} < V_{il}$. That is, any signal degradation from the line or additive interference must be small enough to ensure these conditions are met.

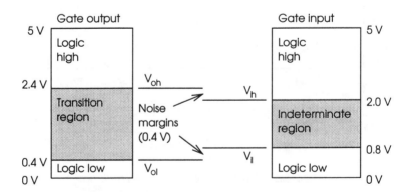

Figure 2.26 *Voltage levels for TTL*

Additive voltages can occur in two ways. Firstly, interfering radiation can be picked up from nearby electrical activity. This is marked as e_n on Figure 2.25. Secondly, the receiver input voltage is sensed relative to its local earth, B, which may not be at exactly the same potential as A. The difference could amount to several volts if the driver and receiver are some distance apart and energized from different points in the power distribution system. This effectively puts a large offset on the received signal and can easily cause the receiver to give an incorrect output.

Larger margins give more freedom from interference. The specification of the EIA-232D standard (a development of the earlier and well known RS232 specification) is shown in Figure 2.27. The CCITT recommendation V28 is very similar. A driver is required to convert logic levels to EIA-232 levels for transmission and re-conversion by a receiver. This standard specifies a limit on the capacitance of the line, 2500 pF, which may represent as little as 20 m of 125 pF/m cable or as much as 60 m of 40 pF/m cable; the RS232 specification gave a maximum length regardless of cable type.

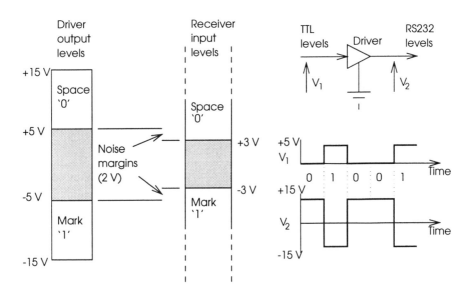

Figure 2.27 *Voltage levels for EIA-232D*

Whilst not within the specification, practitioners know very well that they can use the relationship of Figure 2.23 to allow communication with lower data rates over very much longer lines than is strictly permitted. Satisfactory operation at these extended distances depends on local conditions, low noise levels etc. and cannot be relied upon.

2.7.3 Differential Receiver

Differential receivers have two input terminals and sense the difference in voltage between them; neither terminal is required to be connected to a local earth. (Single-ended receivers detect a voltage difference from a local earth level.) When used as shown in Figure 2.28 two of the difficulties of single-ended receivers can be overcome. Firstly, the transmitter earth is conveyed to and used by the receiver; any difference between local earth levels is ignored. In practice, there is a limit to the ignorable signal between the inputs and the local earth, B. This difference is usually known as the *common-mode input voltage* and an acceptable range is specified in the device data sheet. For simple comparators this may be less than the supply voltage for the receiver but for purpose-designed line receivers it is often much greater; for example the AM26LS33 can accept up to ±15 V whilst operating on a single 5 V supply. Secondly, provided the two lines are laid close together or, better, formed as a twisted pair of lines, any electrical interference will induce almost identical voltages, e_n, into each line. At the receiver $V_1 = V_t + e_n$ and $V_2 = e_n$, but the receiver senses the difference between these,

$$V_r = V_1 - V_2 = (V_t + e_n) - (e_n) = V_t, \qquad (2.1)$$

which is independent, ideally, of interference.

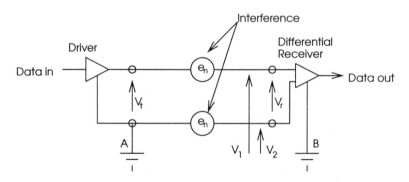

Figure 2.28 *Differential line receiver*

This type of driver and receiver combination is specified by EIA-423 and allows transmission at higher data rates than the single-ended scheme, EIA-232.

2.7.4 Balanced Transmission

Balanced drivers provide two outputs, as shown in Figure 2.29, with each output being similar to a single-ended driver output. The driver arranges that the two outputs have opposite levels, when one sends a *mark* the other sends a *space*. This is indicated in the diagram by $+V_t$ and $-V_t$. A differential receiver is used.

Figure 2.29 *Balanced driver and differential receiver*

One advantage of this scheme is that the effective voltage between the lines is twice that produced by a single-ended driver. A greater signal attenuation can be tolerated and hence longer lines used.

Radiation of interference is reduced because the complementary electromagnetic fields will tend to cancel out. This is beneficial not only in reducing pollution but also by reducing *cross-talk* between closely spaced lines, again increasing the maximum usable line length.

EIA-422 defines a balanced transmission standard using these principles.

2.7.5 Current-loop Transmission

Serial data may be transmitted by switching a current rather than a voltage, such a scheme is known as a current loop. The two states are no current flowing (the *space* condition) and a specified current flowing (the *mark* condition). When electro-mechanical peripherals were common so was the 20 mA current loop (i.e. the *mark* current was 20 mA). Nowadays this scheme is very rarely used.

One form of current loop still in regular use is the *musical instrument digital interface (MIDI),* a 31.25 k baud link, see Figure 2.30. This uses approximately 5mA to represent a *mark* condition. The resistance used to set this current is formed from three actual resistors so that some measure of protection against incorrect connection or signals is provided. The diode in the receive side is also for protection.

The opto-isolator is used to isolate the sending and receiving systems to prevent stray signals from affecting the audio signals produced, in particular to prevent the formation of an *earth loop (ground loop)* between separate amplifiers which can cause a line frequency 'hum' to be induced into the audio signal path.

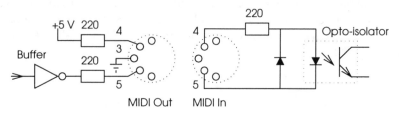

MIDI Out   MIDI In

Figure 2.30 *MIDI current loop*

2.7.6 A Comparison of Standards

Major features of the four most commonly used standards for line driving are shown in Table 2.7. There is a clear improvement from left to right.

A single-ended transmitter and receiver as used by EIA-232 supports relatively slow communication over short distances, perfectly satisfactory for most computer peripherals and relatively very cheap.

Using a differential receiver, as in EIA-423, improves the distance considerably and the speed by a useful amount. The cost of cable is increased and this would be used for long runs or fast peripherals such as plotters or laser printers.

Differential transmitters and receivers, together with properly impedance-matched cable, increases the maximum data rate dramatically. The difference between EIA-422 and RS-485 is that the latter allows up to 32 transmitters to drive the line (one at a time) for implementing local networks.

Table 2.7 *Some common serial transmission standards*

	EIA-232D	EIA-423A	EIA-422A	RS-485
Driver	Single-ended	Single-ended	Differential	Differential
Receiver	Single-ended	Differential	Differential	Differential
Cable length, max	about 100 m	1200 m	1200 m	1200 m
Data rate, max	20 k bits/sec	100 k bits/sec	10 M bits/sec	10 M bits/sec
Driver output voltage	±5 to ±15 V	±3.6 to ±5.4 V	±2 to ±5 V	±1.5 to ±5 V
Receiver input sensitivity	±3 V	±200 mV	±200 mV	±200 mV
Receiver input range	±25 V	±12 V	±7 V	-7 V to +12 V

3

Display and Printing Devices

▶ 3.1 Introduction

Printing devices, printers, were initially based on typewriter technology. A character shaped piece of metal was moved into contact with an inked ribbon in contact with the paper so that ink was transferred. The characters were found on the surfaces of drums and spheres (the popular and high quality *golf ball* printers).

Development of this technology culminated in the *daisy wheel* printer, a relatively low cost yet high quality device. The name derives from the shape of the character container, see Figure 3.1. Each character is placed on the end of a flexible arm and a complete set arranged around a central hub. This collection spins around and a hammer behind the wheel is triggered at the correct time to force the required character into contact with the ribbon. The flexible arm allows the character to stop momentarily to prevent smearing. The wheel mechanism is placed on a carriage which moves along a line of text, as shown in Figure 3.2.

Displays have never been required to provide such high quality and have thus used stylized character sets. Applications requiring only a limited set of characters are able to use simple (and therefore cheap) combinations of indicator. A very frequent requirement is for the display of numerals in test and measuring equipment, cash registers, etc. Stylized representations of the 10 digits (and some letters) is possible with a *7-segment display,* see Figure 3.3.

Each of the seven segments, conventionally labelled from 'a' to 'g', can be made from any suitable indicator; commonly light emitting diodes (see Section 3.4) or liquid crystal displays (see Section 3.6). By enabling suitable combinations of segments the required numeral can be displayed.

A complete alphabet, with numbers and a few other symbols, can be obtained with a *16-segment display,* also known as a *starburst* display, see Figure 3.4. This type of display is not often seen, being rapidly displaced by dot-matrix types which have even larger possible character sets.

General purpose displays and printers that can produce graphics as well as characters are now becoming the normal requirement. The trend is towards devices that provide control over a relatively large number of regularly arranged dots that can be used to form the lines of ·pictures and shapes of characters. These are generically known as *bit-mapped devices.*

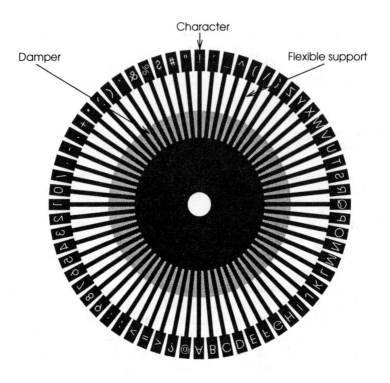

Figure 3.1 *A 'daisy wheel' (full size)*

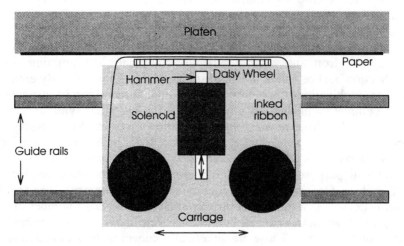

Figure 3.2 *'Daisy wheel' printer mechanism (viewed from above)*

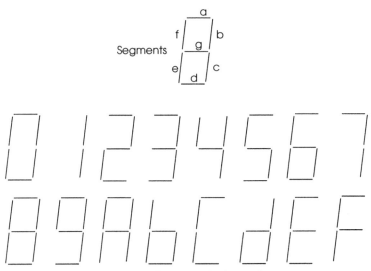

Figure 3.3 *7-segment characters.*

Many different technologies have been used to form the dots of bit-mapped displays, including impact devices such as dot matrix printers, non-impact devices such as laser printers, reflective devices (LCD's) and illuminated devices using incandescent lamps, LEDs and plasmas (similar to neon lamps).

▶ 3.2 Bit-mapped Devices

3.2.1 Introduction

Bit-mapped devices are so called because it is possible to control the state of individual points of the display, not just character sized groups. Total control provides great flexibility in that both characters and graphics, lines and other arbitrary shapes may be drawn. Characters have to be created from a number of points according to some pattern that makes a recognizable shape, known as a font.

Dedicated hardware is used to form a bit-pattern that describes the information on a complete page and to allow control of the state of individual points or *pixels*. For a single line display this requires a trivial amount of memory but for a 600 dpi (dots per inch) printer it is in the region of 4 MB for a page using two-level (on/off) pixels (as on most laser printers, for example); a high quality colour device needs nearer 100MB!

Segments

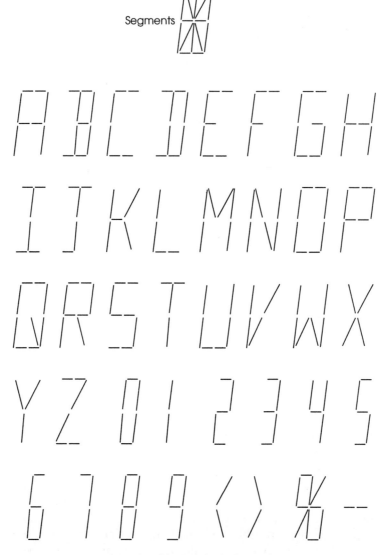

Figure 3.4 *16-segment characters*

3.2.2 Character Fonts

Probably the smallest array of dots used to display a full character set is 5 dots wide by 7 high, usually known as a 5 by 7, or 5×7 array. A sample of the characters possible with this is shown in Figure 3.5. It can be seen that quite a clean representation is possible of these characters; lower case letters are possible but not very attractive.

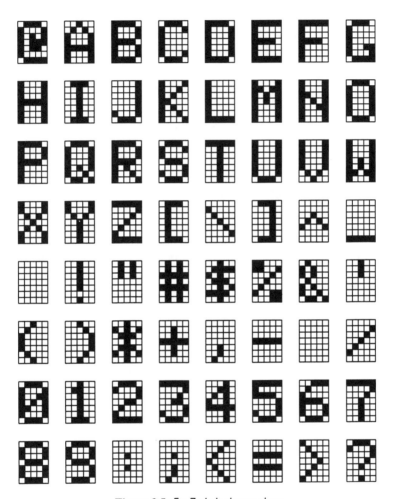

Figure 3.5 *5 × 7 dot characters*

For display purposes slightly higher resolutions are desirable and 7×9 is commonly found on character based computer terminals. Printers, on the other hand, need a much higher resolution to give good results and a dot-matrix printer will use something around 27×18 dots and a laser printer nearer 100×100.

3.2.3 *Implementation*

Devices, such as printers, that produce an image after it is formed can be driven by software that uses standard memory to create the bit pattern. Dynamic devices, such as a computer screen, must be given data continuously, even at the same time as it is being created.

The data rate for a video display device is such that the memory used to form the image cannot be easily shared between the display and the processor. A special form of memory, *dual port memory,* allows access by two different circuits at the same time is used. One port, the standard *random access memory (RAM)* interface, is connected to the computer and the other, a sequential access port, is used by the screen. The sequential access port is well matched to typical displays such as the *cathode ray tube (CRT)* which scans the screen. This special memory device is known as *video random access memory (VRAM)* and usually forms part of a special interface card called a *video adaptor.* The resolution of the display may alter depending on the amount of memory available to an adaptor. With only two brightness levels at each point on the screen, a single bit is needed for each pixel, hence the term bit-mapped. For grey scale or colour images, more bits per pixel are required. Very good grey scales can be obtained with 8 bits per pixel (the eye can only distinguish about 32 shades of grey, 8 bits give 256 shades). Reasonable colour may be obtained with 8 bits per pixel but for photographic quality colour 24 bits are required. Resolutions of around 1000×1000 pixels are common, requiring 1 MB of memory for each 8 bits per pixel.

▶ 3.3 Filament Lamps

Although largely replaced by semiconductor alternatives the incandescent filament lamp still has a few advantages to offer.

Current is passed through a thin metal filament so that it heats up and emits light. In order to obtain a bright, white light the filament must reach 2800°C to 3000°C and tungsten is normally used as it has a melting point of 3387°C. To minimize unwanted heat loss and so that the working temperature can be reached with minimum power input, the filament is usually formed into a spiral. Oxidation (burning) of the filament is prevented by placing it into an evacuated glass bulb. Figure 3.6 shows the general construction.

Glass bulbs and, to a lesser extent, filaments can be formed into a variety of shapes to suit many needs. The connections may be by wires or by push-in, screw or bayonet fittings for easy replacement. The most

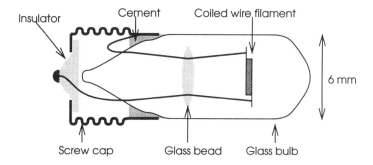

Figure 3.6 *Filament lamp construction*

commonly used types for indicators have either a *lilliput edison screw (LES)* or *midget edison screw (MES)* base, that is they are screw-in types and the base is derived from that used by the inventor of the first practical light bulb, Thomas Edison. Bulbs are usually tubular or globular (round) and are often described by their size as a number after the letter T or G, the number indicates the diameter in eighths of an inch ($^1/_8$" is approximately 3 mm). A typical indicator lamp would be a T1$^3/_4$ LES – a tubular lamp 5.7 mm in diameter with a screw cap.

Filament lamps offer a high brightness source of white light which can be easily filtered to give light of virtually any colour. Large numbers of lamps can be used together to form very large displays. Lamps used for indicating purposes are not normally driven for absolute maximum light output, so that their expected lifetime is typically 5 000 hours and may be as much as 50 000 hours.

▶ 3.4 Light Emitting Diodes

In the 1950's, *Gallium phosphide (GaP)*, formed into a p-n diode, was found to emit red light when forward biased. A great deal of research since then has produced a range of similar devices and the *light emitting diode (LED)* is now a very common indicating device. A range of colours from infra-red, through red, orange, yellow and green, to blue is now available. A pure GaP diode emits green light but impurities change the colour of light emitted, current red light diodes use *gallium arsenide phosphide (GaAsP)*. *Gallium arsenide (GaAs)* is used to produce infra-red light and *silicon carbide (SiC)* for blue light.

Doping of a substrate material is used to form a p-n junction in the chosen material. When a forward current, typically around 20 mA, flows light is emitted sideways from the junction and is reflected forward by a metal bowl in the cathode connection. A fine wire connects the diode anode to the other terminal. The voltage drop across the diode depends on the material used and is typically 1.5 V for an infra-red device, 2 V for a visible red device and 3 V for a blue device. The front of the package is often domed to form a lens to give a brighter light but flat fronted types also exist. Seen from the front the diode package is usually circular but may be formed into other shapes; squares, bars, triangles and pointers are available. The package is a transparent plastic and may be clear or coloured to match the colour of the light emitted. See Figure 3.7.

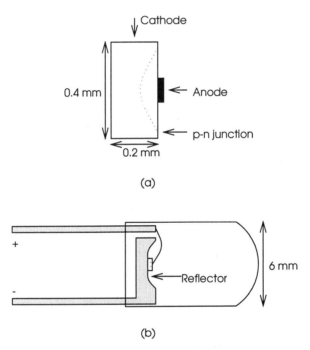

Figure 3.7 *Light emitting diode: (a) chip; (b) packaging*

Several diodes may be fabricated or packaged together for more elaborate displays. Seven-segment displays are formed from seven diodes with diffusers to give bars of light. Thirty-five diodes may be arranged in a 7 by 5 array for general purpose alpha-numeric displays; often a suitable decoder/driver is included so that standard input codes (e.g. ASCII) may be used to control them.

Although not yet as bright, the light emitting diodes have replaced filament lamps in many applications due to their lower power consumption and longer expected lifetime (typically 100 000 hours).

▶ 3.5 Cathode Ray Tubes

Probably the last remaining mass market vacuum tube device, the *cathode ray tube (CRT)*, consists of a glass funnel shaped tube evacuated so that the air pressure is less than 10^{-6}mm Hg. An electron gun produces a fine beam of high speed electrons which is deflected electrostatically or magnetically to strike a spot on the phosphor coated screen to produce light at that point.

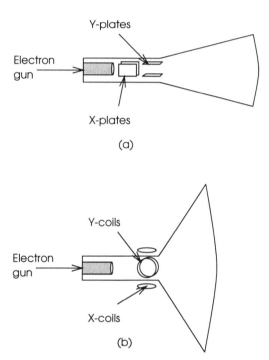

Figure 3.8 *Cathode-ray tube construction: (a) with electrostatic deflection; (b) with magnetic deflection*

Several electrodes form the electron gun, as shown in Figure 3.9. A *cathode,* made from nickel coated with an oxide mixture, is heated indirectly by a filament heater, and raised to a temperature (around 800°C) that causes electrons to be emitted from its surface. The *grid* electrode is situated immediately in front of the cathode and controls the intensity of the beam and hence the brightness of the spot. A negative potential on the grid with respect to the cathode repels the (negatively charged) electrons and reduces the intensity, a sufficient potential (around -20 to -100 V) stops the beam entirely and is known as the *cutoff potential.*

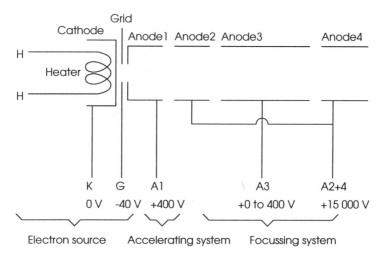

Figure 3.9 *Cross-section of the electron gun*

Anode A1 attracts the electron beam and accelerates it toward the screen. The high potential of the *second anode,* A2, accelerates the beam to a high speed to give it sufficient energy to produce a bright light on the screen. This is connected to the *final anode,* A4, and the inner coating of the tube and screen. The final anode voltage may be only a few thousand volts for a small tube but is typically around 15 kV for a monochrome display and 25 kV for a colour display. Very high brightness tubes for projection systems may require as much as 50 kV but this brings problems with X-ray production requiring careful screening.

Anode A3, between A2 and A4, carries a variable potential. The difference in potential between A2 and A3, and between A3 and A4, produces curved lines of equal potential which act as a lens to focus the electron beam to a small spot on the screen.

Deflection of the electron beam to the required part of the screen may be by either electrostatic or magnetic means.

Electrostatic deflection requires plates within the CRT, between which a deflecting potential may be applied. The resulting electrostatic field attracts the electron beam toward one plate and repels it from the other. The amount of deflection depends on the strength of the field and the time for which it is applied, which in turn depend on the applied potential, the speed of the beam and the geometry of the tube. The deflection is given by

$$\Delta X = \frac{VLD}{2V_{A2+4}d} \tag{3.1}$$

where ΔX is the deflection on the screen
           V is the voltage between the deflection plates
           L is the length of the deflection plates
           D is the distance from the deflection plates to the screen
               (measured from the centre of the plates)
     V_{A2+4} is the accelerating voltage (on A2+4)
           d is the distance between the deflection plates.

Magnetic deflection is obtained by generating a magnetic field from coils external to the tube. Whilst within the magnetic field the electrons move in the arc of a circle giving a deflection

$$\Delta X = lDH\sqrt{\frac{1}{2V_{A2+4}}\frac{e}{m}} \qquad (3.2)$$

where ΔX is the deflection on the screen
           l is the diameter of the coil (and field)
           D is the distance from the centre of the field to the screen
           H is the field strength
      e/m is the electron charge/mass ratio.

Comparing the above equations we see that electrostatic deflection is proportional to $1/V_{A2+4}$ whilst magnetic deflection is proportional to $1/\sqrt{V_{A2+4}}$. At high accelerating voltages it is easier to obtain a useful deflection with magnetic deflection. It is also difficult to obtain wide deflection angles with electrostatic deflection because the deflection plates must be wider apart near the screen to prevent the electron beam hitting them. It is, however, easier to deflect the beam quickly electrostatically; the inductance of the deflection coils makes it difficult to change the magnetic field quickly.

Electrostatically deflected tubes are used mainly for measurement applications, for example in oscilloscopes, where high speed deflection is required, the accelerating voltage is relatively low and the length of the tubes is not a problem.

For data display applications the tube must be physically compact which requires a wide deflection angle. The deflection rate is generally fairly low (a few tens of kHz) and the accelerating voltage needs to be high for a bright display. All these factors indicate the suitability of a magnetically deflected tube.

When the beam of electrons hits the phosphor coating on the inside of the screen it gives up its energy which is converted into light. The phosphor is a mixture of chemicals such as oxides and sulphides of cadmium, zinc and manganese, together with metals such as silver. Particular combinations give particular characteristics such as colour and phosphorescence (emission of light after the beam is removed). For example, the phosphor designated type *P4* is a combination of ZnS, Ag, Zn_8BeSiO_{19} and Mn

which fluoresces with a white light and the fluorescence/phosphorescence characteristic result in the light level reducing to 1% of its excited level in about 5 ms; it is used in monochrome displays.

A thin layer of aluminium metallisation is usually added to the inside of the phosphor layer in high voltage tubes. This has the effect of reducing charge buildup on patches of phosphor and of reflecting the light forward to give a brighter image. Low voltage tubes, those with less than about 5000 V on A3, cannot use metallisation as the electrons do not have enough energy to penetrate it.

3.5.1 Gamma Correction

Screen brightness is not a linear function of electron beam strength and this, in turn, is non-linearly dependent on drive voltage. To a large extent these two cancel each other out but there still remains a less than perfect relationship between drive and brightness. This relationship can be fairly well described by the equation

$$Brightness \propto Voltage^{\gamma} \tag{3.3}$$

with a typical value for γ of 1.2. This is shown graphically in Figure 3.10 which plots percentage drive against percentage brightness; a linear relationship is shown by the dashed line. There is a marked problem at low drive and brightness levels. For example at a drive level of 10% the brightness is 5%, only half that expected! If an image which assumes a linear relationship is sent to a CRT it will appear with a lack of detail in the darker areas where the non-linearity makes things darker than they should be. The difference is small but needs to be corrected for high-quality applications. In broadcast television the correction, known as *gamma correction,* is applied once at the studio rather than on each television set.

When driving CRT's from a computer look-up table gamma correction can be implemented to give uniform increases in brightness. A set of values for a simple 8-level scale is shown in Table 3.1 alongside the values that would have been used assuming a linear relationship.

Values for the look-up table can be derived from the formula

$$Table\ value = R\left(\frac{x}{n}\right)^{1/\gamma} \tag{3.4}$$

where R is the maximum value in the look-up table
x is the brightness level to be encoded
n is the maximum brightness level to be encoded.
For example, for Table 3.1 the values are $R=255$, $n=7$, $x=0$ to 7 and $\gamma =1.2$.

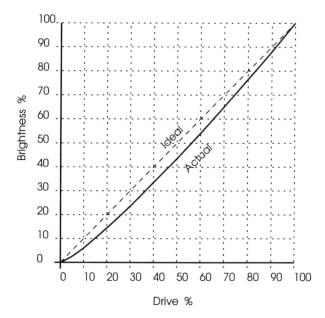

Figure 3.10 *Brightness v. drive*

Table 3.1 *Linear and gamma corrected values for a look-up table*

Brightness step	Linear value	γ corrected value
0	0	0
1	36	50
2	73	90
3	109	126
4	146	160
5	182	193
6	219	224
7	255	255

3.5.2 Colour Tubes

Colour cathode ray tubes are a clever combination of three tubes in one. For a colour display it is necessary to produce three coloured images, one red, one green and one blue, on top of each other so that the eye can merge them to see the desired result.

Three separate electron guns are used to produce three individually controlled beams which pass through holes in a steel sheet to land on three areas of the screen covered with phosphors emitting each of the three required colours. The phosphors are printed in stripes of each colour and it is arranged that the electron beam from the 'red' gun can only fall on the red phosphor, similarly for the green and blue guns. See Figure 3.11.

Correspondence between guns and stripes is ensured by the steel sheet placed just behind the screen. It is arranged that electrons from a gun can pass through holes in the sheet to fall on the correct phosphor but that the sheet casts shadows on the other phosphor stripes. The sheet is therefore known as a *shadowmask* and the complete tube as a *shadowmask CRT.*

Manufacturing tolerances have to be compensated for and some adjustments have to made to ensure that the beams follow the paths they should. These are typically made by adjusting small permanent magnets that move the electron beams. Tolerances are now so good that adjustments can be made at the factory and do not need changing during the life of the tube.

One problem that may occur is that the shadowmask may become magnetized which will result in incorrect colours being shown. To prevent this a procedure known as *degaussing* is carried out each time the display is switched on. By applying a slowly decaying alternating field, via coils around the tube, any permanent magnetism is removed.

Older tubes used phosphor dots arranged in a triangular pattern with a shadowmask containing circular holes rather than stripes and slots. This method is capable of higher resolution displays and is still used in high resolution applications. Unfortunately they require a relatively large number of complex compensating adjustments and circuits to achieve this performance thus adding to the manufacturing cost. Also, the shadowmask intercepts a higher proportion of the electrons and requires higher beam currents for a given brightness, i.e. they consume more power than striped tubes.

▶ 3.6 Liquid Crystal Displays

A *liquid crystal display (LCD)* uses an organic liquid which has a high degree of molecular order to change the polarization of light and this can be changed into a brightness change. An electric field is used to control the alignment of the molecules.

Displays are based on the *twisted nematic (TN)* field effect. The display is manufactured so that molecules are aligned parallel to one surface of the liquid crystal cell and parallel at the other surface but rotated through 90° so that the molecules twist between the surfaces. This has the effect of twisting polarized light through 90° as it passes through the

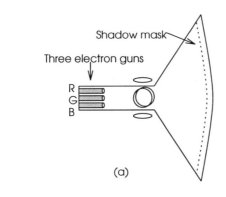

(a)

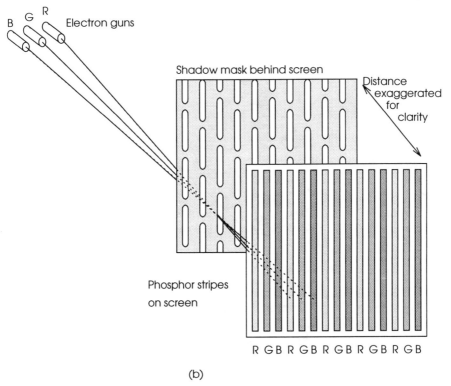

(b)

Figure 3.11 *Shadow mask colour CRT: (a) cross-section (from above), (b) electron beam path*

liquid. Transparent conductive electrodes are formed from a material such as *indium oxide* on the inside of the glass surfaces of the liquid crystal cell. The twisting of the molecules and hence of the light polarization can be removed by the application of an electric field.

Changes in the plane of polarization are made visible by forming a sandwich of polarizing material and the liquid crystal cell, as shown in Figure 3.12. Randomly polarized light is first passed through a *polarizer* so that it is plane polarized, then through the cell where the direction of the plane is rotated, or not, and then through a second polarizer known as an *analyzer.* When no electric field is applied light passes through the combination but when a voltage is applied between the front and rear electrodes the cell ceases to rotate the plane of polarization and the analyzer prevents light from being emitted. Thus we have dark characters on a light background. In practice not all of the light is rotated and the result from the cell is a mixture of direct and rotated light which together form elliptically polarized light. This limits the contrast that may be obtained.

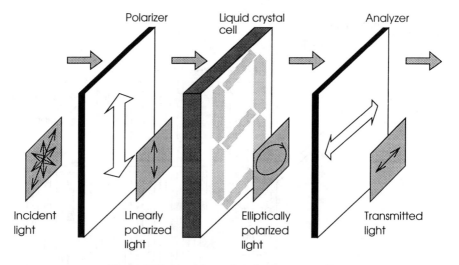

Figure 3.12 *Liquid crystal display operation*

By aligning the polarizer and analyzer, light characters on a dark background may be obtained.

Since light passes through the composite these are known as transmissive displays. The light may come from a LED source or fluorescent panels or tubes.

Replacing the light source with a mirror gives a reflective display in which light from the same side as the viewer is used. This form is no use in the dark but is suited to a wide range of lighting conditions since its brightness always matches the level of illumination.

Deterioration of the liquid crystal material would result if a direct voltage was used across the cell. Instead an alternating voltage is used, the constant changes in polarity preventing deterioration. Only a small voltage is required, typically 5 V to 15 V. It takes time for the molecules to drift back after the voltage is removed (typically around 100 ms) so that changing the polarity of the field has no visible effect. It is possible to use pulses rather than a continuous signal and this is used on larger displays to reduce the wiring and drive circuitry required.

The basic twisted nematic LCD suffers from rather poor contrast ratio (about 3:1 at 15° viewing angle from the normal) and limited viewing angle (20° wide, 60° above horizontal). Both contrast ratio and viewing angle have been improved in the *super twisted nematic (STN)* display. In the STN LCD, the liquid crystal molecules are twisted through at least 180° through the cell. The system still uses polarizers but to create a bire-fringence effect instead of an on-off effect. A contrast ratio of better than 4:1 is possible over a viewing angle 65° wide and 45° above horizontal. The typical response time is slower with STN than TN displays.

Dot-matrix displays are possible and adding coloured filters to cells allows colour displays to be made. For television applications, where moving images are required, slow response times give poor quality images. Small LCD screens with response times adequate for television applica-tions are now becoming available.

▶ 3.7 Electrostatic Printers

3.7.1 Introduction

Electrostatic fields can be used to attract colouring matter on to paper. Oppositely charged bodies, in this case ink and paper, adhere to each other thus causing a transfer of ink. This can be done directly, as the *Versatec* company does, or indirectly via an optical arrangement as in laser or LED printers.

3.7.2 Direct Transfer

Electrostatic printers employ dielectrically coated paper so that an electric charge can be placed on the paper by an array of charging nibs. After a line has been charged it is sprayed with liquid toner containing charged particles, for example carbon particles in an iso-paraffin dispersant. These particles stick to the charged areas of the paper and form an image. Sur-plus toner is removed and the paper dried before handling. The general construction is shown in Figure 3.13 and is essentially a very simple mech-anism.

There is a small air gap of about 0.6 mm (0.025") between the nibs and the paper whilst there is a continuous electrode touching the other side. A voltage of 550 to 750 V d.c. is applied between the electrodes. The higher the voltage the darker the image, and this can generally be adjusted. The paper is negatively charged by the nibs and the toner is positively charged.

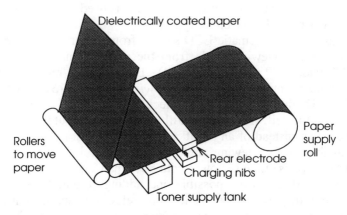

Figure 3.13 *Electrostatic printer*

The spacing between nibs is typically 0.25 mm, giving a resolution of 100 dots per inch. Two rows of nibs staggered slightly can be used to double the resolution.

Colour printing can be obtained by running the paper through several times with a different coloured toner each time.

Unfortunately, the need to provide several hundred high voltage drivers means that these printers are relatively expensive. The similar but cheaper laser printers have replaced electrostatic printers in all but those situations requiring wide or long paper runs.

3.7.3 Laser Printers

Popularly known as a *laser printer*, this device also uses electrostatic fields to transfer toner to the paper. Originally laser printers were made for high speed, high volume production; speeds of many hundred pages per minute are possible.

Referring to Figure 3.14, the critical component is the photosensitive drum. The drum is coated with a selenium based material that is sensitive to light. In the dark it has a high resistance and acts as a capacitor which is charged to a high voltage as it passes under the *charging wire*. A laser beam is reflected off a rotating *polygonal mirror* which causes the beam to scan along a line on the drum. Since the drum is rotating the beam passes over its complete surface. Light falling on the drum causes its resistance to be reduced at the point of impact and the capacitor discharges thus removing the high voltage. By modulating the brightness of the laser, points on the drum can be selectively discharged or left with a high voltage. As the drum passes the toner reservoir the charged areas attract particles of the dry powder which stick to its surface; the discharged areas attract no toner.

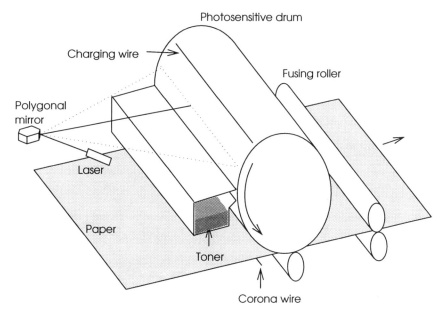

Figure 3.14 *Laser printer*

The paper is given a charge as it passes the *corona wire* so that as it passes the drum the toner is transferred to the paper. A hot *fusing roller* at about 260°C (500°F) melts the toner particles so that, in combination with the pressure of the rollers, they are permanently stuck to the paper. It is also possible to use high pressure rollers without heat.

Instead of using a scanning laser beam, some printers have been made using an array of LED's and are known as *LED printers*. It is difficult to get very high resolutions in this way but 200 to 300 dpi is normal.

▶ 3.8 Ink jet and Bubble jet Printers

Figure 3.15 shows the basic components of one form of ink jet printer. Conductive ink is forced through a very small nozzle to produce a high speed stream or jet of drops of ink. The size and spacing of these drops are made constant by vibrating the nozzle compartment at an ultrasonic frequency with a piezo crystal mounted at one end of the cavity. The vibrating frequency is around 100 kHz, the drop diameter is typically 0.06 mm (0.0025"), and the spacing 0.15 mm (0.006").

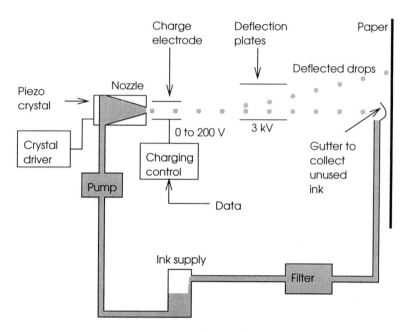

Figure 3.15 *Ink jet printer*

Each drop of ink, after leaving the cavity, is given a specific charge as it passes through a charging electrode located next to the nozzle. The drops are deflected vertically by a second electrode structure and strike the paper. The horizontal position is normally controlled by moving the ink jet system.

The amount of deflection is determined by the charge on the drop. With no charge there is no deflection and these drops are collected in a gutter placed close to the paper. Increasing charge increases deflection so that drops can be placed as desired.

Characters are formed in a dot matrix. For high quality printing approximately 1000 drops are required per character. With 10^5 drops per second released from the nozzle (100 kHz vibration rate), 100 characters can be printed per second.

Continuous flow systems such as that described above are rapidly being superseded by *on demand* systems. A piezoelectric element can be used to produce ink drops only when required and hence there is no need for a collecting gutter. Using a stack of nozzles a vertical line of dots can be produced without a deflecting system and the parallelism increases printing speed.

Rather than controlling the drops of ink with a piezoelectric element it is possible to use thermal means. A small heater in the print head capillary tube is used to vaporize a little ink which causes the expanding gas bubble so formed to push out a drop of ink. These are known as *bubble jet print-ers*. There are typically 24 vertical nozzles and print speeds of several hundred characters a second can be obtained.

▶ 3.9 Dot-matrix Printers

Most printers form characters and graphics using a matrix of dots but the term *dot-matrix printer* is used for impact printers using movable needles to form the dots. A number of hammers and needles in a vertical line are used to print one column of a character and then the print head is moved horizontally for the next column.

The mechanism for each needle is shown in Figure 3.16. At rest the needle is held away from the ribbon and paper by the return spring. When a dot is required a current is passed through the solenoid so that it attracts the hammer which pushes the needle into contact with the ribbon and hence marks the paper. The overrun spring absorbs any excess movement if the print head is too close to the paper or the paper is thicker than expected (multi-part forms, for example). When the current is removed the needle returns to its rest position.

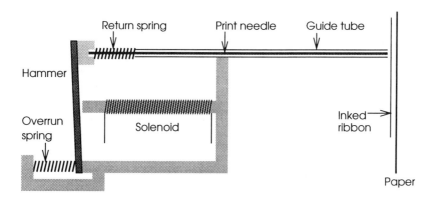

Figure 3.16 *Needle print head: mechanism, side view*

The solenoids are large compared with the needles and must be spaced apart. The needles are guided from the hammer to the required line at the paper by small capillary tubes which are necessarily curved. Any curva-ture is undesirable as it adds resistance to movement and should therefore be kept to a minimum. The solenoids are usually arranged in a circle, as shown in Figure 3.17, to keep the needles as straight as possible.

Printing may take place only on the forward stroke of the carriage con-taining the print head, *uni-directional printing,* or on both the forward and

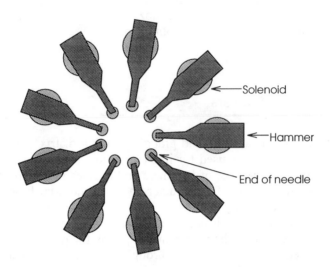

Figure 3.17 *Needle print head: arrangement of solenoids, end view*

reverse directions, *bi-directional printing.* The time taken to return the carriage to the start is quite significant and bi-directional printing considerably improves the printing speed, although more data has to be buffered and processed to achieve this.

Print quality on the early dot-matrix printers was often poor but developments have resulted in modern printers achieving a very high quality. The number of dots used to make up a character determines its quality but the number that can be accommodated on the print head is limited by the size of the mechanism. As many as 27 needles are used in currently available high quality printers. Accurate control of the carriage allows multiple passes to be taken with the dots at slightly different positions each time giving the effect of more pins. It is common to find an option on these printers for single-pass, lower quality *draft mode* printing or slower multiple-pass *letter quality (LQ)* printing. Even very low cost dot-matrix printers may be capable of *near letter quality (NLQ)* printing.

▶ 3.10 Interfaces

3.10.1 Introduction

Character printing devices generally need very little data (characters) to generate a lot of data (the graphic representation of the character, for example a complete dot matrix) which then needs to be transferred to the paper. Graphics devices, on the other hand, need to transfer a complete description of the image; this may be eased by using a *page description language (PDL),* such as PostScript, although this is not the primary aim of a PDL.

3.10.2 Communication

Sequential transmission, as described in Section 2.6, is used for slower devices or where there is a long distance between the computer and the printer. If the distance is short a faster parallel interface (see Section 2.5) can be used. Both of these use the computer to feed data to the interface a character at a time and the amount of time available from the processor limits the maximum data transfer speed attainable.

Reduced processor overhead, as well as increased transfer speed, may be obtained with a *direct memory access (DMA)* connection. This requires much more hardware in the interface so that data can be taken from memory without any processor activity. The processor is free to continue with user programs while the printer gets data. After setting-up the transfer data is moved by the special DMA hardware which generates memory accesses and handles any flow control; the processor is not called upon until all the data has been sent.

Whatever scheme is used, data may be transmitted faster than it can be accepted by a printer, typically due to the relatively slow mechanical operations that must take place. In order not to lose data there must be a method of pausing to allow the printer to catch up; this is normally known as *flow control.* Figure 3.18 shows how this operates. In addition to the wires handling data to the printer there is a connection in the reverse direction indicating when the printer is busy.

Most printers actually print a line at a time and have to buffer data until a complete line has been received. Figure 3.18(b) shows the simplest sequence of events. As each character is received the printer is busy for a short time while that character is placed in the buffer. When the line is complete the printer is busy for a much longer time as the text or graphics is printed and the mechanical operations take place.

Sequential data reception and printing can waste quite a lot of time and most printers *double buffer* the data – incoming data is placed in a buffer until the line is complete and is then transferred to a second buffer. Data from the second buffer is used to control the printer mechanism and, at the same time, the first buffer becomes available to receive the next line of data. This gives virtually continuous printing but may still require pauses in the data flow if the data is supplied too rapidly by the computer.

In practice, memory is so cheap that printers have quite large buffers, typically enough to hold a page of data. If the flow control is not working it may still be possible to print small files without error but large files overflow the buffer and produce garbage – a common problem when setting up a new printer!

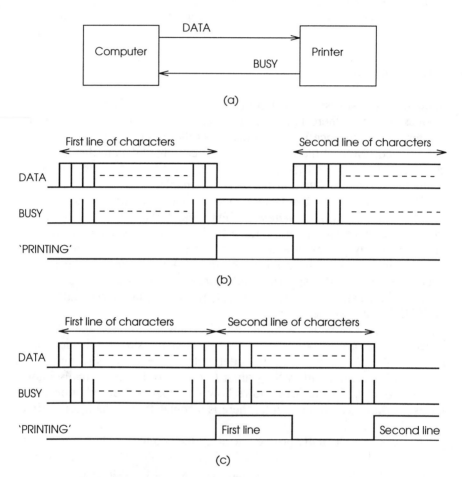

Figure 3.18 *Data transmission with flow control: (a) interconnection; (b) signals with single line buffer; (c) signals with double line buffer*

3.10.3 Page Description Languages

Portability between printers allowing them to use output data in some common format is an attractive characteristic, but the number of different printers is large. It is not practical to describe the desired result at the bit level since different printers work at different resolutions, from less than 70 dpi to over 2000 dpi.

As in portable programming languages, a higher level of description is required. A *page description language (PDL)* such as *PostScript* specifies what is required in terms of lines, shapes, fonts and characters and leaves it to the printer to map this to its own characteristics. PostScript was developed by *Adobe Systems Incorporated* and is a device independent programming language specifically aimed at describing text and graphics. An example is shown in Figure 3.19. The complete set of facilities provided is far too large to be described here and the reader is referred to the books in the further reading section of this chapter.

```
0   0 moveto
0  40 lineto
90 40 lineto
90  0 lineto
closepath
stroke
/Times-Roman findfont
12 scalefont
setfont
10 15 moveto
(Resulting text) show
showpage
```

(a)

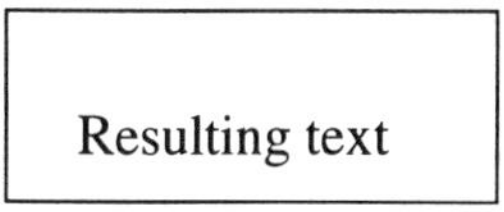

Resulting text

(b)

Figure 3.19 *PostScript: (a) source text; (b) what it produces*

▶ 3.11 Three-dimensional Displays

Our sense of depth is caused by two phenomena, *perspective* and *stereoscopic vision.*

Perspective, the effect whereby objects look smaller the further away they are, together with our learned knowledge of the actual size of an object, enables us to judge the distance to an object. This effect is less certain when the objects are not familiar, as may occur when the computer is used to create fantasy images. It is more convincing when there are several copies of an object of differing sizes; smaller copies then appear to be further away.

Stereoscopic vision comes into play with objects close to the eyes, up to only a few metres distant. Our two eyes, separated as they are by a small but significant distance, each see a slightly different view of an object. These differing views are combined by the brain and the differences converted to distances. Simulating this effect by presenting different images to each eye gives a very convincing 3D effect and is an essential component of *virtual reality* systems.

A demonstration of stereoscopic vision is provided by Figure 3.20. Two copies of an image are given, one for each eye. It can be seen that there are differences between the images. To view the effect it is necessary to look at the left image with the left eye and the right image with the right eye. With practice this can be done with the diagram as it is. It is, however, easier with the aid of a sheet of cardboard about 30 cm long, an A4 sized piece is ideal. Place the board between the images and rest your nose on the other end, about 30 cm from the page; this masks the images so they can only be seen by the appropriate eye. Next it is necessary to alter the usual co-ordination between the eyes and look at the page as though it were further away than it actually is. This is best done by relaxing and not looking too hard at the page, look through the page and after a while the images should merge to a single object. It is now possible to concentrate on what you see and observe the three-dimensional effect.

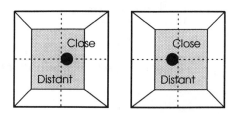

Figure 3.20 *Three-dimensional image demonstration: see text for instructions on viewing*

Calculating the images to present to the eyes is relatively straightforward, but the presentation of those images to the eyes requires special peripherals.

Using a single display screen it is necessary to present the two images alternately and arrange that only one eye sees each. Provided the rate of change is fast enough, more than 50 times a second, the eye will see the result as two constant images and the brain will combine them to one three-dimensional scene. Switching between images to be displayed is a simple electronic operation involving two video memory buffers and is arranged to take place between display frames so that it is invisible. The user wears a pair of spectacles with an electronically controlled shutter over each eye; the shutters are opened in turn in synchronism with the display switching between images. The shutters use liquid crystal technology and are connected by wires to the display.

An alternative switching technology places a polarizing filter over the display; the direction of polarization is controlled by the display so the images are produced with different polarization. The user then only requires spectacles with polarizing filters (as found in sun-glasses) set at the appropriate angles to separate the images. This system has the advantage that the user-worn part of the system is cheap and does not require connection to the display. It is also possible for many people to look at the display at the same time.

When a single user interface is required with intimate interaction, such as in virtual reality systems, a lightweight headset with two miniature display screens, one for each eye, can be used.

▶ 3.12 Colour

Colour reproduction relies on the characteristics of the human eye/brain to give the appearance of most, but not all, of the colours in nature. It has been found that combinations of only three colours, at varying intensities, are required to reproduce a wide range of colours. The three colours used depend on whether the image is a source of light of a reflector.

Sources of light, such as display screens, can use the three *additive primary colours* red, green and blue. With appropriately chosen shades, a combination of equal intensities of all three appears to be a shade of grey. Obviously, zero intensity causes no light to be emitted and the result is black; at maximum brightness the result is white. For other colours the relative intensities of the three primaries is adjusted. Used alone we obtain red, green and blue. Red and green together appear as yellow and we can obtain colours in the range from red, through yellow to green with a suitable mix. Red and blue give magenta, whilst blue and green give cyan.

Reflective images, such as those on paper, must use pigments to absorb light. They use the *subtractive primary colours* yellow, cyan and magenta on a white background. When none is present the result is white and when all are together all light is absorbed to become black. As might be obvious, yellow and cyan together give green; yellow with magenta gives red and cyan with magenta gives blue. The mix of all three usually gives a rather poor black, more like muddy brown. Since text is most often printed using black this looks rather poor, and printers often incorporate the ability to produce pure black as well, the software switching to this automatically when required. The commonly used chart used to depict these relationships is shown in Figure 3.21.

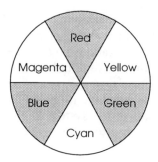

Figure 3.21 *Colour chart showing primary colours (additive colours are shaded)*

In fact the situation is rather more complex than this since the eye/brain does not work with absolute intensities but uses surrounding colours to modify its perception. It is possible to see colours accurately when the illumination is not white light but tinted, and colours can change with intensity, for example orange is seen as brown at low levels.

▶ 3.13 Further Reading

Richard Rubinstein *Digital Typography,* Addison-Wesley, 1988

Adobe Systems Inc. *PostScript Language Reference Manual,* Addison-Wesley, 1987

Adobe Systems Inc. *PostScript Language Tutorial and Cookbook,* Addison-Wesley, 1987

4

Input Devices

▶ 4.1 Introduction

This chapter is concerned with the more common input devices associated with a computer system. These include the keyboard, used for entering text, and the mouse, trackball and joystick which are often used in graphical systems to control on-screen movements. The input of detailed positional information such as digitizing schematics or maps is covered by the section on flatbed input devices, which also discusses methods of optically scanning information directly from an image. Three-dimensional digitizers are then described as, largely, an extension of their two-dimensional counterparts. Their use in graphics and in the fast expanding world of *virtual reality* is mentioned and this topic is described in Chapter 7. Finally, two methods of directly interacting with the screen display are introduced.

This chapter is concerned with the 'main' input devices, although making such a distinction is difficult. Other input and output devices and media are the concern of Chapter 7.

▶ 4.2 Keyboards

Keyboards are widely used to enter information into computers. A keyboard is, at its simplest, a bank of switches whose individual states can be detected by the computer system. By that definition, a series of single state switches on any domestic electrical appliance can be regarded as a keyboard, but the name is most closely associated with the typewriter style alphanumeric keyboards such as the examples shown in Figure 4.1.

Figure 4.1(a) shows the simplest alphanumeric *QWERTY* keyboard and its style is adapted directly from the typewriter. This example uses the English alphabet, but keyboards are adapted to most languages. This keyboard, by using combinations of keys, can produce all characters in the common character sets such as ASCII. In the central and largest section are 26 keys representing the letters of the alphabet. These keys alone produce the lower case letters. The upper case letters are produced by holding down either of the *shift* keys while pressing the alphabetic key.

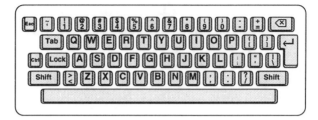

(a) Alphanumeric typewriter style keyboard

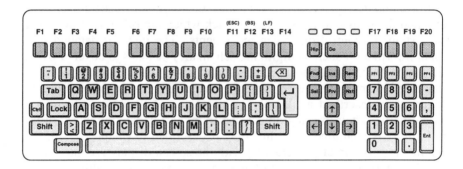

(b) Typical terminal keyboard

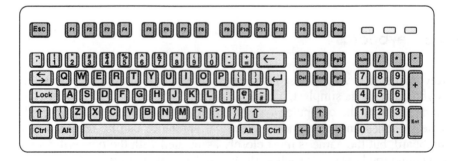

(c) Typical PC keyboard

Figure 4.1 *Keyboard layouts*

Alternatively, the key marked *lock* can be pressed and, until it is depressed again, the 26 alphabetic keys will now produce upper case alphabetics instead. Alongside these are several keys for punctuation characters. They each represent two characters which are shown one above the other on each key. Pressing these keys inputs the lower of the two characters. The other character is produced by holding down either of the shift keys while pressing the key. The top row consists of thirteen more punctuation and digit keys. Again, they can produce either of two characters depending upon whether the shift key is currently depressed. This row of keys includes the ten digits. Note that the state of the lock key does not affect punctuation or digit keys. The bottom row contains one large key, the space bar.

The main difference between this keyboard and a typewriter keyboard is the inclusion of the *CTRL* key. This acts in a similar manner to the shift key in that, when it is held down, the meanings of the remaining keys are altered. It is used to produce *control codes* such as the first 32 characters in the ASCII character set. These codes include characters such as tab, return, escape and backspace. These four particular control codes are, in fact, so commonly used in computing that they additionally have their own dedicated keys. In the example shown, the escape key (ASCII code 27) and the backspace key (ASCII code 8) are at either end of the top row. The tab key (ASCII code 9) and the return key (ASCII code 13) are at either end of the second row of keys in a similar position to their type-writer equivalent keys. These four characters can also be produced by holding down the CTRL key and typing [, H, I and M, respectively. (Note that, on many keyboards the *backspace key* actually produces the function-ally similar *DEL* character (ASCII code 127). The computer system nor-mally interprets these two codes to mean delete the last character typed.)

The keyboard described above and illustrated in Figure 4.1(a) is a min-imal computer keyboard and, in practice, computer keyboards include many more keys. A terminal is a combination of a visual display unit (VDU) and a keyboard which normally communicates with a computer system bidirectionally along a serial line. Figure 4.1(b) shows a typical terminal's keyboard layout. Keyboards also can be detached from the dis-play unit and communicate directly with the computer system, and a typi-cal keyboard for a personal computer is illustrated by Figure 4.1(c)

In these two illustrations, four extra sections have been added. First is a series of *function keys* which are arranged in a row above the normal array of keys. Some of these have predefined purposes or, more com-monly, they are interpreted by programs which take special actions upon receipt. Function keys can be used either to produce codes outside of the normal character set or to produce a short sequence of two or three codes which is interpreted accordingly. Typically the first character of such a sequence is the escape character (ASCII code 27) whose original intention was exactly for this purpose – *escape from the standard code and interpret the following character(s) specially.* Unfortunately the escape character, because of the prominence of a key in its own right, has often been bor-rowed by many software writers to perform other functions and confusion can arise if a fast typist coincidentally actually types in the same escape sequence that a function key produces.

Second is a bank of cursor/screen positional keys immediately to the right of the main array. These are normally used by word processors and similar programs for convenient movement of the cursor position on the screen, to move the text displayed on the screen back and forward by whole screenfuls and to perform other common editing tasks such as inserting, removing and searching for text. As with the function keys, these keys normally produce a short sequence of two or three characters.

Thirdly, a similar shaped bank of keys on the far right of the keyboard comprises the *numeric keypad*. Most of these keys simply reproduce the same actions of some of the keys in the main pad such as the digits and some arithmetic symbols. They can be more convenient to use when inputting numeric data or performing calculator type functions. Some of them may be function keys.

Fourthly and finally, a row of indicator lights is often incorporated. These lights may display the current state of the keyboard such as whether the lock key is active. In general they may be lit for any informative purpose by the computer system.

Desirable features of a keyboard, in addition to layout, include reliability and the *feel* of the keys. These features depend upon the construction and design of the individual keys themselves. Each key is used to operate a simple electrical switch.

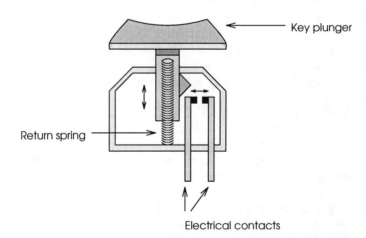

Figure 4.2 *Contact type keyboard switch*

4.2.1 *Key Switches*

Although effort has been taken to obtain better methods, contact switches as shown in Figure 4.2 are widely used. Pressing the key plunger causes the contacts to touch (or maybe separate) and thus one of two voltages can be produced. The contacts may *bounce* when the plunger is depressed giving the appearance of several rapid key depressions. This effect is known as *key bounce* and must be eliminated by special circuitry which effectively ignores the key after its first depression for a very short period of time. A contact switch has a small electrical resistance of the order of 0.1 ohm and this will gradually increase over the operating life.

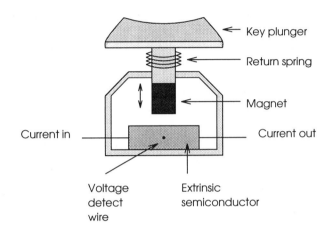

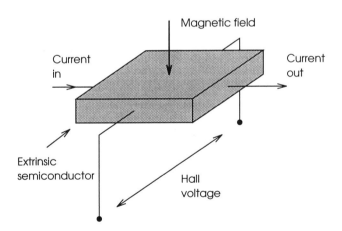

Figure 4.3 *Hall effect key switch*

Another form of contact switch is the *membrane switch*. This switch generally contains three layers of a material such as polyester or polycarbonate film which are separated by spacers. The whole assembly is often less than 1 mm thick. The bottom layer is fixed, the middle layer is flexible, and the top layer, which is also flexible, contains the legends. The switch contacts are between the inner surfaces of the bottom layer and the middle layer. Pressing the top layer causes the middle layer to press against the bottom layer and form an electrical contact. When the top layer is released the contact is broken.

Membrane switches are inexpensive, thin, inherently sealed and can be waterproof. The legends can be illuminated from the back, and some designs can include tactile feedback with an appropriately shaped dome. The switches are often used for control switches on peripherals such as printers. Complete keyboards can also be manufactured using them.

Of the non-contacting switches, Hall effect switches are popular. The Hall effect is the generation of a voltage across a slab of semiconductor when current is flowing through the semiconductor and a magnetic field is present at 90° to the direction of current flow. The voltage generated is at 90° both to the magnetic field and the current flow as illustrated in Figure 4.3. The key plunger of the switch brings a small permanent magnet close to the slab of semiconductor. The Hall effect voltage is then amplified and detected as a key depression.

Another form of non-contact key switch is the capacitive switch as shown in Figure 4.4. Two plates are mounted on the base of the switch. The key plunger holds a third plate which is brought close to the two fixed plates when depressed. An alternating current is applied to one fixed plate and sensed on the other fixed plated when the plate on the key plunger is in close proximity.

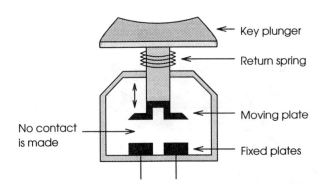

Figure 4.4 *Capacitive key switch*

The key switches described above are amongst the most common in use but there are several other types employed. These include reed switches and mercury contact switches. With the reed switch a magnet is attached to the key plunger in a similar fashion to the Hall effect switch. The magnet attracts the lower of two contacts to make an electrical connection. With the mercury contact switch the key plunger causes two contacts to be immersed in the mercury. Because mercury is an electrically conducting liquid, a connection is made in a similar fashion to a contact switch but with no problem of contact wear.

4.2.2 *Keyboard Scanner*

Most keyboards have around 100 key switches. The computer system must react to each of them independently. It is not practical for the computer system to have a separate communication channel for each switch and, in any case, it is rare that more than one or two switches are depressed simultaneously and so a shared channel is employed. The switches are arranged in a matrix and connected to a keyboard scanner as shown in Figure 4.5(a).

The matrix usually contains five or six rows and around twenty columns. At the intersection of each row with each column is a key switch which, when depressed, makes electrical contact between that row and column. The columns are continuously scanned in turn by placing a voltage on each in turn. The rows are then sampled and, because only one column is active at a time, any key(s) depressed are uniquely detected. The columns must be scanned rapidly so that each is scanned within a time much less than that between the key depressions achievable by a fast typist. In practice the whole keyboard is scanned in far less than a millisecond.

When a key depression is detected, the key in question is reported by the keyboard scanner as either a row and column pair of numbers or a single number. The state of such keys is noted by the scanner which, on subsequent scans, will not report the key as depressed until after it has been released. When the key is released this event is similarly reported. In order to cater for the key bounce effect described earlier, the keyboard scanner may choose to ignore the state of a key for a short time after it has been depressed.

While this scan method can report any number of key depressions and releases, there is one problem that can arise. If three keys are depressed on three corners of any square in the matrix there will be conductivity at the fourth corner and it will appear to the keyboard scanner that the fourth key is also depressed. To eliminate this effect the switches must only pass current in one direction and this is achieved by inserting a diode along the columns between each switch as shown in Figure 4.5(b).

4.2.3 *Keyboard Controller*

The keyboard scanner produces a series of key depression and release messages identifying the key by its position in the matrix. While in some cases this information may simply be passed directly to the computer system reading the keyboard it is usual for more processing to take place. The object performing this processing will be called here a keyboard controller. A keyboard controller may be a circuit or small processor physically located in the keyboard housing. It may, in the case of a personal

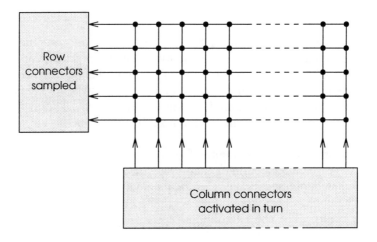

(a) Keyboard matrix scanner

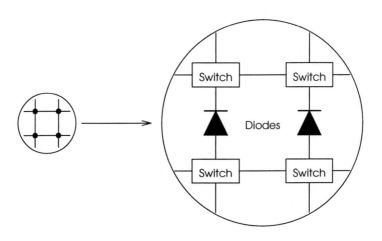

(b) Expanded detail of keyboard matrix connectors

Figure 4.5 *Keyboard matrix scanner*

computer, be located in the main system unit. Its functions may, in fact, be undertaken entirely by a program residing within the main computer system.

The role of the keyboard controller is illustrated in Figure 4.6. There are three principal functions to be performed. First the key, identified by its position in the matrix, must be translated to a code for that character such as its ASCII code. This can be performed using a look-up table.

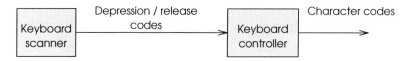

Figure 4.6 *Keyboard controller interface*

Secondly keys such as the shift, shift lock and control keys must be interpreted. These keys do not result in a character being sent but affect the interpretation of the other keys. When the shift key is depressed, for example, a different look-up table will be used until the shift key is released. When the shift lock is depressed, the shift look-up table for the 26 alphabetic keys will be used until the shift lock key is depressed again.

In the discussion on keyboards it was noted that some keys can produce a short sequence of characters instead of a single one. Typically this is the case with function keys and cursor control keys. Also, a common feature is to produce a character repeatedly while a key is held down. This is commonly referred to as *typeamatic* and is produced by the controller when a key has been held down for longer than a set time – usually of the order of a second. These productions of multiple characters for a single key depression form the third principal function of the keyboard controller.

So it can be seen that the controller receives a series of events relating to key depressions and releases and sends a series of character codes in response. In a terminal which includes a keyboard and a screen the controller will exist inside the terminal which is then connected to the computer system by a serial port. The controller for the screen will also be self-contained. In a personal computer or workstation the controller may exist inside the system unit allowing any program to interact directly with the keyboard. This gives the flexibility to ascribe different meanings to the keys.

▶ 4.3 The Mouse, Trackball and Joystick

The mouse, trackball and joystick are positional input devices. The mouse is the most common and is usually associated with an on-screen cursor which follows the mouse's movements. The trackball is used similarly and is, functionally, a stationary mouse upside down. The joystick operates like an aircraft joystick and returns to a central position when released. The mouse especially is the main input device associated with a *graphical user interface (GUI)* where most actions are taken by *clicking* a button on the mouse when its associated cursor is over a particular area of the screen.

4.3.1 *Mouse*

The mouse is a small hand-operated device which is moved over a surface. When it is moved, the distance it has moved in both the X and Y directions is sent to the computer system. It achieves this by having a tracking device on its underside. The mouse also has buttons – usually one, two or three – which, when pressed or released, act as another *event* input. A typical mouse is shown in Figure 4.7.

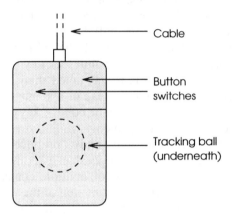

Figure 4.7 *Top view of a mouse*

The mouse is connected to the computer system by a cable which leaves the mouse from the more distant edge and it is this *tail*, along with the scampering effect of the mouse in use, that accounts for the device's name. Not all mice have a cable to communicate their information. Some are not physically connected at all and, instead, communicate using sound or light beams like a television remote control.

The mouse sends relative positional information which is normally used to move a cursor on the screen. The absolute position is governed by this cursor. The operating system will read the mouse and update the cursor accordingly. Programs which use the mouse will then actually interrogate the position of the cursor. The mouse can be picked up, moved and then put down and, because its tracking mechanism is only engaged when it is near to a surface, no positional information will be sent. This feature is extremely useful and, rather than moving the mouse a long distance, the cursor may be moved by moving a short distance, picking the mouse up and returning it to its original position and repeating the gesture several times. This action is often called *stroking the mouse*. Due to this feature, the mouse need not occupy much desk space and may always be returned to a favoured location.

The mouse also has one or more buttons which, both when pressed and when released, send a signal. Despite the apparently small number of events that can be input with these limitations, the creativity of programmers make the mouse a very powerful input device. It is up to the program using the mouse to interpret the buttons and many gain additional functionality by looking for two clicks of a button in rapid succession and treating this as one different event. The near simultaneous depression of two buttons can also be given a separate meaning. In addition, a button may be pressed and held down while moving the mouse and then released. This action can be interpreted differently from moving the mouse with no button depressed. The communication between the mouse and the computer system typically consists of messages in the following form:

- button n pressed
- button n released
- mouse moved by (X,Y) units.

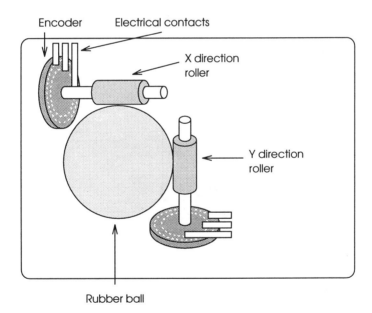

Figure 4.8 *Electromechanical mouse*

Mice differ largely by the type of tracking method employed. Both mechanical and optical tracking systems exist. The mechanical tracking systems employ a small rubber ball as shown dotted in Figure 4.7. When the mouse is moved and the ball is in contact with the surface the ball movements reflect the mouse's movements. This movement of the ball is then measured separately for the X and Y directions (relative to the mouse) by two rollers at right angles to each other and in contact with the ball. This arrangement can be seen in Figure 4.8 and Figure 4.9.

Attached to the end of each roller is a disc. The movement is measured by measuring the rotation of these discs and there are two common methods of doing this. In Figure 4.8 which depicts an *electromechanical mouse,* the discs have several sets of contacts arranged in two circles. The two sets of contacts are slightly offset. The number of contacts in each circular set dictates the resolution of the mouse and about forty is typical.

The two sets of contacts are detected by three metal strips – one on each of the two sets of contacts and the third (middle) one is in contact with both sets of contacts. The middle strip provides a voltage which is then detected on the other two whenever a contact is reached. One unit of movement is then recorded each time both detecting strips receive a voltage. Because the two sets of contacts are offset, there is a slight delay of receiving this pulse on the two strips and the order of the two pulses senses the direction of the movement.

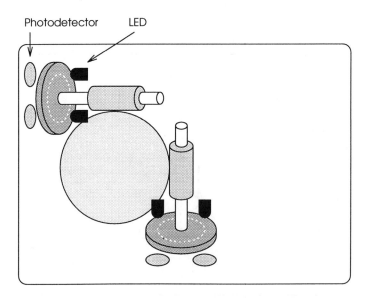

Figure 4.9 *Optomechanical mouse*

An alternate method of sensing the rotation is used by the *optomechanical mouse* as shown in Figure 4.9. Here the discs have a set of holes in them and two sets of LEDs and photodetectors detect these holes. The pulse on each detector measures one unit of movement and, similar to the electromechanical mouse, a slight offset of the two LEDs enables the direction of movement also to be determined. With this method there is no wear on moving electrical contacts.

A less common tracking method dispenses with the ball and instead has two fixed cylindrical rollers at right angles to each other protruding beneath the mouse. These two rollers are functionally equivalent to the two internal rollers in the mechanical mice just described and their rotations can be measured in similar ways.

The second main tracking system used has no moving parts and is the optical mouse. Its tracking system is shown in Figure 4.10.

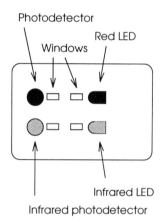

Figure 4.10 *Optical mouse*

This mouse has two LEDs inside which shine down onto the work surface through two small windows in the casing. A second pair of windows allows the reflected light to return into the mouse where it is detected by two photodetectors. One LED is the normal red visible variety, the other produces infra-red light. This mouse requires a special mouse mat which has a series of alternate black and blue lines printed on it in both the X and Y directions as shown in Figure 4.11.

The blue lines absorb red light but not infra-red light. The black lines absorb the infra-red light. The red LED will then receive pulses due to every line while the infra-red detector receives pulses on alternate lines. In a similar manner to the optomechanical mouse, a slight offset in the spacing of the lines can be used to determine the direction of movement.

These mice have no moving parts and therefore should be more reliable. The ball in a mechanical mouse picks up dust and has to be cleaned periodically although the use of a suitable rubber mouse mat can reduce this effect. The disadvantage of the optical mouse is that, unlike its mechanical counterparts, it must use a special mat.

As mentioned at the beginning of this section mice communicate messages to the computer system whenever the mouse moves or when a button is sensed. This communication can utilise a special piece of circuitry within the computer system which also provides power for the mouse's

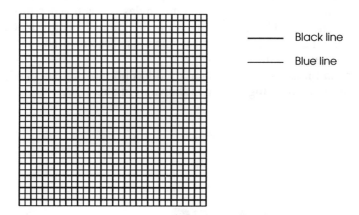

Figure 4.11 *An area of the mat required for an optical mouse*

own circuits. More commonly, a mouse can communicate directly with a standard serial interface such as RS232. Each message is a short sequence of bytes which are then interpreted by the operating system. A standard serial interface, when active, will set a 12 v signal on its RTS (ready to send) line and this is used as a source of power for the mouse.

4.3.2 Trackball

The trackball is used for similar purposes as the mouse. Its internal design is almost identical to a mouse and can be regarded as a mouse on its back and left in a stationary position. The trackball pre-dates the mouse and it is popularly believed that the mouse was conceived by turning a trackball upside down and moving it across a table surface. The main features of a trackball are shown in Figure 4.12.

The ball is completely free to rotate within its socket. It is operated by the palm of the hand and the movements sensed by the ball being in contact with two rollers inside the casing in the same manner as a mechanical mouse. The rollers' movements again are detected by sensing the rotations of discs attached to their ends. This sensing can be achieved by electrical contacts or by LEDs and photodetectors. Like the mouse, a trackball unit will usually include some buttons which can be reached by the tips of the fingers while the palm of the hand is resting on the ball.

For most purposes the mouse is more popular than the trackball but in situations where space is tight or no suitable surface is available the trackball is used. Currently it is commonly integrated into the casing of most laptop personal computers.

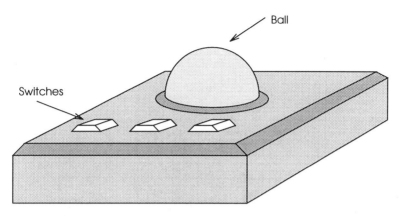

Figure 4.12 *A trackball*

4.3.3 Joystick

The joystick is also a positional device which can be used to control the position of an on-screen cursor. It is a short stick which, like the eponymous aircraft control, is either gripped or operated by the tips of the fingers and can be moved in all compass directions. An example of a joystick is given in Figure 4.13.

Because small movements of the stick become enlarged when translated to a cursor, it is difficult to achieve accuracy in this manner. The stick may also fall slightly if it were left tilted. For these reasons the joystick is not used to give absolute positions but relative ones. It is also sprung so that it returns to its central position when released. The movement of the stick can be used to cause the cursor to move in the same relative direction and to stop moving when the stick is back in the middle. The movement of the stick is used to give a direction and the size of the movement is used to control the speed that the cursor moves. In this manner accurate positioning is possible.

A common use of joysticks on personal computers is to control features in games – particularly flight simulations – where the movement of a character or object is controlled in a similar manner to that just described for cursor control.

Some joysticks employ a third degree of movement in that the joystick can be twisted. Like the normal movements, the twisting can be absolute, like turning an ordinary rotary control, or it may return to a central position upon release. Most joystick units, like mice and trackballs, will also sport one or more buttons.

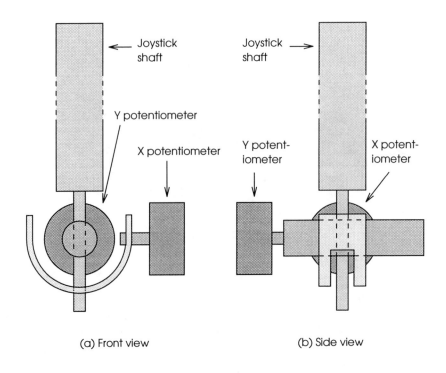

(a) Front view   (b) Side view

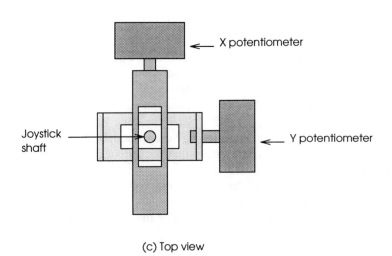

(c) Top view

Figure 4.13 *A joystick*

Many joysticks work by turning two potentiometers which are at right angles to each other. These are analogue joysticks. The two potentiometers are read to obtain X and Y coordinates. The mechanics of achieving this are shown in Figure 4.13 which displays three views of the way in which the joystick shaft connects with the two potentiometers' controlling spindles. The shaft narrows when it enters the joystick unit's casing so that it can pass through the (enlarged) spindle of one of the potentiometers. In Figure 4.13 this is the spindle of the Y potentiometer. Looking at Figure 4.13(a) left/right movements of the shaft will turn that Y potentiometer's spindle. The narrowed joystick shaft then continues through a semicircular strip which has a hole in it sufficient to allow the movement just described.

The view in Figure 4.13(b) is at ninety degrees to that in Figure 4.13(a) and looks directly down the spindle of the other potentiometer – the X potentiometer. In Figure 4.13(b) a left/right movement will move the X potentiometer's spindle and, as is more clear in Figure 4.13(c) which is a view from the top, the first hole that the shaft went through is sufficiently long to permit this movement. This left/right movement in Figure 4.13(b) moves the semicircular strip which is connected to the (shortened) spindle of the X potentiometer.

Movements of the joystick shaft in any direction will, in general, cause both potentiometers' spindles to turn, as is perhaps clearer in the view down the joystick shaft from above in Figure 4.13(c). A voltage is presented to the centre terminal of both potentiometers. The two end terminals of each potentiometer are read to obtain the X and Y values. If a button is present then this same voltage is applied to the button's switch and the other side of the switch is read. Then the cable to the joystick contains:

- voltage out
- two X voltage returns (analogue values)
- two Y voltage returns (analogue values)
- one voltage return for each button (digital on/off value).

The joystick just described is an analogue joystick, as it provides an analogue (continuous) voltage to specify the X and Y positions. Digital joysticks also exist and, instead of moving the spindles of two potentiometers, they operate discrete switches. For this reason they are sometimes referred to as *joyswitches*. The joystick shaft is moved in the same way as before but now makes contact with four switches positioned at the top, bottom, left and right locations in the unit's case. Some have eight positions for greater resolution of direction. The types with four switches are arranged so that, for example, in the North-West position, both the North and the West switches are activated and so eight different directions are possible. A similar arrangement with the eight switch variety gives sixteen discrete values for the joystick direction.

This digital joystick facility is alternately provided by a pad of four pressure switches arranged at the four compass positions. This produces the same information as the digital joystick and, by pressing two adjacent switches simultaneously, a total of eight directions can be input.

▶ 4.4 Flatbed Input

The previous section discussed devices which give relative positional information. This section is concerned with tablet or *flatbed* devices which are generally used to give absolute positional information. First a variety of tablet writing devices is discussed, and then scanning devices which input existing graphics are described.

4.4.1 Tablets

A tablet is a flat surface whose area is addressed as a series of discrete regular X and Y coordinates. The area varies from the order of a few inches square, suitable for an electronic notebook or laptop computer, to the size of a large desk. The larger tablet may be used for inputting maps or architectural designs. In between are tablets just under two feet square which are popular with computer graphics designers.

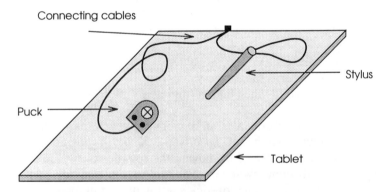

Figure 4.14 *A tablet and locating devices*

The general features of these devices are shown in Figure 4.14. In that figure are the two main locating devices – the *stylus* and the *puck*. Although both are present in the figure, only one would normally be used for a particular application. Both the stylus and the puck include buttons which, when pressed, cause the tablet coordinate of the current location to be transmitted. In some systems, pressing the stylus into the tablet causes a signal to be sent and even the height of the stylus above the tablet can be detected. The stylus points to a position on the tablet. The puck, which resembles a mouse, has a small window with cross-hair locators.

The tablet can be used alone and then the locator would control a screen cursor which mirrors the locator on the screen. This use is common with a stylus for *paintbox* graphics design applications where the computer artist can *draw* on the tablet while watching the result on the screen.

Alternatively a picture on a piece of paper can be attached to the tablet and the locator used to trace the strategic points on the picture so that a computer reconstruction can be made. This is the most common application for the puck and is known as digitizing. With most applications a small region of the tablet is set aside for control functions. A set of small rectangular legends are placed in this area and, when the program which is using the tablet receives a hit in one of these areas, it performs a certain action – such as change the current drawing colour – instead of interpreting the hit as data. This gives the user the freedom to use a a stylus on a tablet almost exclusively with a package, so avoiding the distraction of turning their attention to another device such as the keyboard.

The differences between tablets is how the locator senses its position. The locator normally transmits or receives some signal and is electrically connected to the tablet by a cable. If the locator only transmits then the cable can be dispensed with and a battery used in the locator.

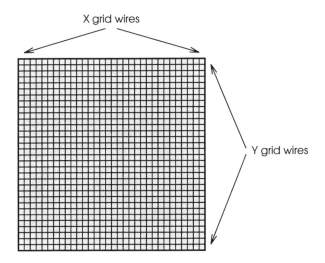

Figure 4.15 *Electromagnetic tablet*

The three main methods used for determining the position of the locator are electromagnetic, sound and pressure. These will now be described in turn, followed by a short discussion on some other less common techniques that are also employed.

The electromagnetic tablet is shown in Figure 4.15. Inside the tablet is a grid of wires. Sequences of electrical pulses are sent down the wires and these induce a voltage in a coil housed inside the stylus. The strength of the induced voltage is used to determine the location of the pulse from each wire and, hence, its absolute position. The overall strength of the induced voltage can also be used to determine how far above the tablet the stylus is. In this way it is possible for the stylus to be swept over the tablet without necessarily coming into contact with it. This feature is useful for computer artists. If the distance is too far – more than about half an inch – then the stylus would be ignored. It can be arranged that signals received in the special areas mentioned above that may be used for control purposes will only be accepted if the stylus is pressed onto the tablet, giving maximum strength signal.

The grid need not be spaced closely in order to obtain high resolution as the exact distance from a wire can be measured quite accurately with this method. A fine grid can, on the other hand, be employed to permit cheaper and less accurate circuitry. Grid spacings typically range from around 0.25 mm to 10 mm.

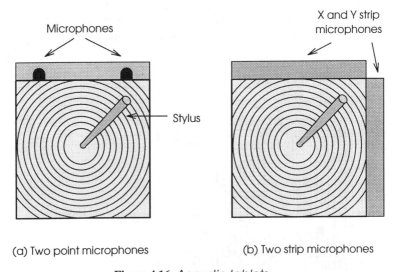

(a) Two point microphones   (b) Two strip microphones

Figure 4.16 *Acoustic tablets*

The second type of tablet described here is the *acoustic tablet* which is also known as the *sonic tablet* and two forms of it are shown in Figure 4.16. With this approach the stylus transmits *ultrasound* information which the tablet receives and so it is possible to use a cordless battery powered stylus. Also, because the tablet itself is not actively participating, any work area will suffice. Ultrasound is sound at frequencies above the human audible range and typical frequencies used are around 40 000 Hz. The stylus regularly emits ultrasound which is picked up by two microphones which are either point microphones as in Figure 4.16(a) or strip microphones as in Figure 4.16(b). The first approach receives the sound from one edge only. The relative strength of the sound in the two microphones is used to pinpoint the source using a triangulation technique. The second approach uses the two strengths of signal received by the X and Y microphones independently to calculate X and Y coordinates.

This form of tablet is convenient for two reasons. Firstly as mentioned above, it is not dependent on a special work area and so can be installed around an object. Secondly it can be used to trace the surface of a thick object such as a book. The book or other object may be too thick for the electromagnetic tablet to respond.

The third type of tablet described here is the pressure tablet. This has a layout similar to the electromagnetic tablet in that there is a grid of X and Y wires. The method used to locate the stylus is similar to that of a keyboard described earlier in this chapter. The grids are separated by a thin perforated membrane and enclosed by a rigid bottom surface and a flexible top surface. The pressure of the stylus on the top surface will cause an X wire to contact a Y wire. The Y wires have a voltage placed on them in turn in a rapid sequence. The X wires are read in order to identify the point in the grid where contact has been made.

Other forms of tablet exist or have been used. One tablet maintains a voltage gradient across the tablet alternately in the X and Y directions. The tablet is made of a resistive (partially conducting) material such as Teledeltos paper. The voltage gradient is rapidly switched between the two X edges and the two Y edges and the two voltages measured on the stylus at those times indicate the X and Y coordinates. For this tablet the stylus must be in electrical contact and so it cannot be used for tracing a diagram on paper. Yet another tablet – the Sylvania tablet – uses a conducting surface. Two high frequency signals are passed across the tablet surface one in the X direction and one in the Y direction. They are different and so distinguishable from each other and they are of the order of 100 kHz. The signals are modulated so that two distinct sequences pass over the surface repeatedly. The stylus contains a coil which picks up the signals and, by reference to the parts of the sequences currently at the transmitting edges, the location of the stylus is obtained.

4.4.2 Scanners

The flatbed input devices just described require manual operation of a stylus or puck to draw an image. Scanners take an image and automatically transform it into a digital bitmap. The scanner is effectively a tablet which senses the intensity and, possibly, colour at each of many points in a rectangular grid. This bitmap can then be manipulated and/or reproduced on a bit-mapped screen or printer.

In addition to a flatbed scanner a cheaper hand held scanner scans one small row of the image at a time and is manually rolled across the picture collecting each row as it is traversed. An even cheaper alternative is a small detector mounted to the printing head of a raster scan printer such as a dot-matrix printer which is capable of printing in graphical mode. The printer is instructed to *print* the page to be scanned with a blank graphical image. The scanning unit is synchronized to the printer's printing action and scans each of a small array of pixels as the printing head *prints* a blank grid. The flatbed scanner and the hand-held scanner will now be described.

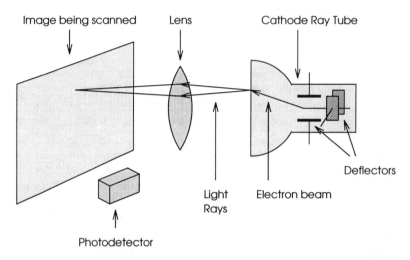

Figure 4.17 *Cathode ray tube scanner*

A flatbed scanner looks similar to a photocopier machine. The image on paper is placed on a glass screen and then the whole page is scanned. One such type of scanner is shown in Figure 4.17. This is a CRT scanner and uses the existing scanning mechanism of a cathode ray tube to scan the image. The image is scanned row by row and each row is divided into a number of pixels. The light of the tube is focused onto the image and, in synchronization with the tube's scanning circuitry, the intensity of the reflected light is measured as each pixel in turn is illuminated.

This scanner is now rarely used and has been all but superseded by other means. One alternative uses the technology of the laser printer, where a laser beam scans the image which is either laid flat or wrapped around a cylinder. The existing laser printer mechanism is readily adapted to make such a scanner. As with the CRT scanner, the intensity of the reflected light is measured as the beam illuminates each pixel.

A more common flatbed scanner is a line scanner whose operation is illustrated by Figure 4.18. This scanner illuminates the whole image and then focusses the light reflected at each pixel onto a photodetector. One whole row or line is scanned at a time and this requires a row of photodetectors – one for each pixel in a row. This row of photodetectors is then used on each row in turn by adjusting the optical system. To achieve dense

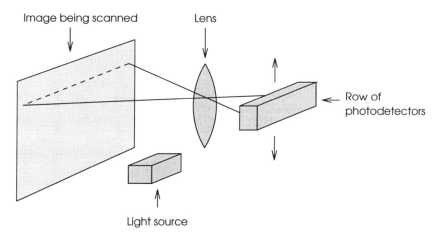

Image being scanned   Lens

Row of photodetectors

Light source

Figure 4.18 *Line scanner*

concentration of pixel scanning, each row may be scanned several times with the row of detectors shifted slightly to one side on each scan.

The scanners described so far have measured the intensity of each pixel. The quality of the scan depends upon two features. Firstly the resolution which is measured in dots (pixels) per inch. The higher the resolution the better the detail that can be stored. Secondly the range of intensities that can be distinguished dictates whether subtle changes in intensity are detected. The intensity is recorded as a digital value and the number of different values used determines this aspect of the scanner's quality.

This intensity is usually quoted as a bit value which is the number of binary digits in the word which contains the intensity. Thus an 8-bit scanner can distinguish 256 (2^8) different levels of intensity – usually referred to as a grey scale. It is generally regarded that a 256 grey scale is sufficient for most purposes as the human eye is believed not to be capable of detecting more levels.

A colour scanner will describe the colour by splitting it into three primary colours and recording the intensity of each primary colour separately. The usual approach is to measure the red, blue and green components for each pixel. This can be done either by scanning the image three times and placing an appropriate colour filter on the photodetectors or replacing each photodetector with three – each with an appropriate filter placed over it permanently.

Using the same argument as was used for grey scale levels, each of the three colour intensities occupies an 8-bit value in order to take a *perfect* recording in colour. Each pixel then requires a total of 24 bits to represent its colour faithfully.

Many colour scanners will use a full 8-bit scale for monochrome and a 24-bit scale for colour but cheaper ones will compromise these values. This is not important for some purposes when, for instance, a grey scale of only a few values is perfectly sufficient. A scale of just two values – black and white – is all that is needed if the only images to be scanned are text.

The resolution of the scanner measured in bits per inch varies with the quality of the unit but is typically in the range of 300 to 2000.

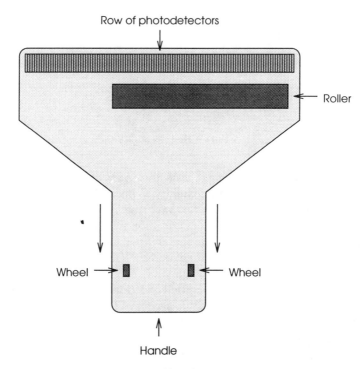

Figure 4.19 *Hand scanner*

A cheaper scanner is the hand scanner as shown in Figure 4.19. The figure shows the underside of the scanning unit. The unit is placed on an image and then moved along it. The width of image that can be scanned is restricted to the width of the scanner. There is a row of photodetectors at the head of the unit and an internal light which illuminates the image. Each photodetector measures a separate pixel on the current row. This can be achieved either with an optical arrangement or by placing each detector at the end of short tube.

Parallel to this row of detectors is a roller and this rotates as the scanner is drawn along the image. Its position is measured in the same manner as the rollers in a mechanical mouse. As each small unit of rotation is measured, this correspond to a row of the image and the photodetectors are quickly sampled. Given the *snapshot* effect of this process the speed with which the scanner is moved can be varied but, as a finite time is taken to record each of the photodetectors' values, there is a maximum rate that the scanner can handle. A photograph may be scanned in a matter of about a second or less. The resolution of hand scanners is restricted by how close together the detectors can be placed, and 300 dots per inch is typical. The flatbed scanners, as mentioned above, can scan down the image several times after moving the detectors slightly and hence achieve higher resolutions.

Very high resolutions are often quoted for scanners but often this is a result of software enhancement and the true physical resolution is actually much lower. The enhancement is achieved by techniques which interpolate between pairs of pixels to fill in some more pixels between them.

▶ 4.5 Three-Dimensional Input

The previous two sections describe two-dimensional positional input devices. This section is concerned with devices which can be used to convey three-dimensional positional information. The two-dimensional digitizing devices such as the puck and pen have their three-dimensional digitizing partners which use similar methods of conveying the information. Some of the main devices are now discussed.

4.5.1 3D Pen Position Sensor

A 3D pen position sensor operates like the pen on a digitizing tablet in that its tip is placed on a location of interest and then a button pressed to activate the capture and input of the coordinates of the tip. It is used to input the three-dimensional coordinates of any solid object so that object can be reconstructed in the computer, manipulated and displayed.

A common device is the Polhemus sensor which uses electromagnetic sensing. Three electromagnetic transmitters are arranged in mutually orthogonal directions. Similarly there are three orthogonal receivers – usually in the pen but the roles can be reversed. The three transmitters can use different frequencies to distinguish their signals or they can be pulsed repeatedly in turn. The strength of the three received signals is then used to determine the location of the pen.

Ultrasound can also be used as the locating medium, and such a pen operates in a very similar manner to the ultrasound tablet described in an earlier section, but employing three microphones instead of two.

4.5.2 Data Glove

Three-dimensional sensors are used to sense the position of a variety of objects and their popular applications currently are in the areas of virtual reality. They are used, in combination with other position sensing devices, to produce the data glove.

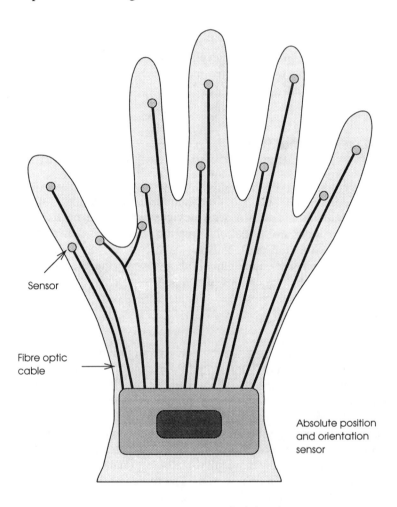

Figure 4.20 A data glove

An example of a data glove is given in Figure 4.20. The data glove transmits positional data about the wearer's hand movements. The user can then manipulate a virtual environment in a truly manual way. In Figure 4.20 the wrist section contains a combined location and orientation sensor. This is a combination of absolute three-dimensional locators which operate using, typically, magnetic or ultrasound signals. The absolute position of the hand can be deduced along with its orientation.

In addition the position of the individual fingers can be transmitted. This requires measuring the angles of the finger joints, and in the example there are twelve sensors measuring these angles. Each finger and the thumb has two sensors measuring two joints on each digit. Two further sensors sense whether the thumb is positioned over the palm and across the first finger or not. There are two popular types of sensor used to achieve this. The example in Figure 4.20 uses fibre optic position sensors. Light is sent down each fibre optic cable from the wrist unit and received at the other end by an optical sensor. Fibre optic cables transmit light even when they are bent, due to internal reflections of the light signal. There is, however, a small loss of light at a bend – especially at a tight bend – and this loss can be measured and translated into a finger movement. In order to achieve greater sensitivity the fibre optic cable can be deliberately down graded at the joints to exaggerate the loss of light.

A second common approach uses a resistive strip of plastic in place of the optic fibre. When bent the resistance increases and a current sent down the strip is used to measure this change of resistance. The material used is mostly mylar which has been painted with a resistive ink.

There is a lot of development in data glove technology, due to its uses in the fast evolving world of virtual reality. Examples of some data gloves in use are the DataGlove from VPL research, the CyberGlove from Virtual Technologies and Mattel's PowerGlove. The first two use fibre optic cables to detect finger movements while the PowerGlove uses resistive strips.

Positional sensors in the world of virtual reality can also be used to detect the location and orientations of the user's head. A combination of these sensors along with the appropriate graphical feedback information creates the illusion of being in a different world or *virtual environment,* and this is discussed further in Chapter 7.

▸ 4.6 Screen Input

This section is concerned with input produced by some sort of interaction with a display screen. In many ways some of the devices described in the previous section, such as the mouse, involve screen interaction as they usually control an on-screen cursor, but the devices described here involve direct physical contact with the screen. The input received is the coordinates of the area of the screen that is chosen. The two common methods are to use a pointing device to touch the relevant small area of the screen and to touch the screen with the user's finger(s).

4.6.1 Light Pen

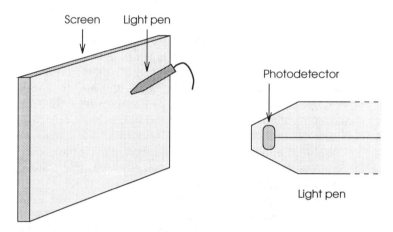

Figure 4.21 *Light pen*

The operation of a light pen is shown in Figure 4.21. The pen contains a photodetector at its tip and detects the light emitted from the screen. It will normally also incorporate a button which, when pressed, causes the current screen position to be read. The circuitry which controls a light pen is connected to the scanning circuitry of the screen. A screen is scanned 50 or 60 times a second and each pixel is refreshed once on each scan. The refreshing of a pixel causes a brief change in intensity and it is this change which the light pen circuitry detects. As it is synchronized to the screen's scanning circuit, the pixel which was just refreshed can be identified and the screen coordinates of the pen are produced.

A problem arises if the area pointed at has no information displayed there. In that case, the light pen cannot work using the method just described. There are three approaches to this. Firstly, the use the pen is put to can dictate that it always refers to a displayed object on the screen. The object in question can be deduced by the underlying user program from the screen coordinates. In this case, valid areas will always be illuminated when pointed at. Secondly, the pen can be used to control a cursor, like that used with a mouse, and the cursor will follow the pen. The cursor is always illuminated and so the pen will always work. Thirdly, when the light pen's button is pressed, a short temporary frame of low intensity can be displayed so that the whole screen is illuminated. This frame will only last for about 1/50 of a second and will hardly be noticeable.

For all practical purposes the light pen has almost been completely superseded by devices such as a mouse. It still finds some applications on large vector graphics screens but its days appear to be numbered.

4.6.2 *Touch Screen*

A touch screen is an ordinary display screen which has something attached so that, when a finger touches the screen, the X and Y coordinates on the screen can be detected. The resolution is clearly low and it is most often used to identify one of a few objects which have been displayed on the screen. Note that, unlike the light pen, there is no direct communication between what is actually being displayed and what the finger touches but simply an X and Y coordinate in a range of up to around 50.

The methods adopted for detection are almost identical to those used in the tablets described in the previous section. Simple touch screens may impose transparent layers of conducting material over the screen which rely on a resistive or capacitive connection to be made by the finger. Such layers will often distort the clarity of the screen and so more sophisticated techniques employing infra-red or ultrasound are used in more sophisticated touch screens.

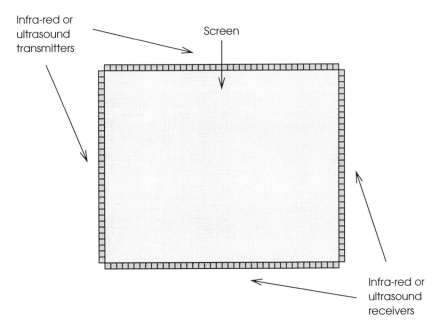

Figure 4.22 *Touch screen*

These touch screens employ a row of transmitters on one side of the screen and a corresponding row of receivers on the other side. The transmitters are continuously sending a signal to their receivers. When the finger touches the screen, one or more receivers no longer receives the signal and the row touched is identified. A similar set of transmitters and receivers is used along the top and bottom edges of the screen in order to identify the screen column. This arrangement is shown in Figure 4.22.

Such screens can be accidentally activated by foreign objects such as insects. A finger perusing the screen prior to selection may activate the screen if it is too close. Because of this, some screens incorporate an additional mechanism akin to the control button on a light pen, where positive pressure is required on the screen in order to be effective. This pressure can be detected by a simple membrane overlaying the screen. Because it only has to detect pressure anywhere on the screen, it can be thin and fully transparent. Unlike the screens described at the start of this section, which also employ overlaid membranes, this simply overlay can be completely unobtrusive.

Touch screens are often employed when a mouse is either inconvenient or too slow. Common uses include displaying keys on the screen to make a simple keyboard which can be readily changed. There may be a set of calculator keys or a list of telephone numbers to select. Some retailers use a touch screen with a variety of menus to allow a single unit to be used as an ordering device and a till. Other applications include selecting items such as stocks or foreign currency to buy or sell. The touch screen lends itself well to the sometimes frenetic activity in such dealing rooms.

5

Disc and Tape Storage

▶ 5.1 Introduction

From the earliest computers of the late 1940s, the store which holds programs and data has been divided into a main store and a backing store.
The main store is typically semiconductor memory and is fast but relatively expensive. It normally only retains its information while power is
connected. Backing store is slower, usually much larger, and retains its
information even when the power is disconnected. Backing store usually
consists of disks and tapes, on which information is recorded either magnetically or optically. The first type of backing store was the *magnetic
drum* as shown in Figure 5.1.

The magnetic drum is not in use in modern computer systems but its
simplicity serves as a useful introduction to modern magnetic stores which
use the same principles. The drum has a magnetic surface formed from
material such as iron oxide and revolves continuously. Local areas of magnetism are produced on the surface by small electromagnets known as
read/write heads. These heads can later read back the magnetically coded
information. The magnetization can be in one of two directions – north or
south – and these can be used to represent 0s and 1s. Each head covers
one small area around the circumference of the drum which is known as a
track. The example shown in Figure 5.1 has fixed heads – each permanently covering one track. Drums can also use just one read/write head
which can move up and down the drum's length. It is moved to the desired
track prior to writing to or reading from the drum. Movable heads are common on modern disk drives. This reduces the cost of the unit, as fewer
heads are required, but it introduces a time delay while the head is positioned on the required track. Another reason for employing movable heads
is that modern magnetic surfaces can cope with a very small track width,
which is much smaller than the head and its associated mounting, and so it
is not physically possible to dedicate a head to each track unless the heads
are arranged in a staggered manner.

Nowadays the most common formats for storage are disks and tapes.
Their shapes are very similar to audio records and tapes. It was from the
audio industry's existing technology that the equipment and expertise to
design digital magnetic tapes and disks first became available. While the
evolution of magnetic disks and tapes then continued separately from the

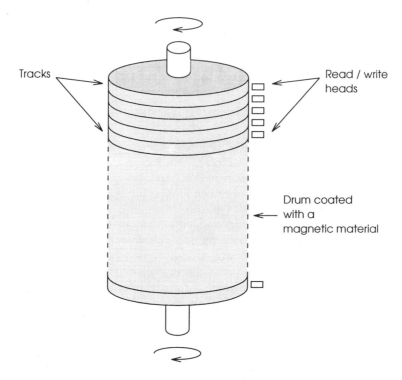

Figure 5.1 *Old style magnetic drum storage*

audio industry, the two have subsequently rejoined forces, with the use of compact discs to provide storage on *CD-ROMs,* and the use of both 8 mm video tape and digital audio tape (DAT) for mass storage of data for archiving purposes.

In the following sections there is an account of recording methods and coding techniques. Following that, the physical formats of disks and tapes will be described. It is convenient to describe magnetic devices first and then optical devices. Within these two groups, the physical forms of disk and tape are dealt with separately. In order to avoid repetition where possible, those methods and techniques which apply to more than one format will be described in the first appropriate section and then only referred back to in subsequent sections. Magnetic and optical storage devices require sophisticated interfaces to a computer system and the more common interfaces are explored. Finally, file formats and storage performance enhancers such as *caches* and *compression* techniques are explained.

The naming convention used for disks should be explained here. The word *disk* is used when the unit (which is disc shaped) is a computer storage unit. The word *disc* is used in the audio context such as 'compact disc' and as a more general physical description.

▶ 5.2 Recording on a Magnetic Surface

Information is stored on a magnetic surface as a sequence of magnetized *cells*, with each being magnetized in one direction (north say) or in the opposite direction (south). The process is illustrated in Figure 5.2.

To start with, it is convenient to consider the recording as being a sequence of fixed sized cells. The full truth is that a cell as described here, is the minimum distance achievable before a change in magnetic direction between north and south (a *flux reversal)* can occur. Both the writing head and the reading head consist of a circular *core* made of a material with a low *magnetic reluctance.* Magnetic reluctance is a measure of how much resistance there is for a *magnetic flux* to flow. It is alternatively described as having a high *magnetic permeability.* Permeability is simply an alternate measure and is inversely proportional to reluctance. A coil of wire is wrapped around the core. If a current is passed through the coil then a magnetic flux flows around the core. The direction that the flux flows in depends upon the direction of the electrical current. Similarly, if a flux is produced in the core by passing the head over a magnetized surface then a current is induced in the coil. Again, the direction of the magnetization and electrical current are directly related. In order to interact with the magnetic surface, a small gap is required in the core. This gap can be simply left open to the air or, more usually, filled with a material of high magnetic reluctance. Without this gap, flux would flow almost entirely within the core and would not be induced by passing the core over a magnetized area.

Figure 5.2(a) shows a writing head in the process of magnetizing the surface. Magnetic flux is produced by passing a current I_w through the coil. At the gap, the high magnetic reluctance causes the flux to spread out slightly and flow through the surface. This magnetizes a small area of the surface known as a cell. If the current I_w is reversed, then the cell is magnetized in the opposite direction. The surface is moving and a sequence of cells are written by sending a rapid sequence of current flows through the coil. The spacing of these cells is critical. They should be as small and as close together as possible in order to record a high density of information on the surface. This requires a small head placed very close to the surface. If the cells are too close together, however, then they will interfere with each other. Two adjacent cells with opposite magnetization will try and demagnetize each other if they are sufficiently close. The strength of the magnetization also comes into play here. If the magnetization is weak then cells can be closer before the interference effect is apparent. However, the problem with very low magnetizations is that they are more difficult to detect when the information is subsequently read back.

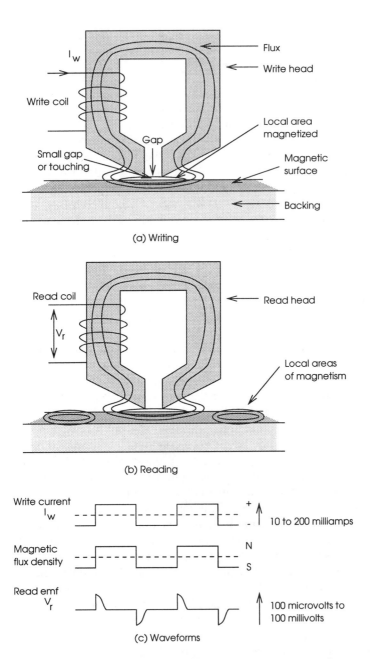

(a) Writing

(b) Reading

(c) Waveforms

Figure 5.2 *Recording on a magnetic surface*

Figure 5.2(b) shows a reading head detecting a magnetized cell. As the surface moves, a flux change in the core is detected by its induced voltage in the coil. The induced voltage V_r is proportional to the rate of flux change, according to Faraday's law. The resulting voltage pulses, as shown in Figure 5.2(c), are then interpreted to give the magnetization direction of each cell as it passes under the reading head.

For writing, the head should have a relatively large gap so that smaller writing currents can be used. The coil should have few turns in order to reduce its inductance and, hence, to permit fast current changes. For reading, a large gap is also desirable for higher efficiency but a large number of turns of the coil is required to maximise the detection of flux changes. A large gap, however, produces larger cells and so a compromise is made between head efficiency and the density of cells on a track. For the size of the coil either a compromise is made, or separate reading and writing heads are used. Most magnetic disk drives use a combined head, while separate heads are more common on magnetic tape units. A typical hard disk core will have a coil with between about 5 and 500 turns and a common gap size is of the order of 50 μm.

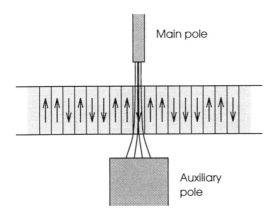

Figure 5.3 *Vertical recording*

This process of recording is known as *horizontal recording* because the cells are magnetized with north and south poles lying across the surface. An alternative process is known as *vertical recording* (or *perpendicular recording)* and this creates magnetic cells through the thickness of the medium, with the north pole on one surface and the south pole on the other. The magnetized columns are substantially narrower than the cells obtained by horizontal recording – typically up to 30 times narrower. However, horizontal recording permits both surfaces to be recorded upon independently, and is technically simpler and cheaper. Vertical recording can be achieved by using two poles, one on each side of the surface as shown in Figure 5.3 or a head can be designed to operate from one side only. Vertical recording is not commonly used as yet because a suitable magnetic medium is difficult to produce, and so no hard disks currently employ this technique. It has been used on some flexible media to create high grade floppy disks and magneto-optical disks.

▶ 5.3 Magnetic Recording Codes

The manner in which information can be recorded onto a magnetic surface was described in the previous section. Information is stored as a sequence of cells on the surface each of which is magnetized either in one direction (north) or in the opposite direction (south). These two states can be interpreted as 0 and 1 respectively and used directly to store digital data with each cell representing one bit. In practice a number of different *recording codes* are used to translate between digital data as a sequence of 0s and 1s and magnetic data as a sequence of norths and souths. Codes are also in data communications as explained in Chapter 8. Indeed there are many similarities between recording and reading data on backing store and sending and receiving data over a communications line. In both cases data is sent at a rate which needs to be synchronized at both ends of the communication.

The reading process must sample the surface at a known rate in order to read each cell. The speed that the surface is moving is known to a high degree of accuracy and the cell density in number of cells per inch is also known accurately. Unfortunately neither is known sufficiently accurately to rely on this information alone. In any case the speed of the surface will vary and it may well be slightly different when data is read from that when that same data was written. This difference will be very small, but when several million cells are stored on one platter only a few inches in diameter, even a very small fluctuation will result in cells being missed or read twice. Figure 5.4 shows the effect upon reading the data if the timing circuitry for sampling cells is running too fast and/or the surface speed is too slow. In this case only sixteen cells have actually been traversed but twenty one have been read as five of them have been sampled twice.

The effect in Figure 5.4 has been grossly exaggerated in order to illustrate it in a small space and, in practice, the discrepancy would be much smaller. The effect would still occur eventually, however small the discrepancy between the timing sample rate and the surface speed. Even a relatively slow device such as a floppy disk drive head, for example, is traversing cells at the rate of many thousands a second and very soon a cell will be read twice or, in the case where the surface is moving at a rate in advance of the sampling rate, a cell will be missed. The way in which this problem is solved is to take the timing not just from some internal electronic circuitry but from the surface itself. The sampling rate is generated

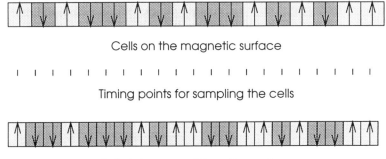

Cells on the magnetic surface

Timing points for sampling the cells

Cell data as read from the surface

Figure 5.4 *Slow surface speed – erroneous data read*

as before but each time a flux reversal is detected – two adjacent cells with opposite magnetization – the clock is resynchronized. The effect of this on the original data from Figure 5.4 is shown in Figure 5.5.

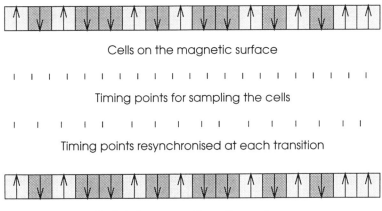

Cells on the magnetic surface

Timing points for sampling the cells

Timing points resynchronised at each transition

Cell data as read from the surface

Figure 5.5 *Data read correctly by resynchronizing the sample rate*

Here the sample rate is corrected and synchronized with the rate dictated by the surface speed whenever a change from north to south or south to north is detected. In the example shown, this results in the data being read correctly, even though there is a large discrepancy between the surface speed and the expected sample rate. The reason that the data appears correctly in Figure 5.5 is that flux reversals occur regularly. There are never any sequences of cells with more then two magnetized in the same direction. If the two states of magnetization directly represent digital data of 0s and 1s then, in actual data, longer sequences of 0s or 1s would be normal. So this method of resynchronization would break down if there were sequences of three or more adjacent cells with the same direction of magnetization. This is shown in Figure 5.6.

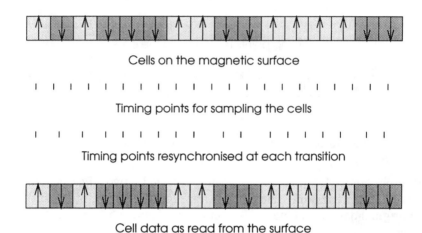

Cells on the magnetic surface

Timing points for sampling the cells

Timing points resynchronised at each transition

Cell data as read from the surface

Figure 5.6 *Data read incorrectly when flux reversals are not sufficiently frequent*

Here the flux reversals do not always occur sufficiently frequently. Even with a small discrepancy a sufficiently long sequence of one direction of magnetization will eventually cause an error in reading. There are two approaches that can be employed to deal with this problem. One is to use a form of encoding which guarantees that a flux reversal will always occur at a minimum frequency that is sufficient to cope with the worst likely discrepancy. The other is to maintain a special track of cells on the surface, running parallel to the data tracks and which contains cells which alternate in direction. This track is a special form of *servo track* and is read by a separate head. The timing can then be taken solely from the servo track. There are three drawbacks to this latter approach. Firstly, it is more expensive to employ two heads and to have them adjusted to stay in exactly the same relative position. Secondly, the servo track is taking up space that could otherwise be used to store data. Thirdly, the surface can deform slightly, leading to a skew between the servo track and the data tracks. While none of these problems is insoluble the servo approach is usually considered too expensive and an encoding method is used in most magnetic backing stores.

There are many possible recording codes, and the more common ones are shown in Figure 5.7. Most of those shown, but not all, guarantee regular flux reversals no matter what the data to be coded is, and so overcome the above problem of synchronization. Those that do are said to be *self-*

clocking codes. Each code is simply a translation of the 0s and 1s which are the bits of the data into norths and souths of the cells. Some codes require one cell for each bit while others require more. For each code shown in Figure 5.7 each column represents one bit but, depending upon the code, up to three cells may be used for each bit. Some of these codes are also used in data communications as described in Chapter 8 and, while only the more advanced ones are now used in magnetic storage coding; the rest are included for completeness. They are described individually below:

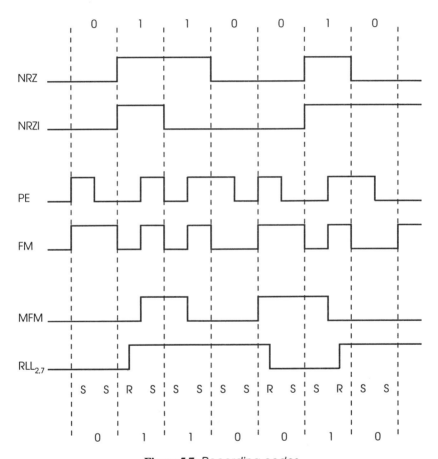

Figure 5.7 *Recording codes*

Non-return to zero (NRZ) is perhaps the most obvious code although it suffers from the fact that it is not self-clocking. A 1 bit is represented by a cell magnetized north and a 0 bit is represented by a cell magnetized south. Its name is based on a similar code called *return to zero (RZ)* where 1s are stored as a pulse of magnetization which quickly returns to no (zero) magnetization.

Non-return to zero invert (NRZI) represents a 1 bit by reversing the current flux direction from north to south or from south to north. A 0 bit is represented by no change of flux direction. Like the NRZ code, it is not self-clocking.

Phase encoding (PE) and *frequency modulation (FM)* are the next pair of codes. Unlike the previous two, flux reversals can occur half-way through one of the *bit columns* of Figure 5.7. They both need two cells for each bit and so can represent only half the data in the same space as the previous two. Their important advantage is that they are self-clocking. It is simpler to visualize each of the columns as holding two magnetic cells each of which can be either north or south. In the illustration then, the PE and FM graphs should be drawn at twice the length to keep to the magnetic surface scale in the NRZ and NRZI graphs. Their names are taken from regarding the information to be stored as a wave which has either its phase or frequency changed.

Phase encoding (PE) represents each bit by both a north and a south flux direction and therefore occupies twice the space of the preceding two codes. A 1 bit is represented by a south flux direction followed by a north flux direction. A 0 bit is represented by a north flux direction followed by a south flux direction.

Frequency modulation (FM) like the PE code requires twice the space of the simpler codes. There is always a flux reversal at the beginning of a bit coding. For a 1 bit there is an additional flux reversal half-way through the bit coding. Put another way, 0 bits are recorded at one wave frequency and 1 bits are recorded at double that frequency.

The final two codes are modified frequency modulation (MFM) and run length limited (RLL). With these codes and especially with RLL, the simplistic view of the surface as a series of discrete magnetic cells is not sufficient. The reading head in practice detects the current flux state (north or south) and the location of reversals. The head circuitry can locate the position of a reversal very accurately. The magnetic media however can only accurately record data if the distance between reversals is no less than a given minimum. This minimum depends both upon the quality of the surface and head and the gap size between the surface and the head. Thus reversals can occur at almost any point on the surface and not at arbitrary cell units as previously described. The only restriction is that the code employed does not require a reversal too soon after the previous reversal. This point will become clearer under the discussion of RLL.

Modified frequency modulation (MFM) as its name suggests is an adaptation of the FM code. It is sometimes called *Miller coding* after its inventor. It is the same as the FM code except that the flux reversal at the beginning of each bit coding is present only if the current and previous bits are 0s. This guarantees that only one flux reversal is required for each bit and so requires only the same space as the simpler NRZ and NRZI codes. MFM and the following RLL codes are the most common codes used on magnetic disks and most magnetic tapes.

Run length limited (RLL) is a general set of codes which specify a minimum and maximum distance – *run* – between flux reversals. The maximum length ensures that flux reversals are sufficiently frequent that the code is still self-clocking. The minimum length can permit high density of coding. RLL code is similar to a coding method called *group coded recording (GCR)*. This groups bits into equal length small sequences and assigns a (slightly longer) code to each sequence. The code assigned ensures that a long sequence of 0s or 1s cannot arise. The newly assigned code can then be recorded using a space efficient coding such as NRZI. For example, each group of 4 bits can be assigned a 5-bit code as shown in Table 5.1. Because each 5-bit code includes at least one 0 and one 1, the code is self-clocking. In the example given there is a minimum run of 0s or 1s of 1 but a maximum length of consecutive 0s or 1s of 8.

Table 5.1 *Group coded recording*

4-bit data	5-bit code
0 0 0 0	1 1 0 0 1
0 0 0 1	1 1 0 1 1
0 0 1 0	1 0 0 1 0
0 0 1 1	1 0 0 1 1
0 1 0 0	1 1 1 0 1
0 1 0 1	1 0 1 0 1
0 1 1 0	1 0 1 1 0
0 1 1 1	1 0 1 1 1
1 0 0 0	1 1 0 1 0
1 0 0 1	0 1 0 0 1
1 0 1 0	0 1 0 1 0
1 0 1 1	0 1 0 1 1
1 1 0 0	1 1 1 1 0
1 1 0 1	0 1 1 0 1
1 1 1 0	0 1 1 1 0
1 1 1 1	0 1 1 1 1

This GCR code is also called *modified NRZI (MNRZI)*. Any code is, in fact, an RLL code. RLL is simply the description of a code in terms of the minimum and maximum distance between flux reversals although the name RLL is usually reserved in the literature to describe the particular coding method described below. The MNRZI code in Table 5.1 has a minimum length of 0s or 1s in a sequence of 1 – sequences such as 010 and 101 can occur. It has a maximum sequence of 8 – for example the 5-bit code 01111 followed by the code 11110 produces a sequence of 0111111110. It can therefore be called a $RLL_{1,8}$ code. Its benefit is that it uses a relatively short maximum length, which keeps it self-clocking. It has an additional benefit in that only 16 of the possible 32 5-bit codes are assigned and an error in reading/writing may produce one of the unassigned codes, which can then be detected as erroneous. GCR is commonly used on magnetic tape cartridges. The particular code normally indicated by the term RLL is an $RLL_{2,7}$ code. It groups bits into sequences of 2, 3 and 4 bits and for each of these sequences a code is assigned which is twice as long. The sequence is described as a series of *S-codes* and *R-codes* to avoid confusion between 0s and 1s. An S-code or *space* code is one of the first two shown in Figure 5.8 while an R-code or *reversal* code is either of the second two in the figure. Which of the two is chosen depends on the current flux direction.

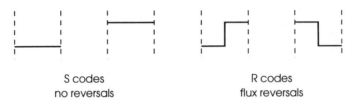

S codes
no reversals

R codes
flux reversals

Figure 5.8 *The four RLL S- and R-codes*

The coding is shown in Table 5.2 where each of the seven bit sequences is expanded to an S/R sequence twice its length.

Table 5.2 $RLL_{2,7}$ *code*

Bit sequence	S/R-code sequence
10	S R S S
11	R S S S
000	S S S R S S
010	R S S R S S
011	S S R S S S
0010	S S R S S R S S
0011	S S S S R S S S

$RLL_{2,7}$ guarantees that there will be at least two S-codes (no reversal) between two R-codes. At the other extreme, there are no more than seven S-codes between R-codes. The former is guaranteed because there are no single S-codes in a sequence and all sequences end in two S-codes. The latter is guaranteed because there are no such sub-sequences within any of the seven sequences and no sequence starts with more than four S-codes nor ends in more than three S-codes. This gives a reasonable self-clocking mechanism. A minimum sequence of two S-codes is shown in Figure 5.9.

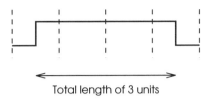

Total length of 3 units

Figure 5.9 *Minimum flux reversal in* $RLL_{2,7}$

Note that, because reversals occur half-way through an R-code, the two R-codes contribute half their length each to the total length occurring between actual reversals. The total minimum length is then the length of three R/S-codes. Thus the length of an S- or R-code can be one-third of the minimum length that the surface allows between reversals – previously referred to as a magnetic cell.

To summarize then, $RLL_{2,7}$ first doubles the apparent length of the original binary data by assigning two S/R codes to each data bit. However, each of these S/R-codes is one-third of the length of a magnetic cell and so three S/R-codes can occupy the space of one cell. As two S/R-codes are needed for each data bit, the length of a magnetic cell is now effectively holding one-and-a-half data bits. The best that any of the other codes can achieve is a data bit for the length of a magnetic cell and so $RLL_{2,7}$ can store 50% more data than NRZ, NRZI or MFM.

Because of the coding used by RLL, any error in reading the flux changes can propagate itself for several bits until the coding recovers. The same is true but to a lesser extent with MFM. RLL controllers use a sophisticated error correcting algorithm as a result, and need to store slightly more redundancy information in the blocks' trailers than would otherwise be required. This fact unfortunately was overlooked in the early days of using RLL on magnetic disks, when an RLL code was substituted for MFM coding without boosting the error detection and correction codes. The problem was not, as some of the literature states, a case of trying to squeeze more flux reversals into the same space. The density of flux reversals in RLL coding is no more than that of MFM coding. It is because RLL coding is more context sensitive that an error has a larger effect and therefore a larger correction scheme is needed. There are other forms of RLL coding than the $RLL_{2,7}$ described here although $RLL_{2,7}$ is currently the most common. Others in use include $RLL_{1,7}$ and $RLL_{3,9}$ which are alternatively referred to as advanced RLL (ARLL).

The codes shown in Figure 5.7 give the relationship between flux reversals and bits. In order to show the space occupied on a magnetic surface, Figure 5.10 shows the same codes scaled appropriately, and also summarizes their features.

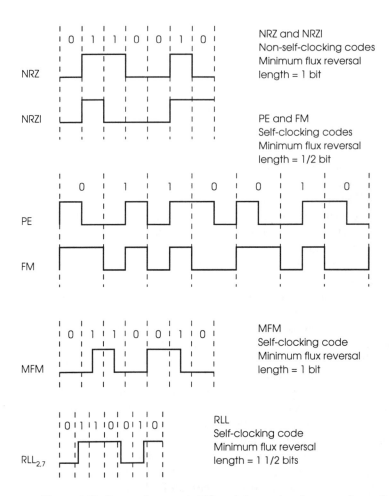

Figure 5.10 *Recording codes shown to scale of magnetic surface use*

▶ 5.4 Magnetic Disks

The two most common types of magnetic disk are *floppy disks* and *hard disks*. Floppy disks can usually be removed from the drive mechanism. There exist hard disks that are also removable, but the most common form has several disk surfaces permanently fixed within the drive mechanism. This is because the critical spacing between a hard disk surface and the read/write head means that a sealed unit is necessary if the unit is to be used in a normal home or office environment. There is also the less common *Bernoulli disk,* which is a hybrid version of the floppy disk and the hard disk. These three types of disk are described in this section. Another form of magnetic disk is the *magneto-optical* disk which, as its name suggests, uses both magnetic and optical techniques. This disk is described after the sections on optical disks.

5.4.1 Magnetic floppy disks

The two common formats of floppy disk are shown in Figure 5.11. Both contain a flexible (floppy) disk made of mylar and coated with a magnetic surface such as ferric oxide.

The first type, in Figure 5.11(a), has a flexible outer sleeving or jacket. The first floppy disk was developed by IBM in the 1960s and was of this type, using a disk which was eight inches in diameter. The size used now is $5^{1}/_{4}$ inches in diameter, and currently these disks have capacities up to 1.2 MB. The disk surface is exposed in three places. Firstly, the centre of the disk is gripped by a mechanism in the drive unit in order to spin the disk. Secondly, the area of the disk that has information recorded on it is accessed through a radial opening. Finally, a small circular hole in the jacket is used to detect the *index hole* which is a small circular hole in the disk itself, which provides a physical index marker for positional information. On the right hand side of the jacket is a notch called the *write protect slot*. This is normally left uncovered and the disk can then be written to as well as read from. If it is covered up, then a sensor in the drive mechanism detects this, and writing will not be permitted. This flexible jacket floppy disk is rapidly being superseded by the rigid jacket shown in Figure 5.11(b).

The rigid jacket floppy disk is totally enclosed and is most commonly $3^{1}/_{2}$ inches in diameter. A typical capacity is up to 1.44 MB but a rarer, more dense, version exists at 2.88 MB. The physical size of this disk was chosen to be convenient for carrying (it is said that its size is based on the typical dimension of a shirt pocket). It is robust because no part of the disk surface is exposed and so, unlike the flexible jacket version, it does not need a separate outer cover. The rigid jacket also prevents damage to the disk from most minor accidents. A further design feature means that it is not possible to insert this type of disk into the disk drive the wrong way round. There is a sliding protective metal cover at the top of the jacket. This is slid back automatically when the disk is loaded into the drive unit to expose the magnetic surface. Instead of a write protect slot there is a plastic slider which can reveal a hole in the jacket on the bottom left. The convention here is that the hole is normally covered. Revealing the hole will not permit any writing to the floppy disk. On the right hand side there can be another hole (with no slider). If this hole is present, then this indicates that it is a high capacity disk, on which information can be stored at a much greater density.

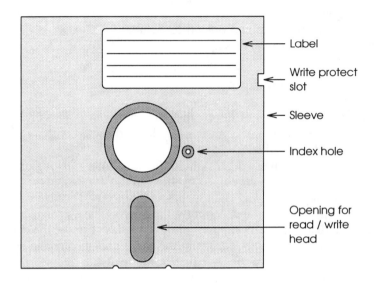

(a) Flexible jacket floppy disk

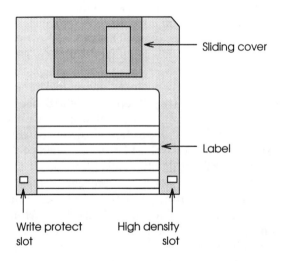

(b) Rigid jacket floppy disk

Figure 5.11 *Floppy disk formats*

Both formats of floppy disk are rotated at around 360 rpm. Their drive units have either one head (single sided) or two heads (double sided). The heads are in contact with the disk surface while the disk is in the drive unit, which makes the floppy disk similar to magnetic tape. In hard disk units a very small gap is maintained between the head and the disk surface. This gap requires an extremely high precision in the manufacture of both the drive unit and the magnetic surface. The contact method used by the floppy disk avoids the higher cost of production, but has two main drawbacks. Firstly, the magnetic surface is gradually worn away by the head. Eventually the floppy disk surface is worn away so much that it can no longer store data correctly, although this would require constant use of the disk for a considerable amount of time. More importantly, the small pieces worn away from the surface stick to the head, and so the head needs regular cleaning. This is usually performed by a special cleaning floppy disk. This drawback is lessened considerably by the fact that the drive unit only activates the motor used to rotate the disk when information is actually being read/written.

When the floppy has not been accessed for a time (typically a few seconds) the motor is turned off. When the floppy disk is next required then the motor is turned back on to spin the disk surface. This results in a small initial delay.

The second drawback is that, with the head in contact with the surface, the disk can only be rotated at relatively slow speeds – about six times a second – and this means that information is read/written much more slowly than on, say, a hard disk drive.

Floppy disks are used on small systems with no hard disk and for distributing software from one machine to another. They are sometimes used for *archiving* where copies of files from the hard disk unit are taken in case of failure, but this task is normally performed using magnetic tape.

5.4.2 Magnetic hard disks

Hard disks or *rigid disks* as they are sometimes called are used in most computer systems as the main form of backing store or file-store. They have much larger capacities than floppy disks and can read and write data at far higher speeds.

A disk surface is usually made of aluminium, coated with either a ferric oxide material or a metal alloy. The metal alloy surface is more precise and thinner than the oxide equivalent, with the main constituents commonly in use being nickel and cobalt.

Hard disks rely on precise engineering to maintain a small gap between the head and the surface. This contact free method avoids the drawbacks of the floppy disk contact method, and permits information to be stored at a very high density and at a much faster speed. The gap between the head and the surface can be as small as around 0.1 μm. This is so small that objects such as hair, dust particles or even fingerprints would seriously interfere with the operation of the disk if they were to come into contact with the surface.

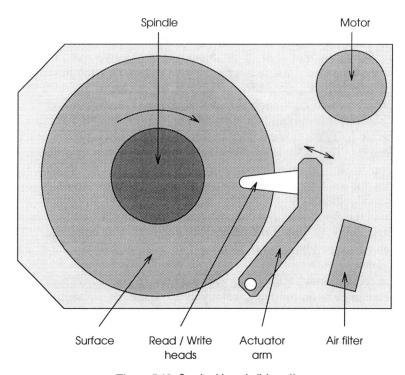

Spindle   Motor

Surface   Read / Write   Actuator   Air filter
                heads   arm

Figure 5.12 *Sealed hard disk unit*

Older disk units permitted the use of removable surfaces as floppy disk drives still do. The surfaces were kept in special dust free containers and the unit itself was kept in a clean air environment – usually in a special machine room. Modern disk units are sealed so that air can only enter through a filter. Such surfaces are not removable but the very high capacities of these units means that this is not so important. A typical layout of a sealed unit is shown in Figure 5.12. The disk has a coating on both of its surfaces and is spun continuously by the motor – there is no *startup* delay with each access of the disk as with a floppy disk. The disk heads (one for each side) are moved by an *actuator arm* to access different tracks. In order to increase capacity, there are usually several platters in the same drive, each with their two heads connected to the same actuator arm. This is illustrated in Figure 5.13.

Typical speeds of rotation for hard disks are 3600 rpm, 5400 rpm and 7200 rpm. These speeds are about ten to twenty times faster than a floppy disk. Typical diameters of hard disks are 5¼ and 3½ inches but even smaller diameters are used for disks which are destined for use in small portable or laptop computers.

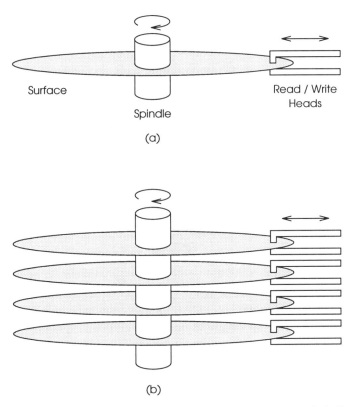

Figure 5.13 *Hard disk surfaces: (a) one platter (b) several platters*

5.4.3 *Bernoulli disk*

The Bernoulli disk combines the advantages of the floppy disk and the hard disk. The disks, like floppy disks, are flexible and removable. Like a hard disks, they are read and written by a head which is close to, but not touching, the surface. This is achieved using the Bernoulli principle which is illustrated in Figure 5.14.

The flexible magnetic disk is held below a rigid metal disc and when stationary, as in Figure 5.14(a), the flexible disk flexes down from the metal disc. When spinning, as in Figure 5.14(b), the disk stays at a small and constant distance from the metal disc. The head is mounted in the metal disc and moves radially. Because the disk surface is flexible, it takes on the shape of the head as it moves so that contact-free reading and writing is possible. The disk surface will also flex over other obstructions such as dust particles without touching, and so a completely sealed unit is not necessary.

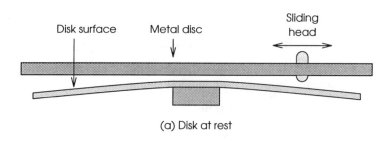

(a) Disk at rest

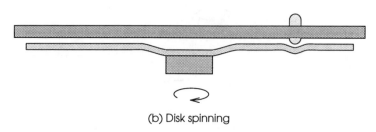

(b) Disk spinning

Figure 5.14 *Bernoulli disk operation*

The disk rotates at speeds comparable with hard disks and the head-to-surface gap is also similar. The disk surface is the same size as a 5¼ inch floppy disk and has a capacity of between 200–300 MB.

▶ 5.5 Magnetic Disk Formats

5.5.1 Surfaces, Sectors, Tracks, Blocks and Cylinders

A disk or platter is a circular object with two surfaces. Normally information is stored on both surfaces although some older floppy disks use only one of the surfaces. Hard disk units usually include several platters as shown in Figure 5.13(b). Each surface is further divided into units in which data and other organisational information is stored. This information is stored on tracks. A track is one or more magnetic cells wide and the disk reading or writing head is positioned over one particular track at a time. The spacing between tracks is usually several times the width of the track in order to facilitate track location. Each track is then further divided into *sectors*. This division is shown in Figure 5.15.

This structure is typical of magnetic surfaces. A series of concentric circular tracks is recorded on the surface. Each track is divided into equal

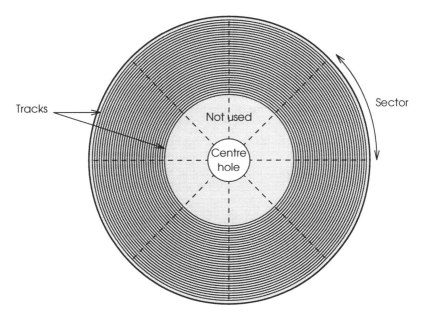

Figure 5.15 *Tracks and sectors on a disk surface*

sized lengths by sectoring. Tracks near the edge of the disk are longer than tracks nearer the centre, but each track, however, stores the same amount of information and is traversed by the head in the same time. This means that the information is packed more densely in inner tracks and the innermost track is coded at the maximum possible density the medium will permit. Conversely this implies that all other tracks are coded less densely than they can accommodate and thus space is wasted. For this reason the innermost track stops well short of the centre of the disk. Later in this section a technique of *zoning* is described which makes more efficient use of the available space.

In the example shown in Figure 5.15 there are 32 tracks and 8 sectors. On a real magnetic surface there would be many more tracks. Typically, a floppy disk contains of the order of 100 tracks and a hard disk over 1000. A floppy disk would normally be split into between 8 and 18 sectors, although some formats use over 30 sectors. Again, a hard disk may well be divided into many more sectors, due to the much greater concentration of recording which a hard disk permits.

A unit of information on a surface then has an address consisting of two components – a track number and a sector number. Within each unit there is space for, typically, 128, 512 or 1024 bytes and this is the minimum sized unit of communication between the computer and the disk. It could be argued that the sector size should be much smaller so that individual bytes could be addressed as with conventional memory. There are two principal reasons why that is not the case.

Firstly, there is the additional control and positional information that is recorded on the surface. This information is required for each track and for each sector. If each byte of data were to have such information associated with it, then most of the disk space would be occupied by control information instead of user data.

Secondly, consider the process of accessing one byte of information. A disk may be able to transfer information at a very large rate but, before commencing this transfer, two processes are necessary. The head has first to be positioned over the required track. This is called *seeking* and the time it takes is the *seek time*. While a head can be moved relatively quickly the seek time is still large compared to the transfer rate. The disk unit must then wait for the required sector of that track to appear under the head. On average, half of a revolution of the surface will occur here. The time lag this creates is called *latency*. The combined time of seeking and latency is several orders of magnitude larger than the time to transfer one byte and dominates the actual transfer rate achievable. If more than one byte is transferred then the effective transfer rate is increased in proportion. That is, given that the dominant time involved is for seeking and latency, a unit of 512 bytes can be effectively read/written in the same time as a unit of one byte.

This unit of transfer – one sector of one track – is often called a *block* although it is also often confusingly referred to as a sector. What is really meant is a particular sector of the current track. A large block size increases the effective efficiency of the surface. However, given that it is the minimum sized unit, space will be wasted when a smaller size is actually required. A file on the disk will occupy a whole number of blocks, and the last block of a file will, in general, be only partially used. On average, therefore, the last block will be half used and so if a surface stores, for example, 1000 files, the equivalent of 500 blocks will be unused.

To summarize, a compromise is made when choosing a block size. A large size makes disk access more efficient, but a small size wastes less space. The equation is not quite that simple because, as described above, there is additional control information stored on the disk for each track and each sector and therefore, for each block. The amount of information is much the same regardless of the block size, and so this moves the strength of the argument more in favour of large block sizes. The most common block size is 512 bytes.

Finally there is one more unit of information that can be referred to when describing disks – the *cylinder*. A disk unit either has one or many platters as shown in Figure 5.13. Even with only one platter there are two surfaces and, normally, each surface can be read at the same time, as each has its own associated head. The heads are moved in unison, so at any given time they are all positioned over the same numbered track on their surfaces. Collectively, all the tracks – one per surface – that are addressed simultaneously in this way are termed a cylinder. This is illustrated in

Figure 5.16, where four platters are shown. Each corresponding set of eight tracks on the eight surfaces make up a cylinder. In the illustration only the four tracks on the four upper surfaces are visible. The other (obscured) four tracks are on each of the four lower surfaces.

A cylinder is a useful notion when considering the efficiency of using a disk. The disk stores individual blocks. The user will store information as a set of files. A file is a sequence of blocks and it is the responsibility of the operating system to keep track of which blocks, and in which order, comprise each file. Access to the disk often involves reading or writing a file sequentially. If large sequences of the blocks of a file can be stored on the same cylinder, then little head movement is needed when reading or writing the file. As head movement accounts for most of the transfer time, this results in a considerable performance gain. Some disk units can read from each surface simultaneously and so the gain can be even greater. The ability to read from each surface simultaneously is, however, rare as it requires the duplication of much circuitry.

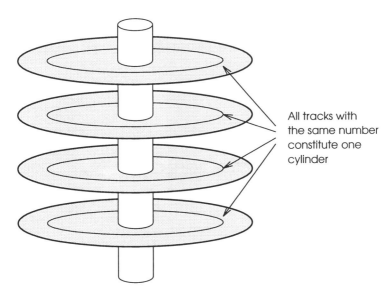

All tracks with the same number constitute one cylinder

Figure 5.16 *A cylinder – each surface's corresponding track*

In order to bring together the relationships between surfaces, sectors, tracks, blocks, and cylinders consider again the example in Figure 5.13(b). This disk unit has four platters and so eight surfaces. Assume that each surface has 2048 tracks and is divided into 32 sectors, then there are 32 × 2048 blocks on each surface or a total in the entire unit of 8 × 32 × 2048 blocks (524 288). Each block contains 512 bytes (half a kilobyte) and so the unit has a capacity of 256 MB. The features of this example disk unit are summarized in Table 5.3.

Table 5.3 *Example of statistics of a disk unit*

4	Platters
8	Surfaces
32	Sectors / surface
256	Sectors
2048	Tracks / surface
16 384	Tracks
2048	Cylinders
65 536	Blocks / surface
524 288	Blocks
512	Bytes / block
256	Megabytes capacity

Note that, in computing circles, 1 k is 1024 and not 1000. Also, 1 M is 1024 × 1024 which is 1 048 576 and not 1 000 000. Most disk manufacturers quote disk sizes in *megabytes* which are actually 1 000 000 bytes. The example in Table 5.3 would therefore be quoted as having a capacity of 268 MB. This means that a disk actually holds almost 5% less information than might be expected. Actually the situation is worse than that because some disk units quoted capacity includes the space required for control information to be stored, so further inflating the apparent size.

5.5.2 *Zoning*

In the previous section it was noted that, because each track is divided into the same number of sectors, outer tracks are coded at a much lower densities than they are capable of. With a spiral track, the density of coding is often kept constant and so the number of sectors in each revolution is continuously reducing as the centre of the disk is approached. This makes the notion of a track a little vague but does make efficient use of the surface. A technique based on this principle is that of *zoning* and is illustrated by Figure 5.17.

In this example, the surface has been divided into three different zones. Within a zone the number of sectors is constant. Outer zones contain more sectors for each track and so more of the surface is utilised. There is an additional advantage to zoning. The outer zones contain more sectors than normal, but each track is still read at the same rate. Sectors in outer zones can therefore be read more quickly, and the most commonly used blocks can be placed in outer zones in order to take most advantage of this feature.

The disk controller needs to be more sophisticated to cope with zoning because information about each sector is no longer appearing at the same time intervals for every track.

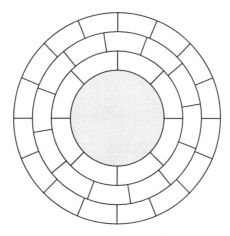

Figure 5.17 *Zoning – three different zones on a surface*

5.5.3 *Interleaving*

The earlier discussion on cylinders made the point that, if successive block accesses are for the same track, then no time is wasted in track seeking. The other overhead in accessing a block is latency. This is the time waiting for the required sector to come around to the waiting head. A file is normally stored as a sequence of blocks and usually accessed in that order. If a sequence of blocks from a file are not only on the same track, but also stored in consecutive sectors on that track, then the reading and writing process can be extremely quick as latency is also eliminated. However, this approach will not work on some systems. Some disk controllers are not capable of reading successive sectors because the delay in processing one sector results in the next one having already passed under the head before the controller is ready again. Even if the controller can keep up, the host computer may introduce delays which produce the same effect. The latency is then at its worst possible value, as almost a whole revolution of the disk is introduced between block reads. To help overcome this situation, the sectors can be interleaved as shown in Figure 5.18.

Figure 5.18(a) is the normal situation where each sector occurs in turn. This is said to have an *interleave factor* of one. In Figure 5.18(b) there are two sectors between each successive sector, and the interleave factor is three. The choice of interleave factor depends upon the usual delay between reading blocks, and is usually set by trial and error for each particular system. Tools exist which can help to determine the optimum interleave factor.

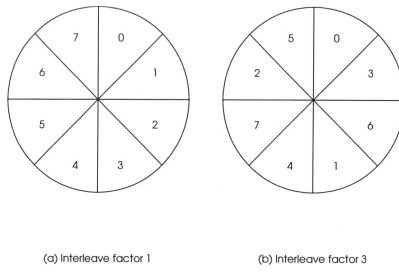

(a) Interleave factor 1   (b) Interleave factor 3

Figure 5.18 *Interleaving of sectors*

When the controller cannot alter the interleave, then this function is left to the computer's operating system which would, for example, use each other successive sector when possible. Many disk controllers always read entire tracks at a time storing the information in their own local memories. With these devices there is no interleave problem and the interleave setting is most efficiently set at 1.

▶ 5.6 Magnetic Disk Organization and Head Positioning

As already described, the process of reading information from a disk consists of three parts. First the head is moved to the desired track. This is called seeking. Secondly the required sector is awaited. This is the latency. Finally the required data is read or written. As mentioned earlier, in order to identify tracks and sectors, positional control information has to be recorded in addition to user data. The writing of this information is called *formatting* the disk and is normally only performed once. Strictly speaking, this process is a *low-level format* because a later *high-level format* process is also performed by the operating system to permit the blocks of a disk to be organized into a file-store.

5.6.1 Control information

Control information is written onto the disk during the low-level formatting process. This consists of positional information which identifies each track and sector, and error checking information to ensure the integrity of the data. The positional information can either be written on a dedicated surface as a series of servo tracks, or it can be embedded within the data on each surface. Error checking information is concerned with each individual block and so must be embedded within the data. The embedded technique is more common than the use of servo tracks.

When servo tracks are used, they are written on one surface such as the top surface as shown in Figure 5.13(b). Each servo track contains the identity of the track and the start of each sector.

With the embedded technique, this information is stored alongside the user data. A typical track may appear as in Figure 5.19.

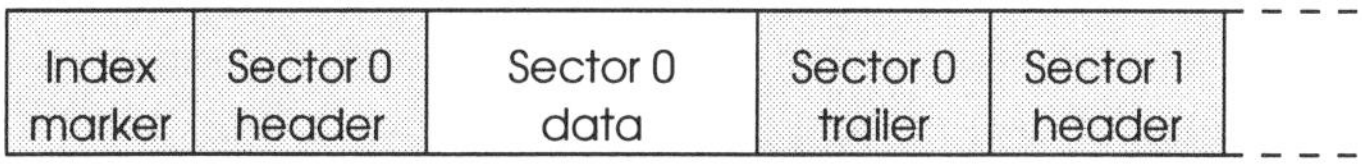

Index marker	Sector 0 header	Sector 0 data	Sector 0 trailer	Sector 1 header

Figure 5.19 *Embedded control information*

At the same location on each track is the track's index marker. This contains the track number but, more importantly, it is used to establish a known starting position on the track. On some floppy disks a hole in the disk announces the arrival of the index marker. Each sector in the track is surrounded by a header and a trailer. The header's main function is to identify the track and sector and hence the block number. The trailer will contain information such as a cyclic redundancy check (CRC) which can be used to check that the sector data was read correctly. For a more detailed description on error checking techniques the reader is referred to the later section on optical recording codes and to Chapter 8 on data communications.

The situation is not quite as simple as Figure 5.19 implies. There will be small gaps in between the index marker, sector headers and trailers and sector data sections. These allow a short breathing space for the disk controller to digest the information. There will also be unique sequences of characters surrounding each piece of control information. These permit the disk unit to identify the different sections. When a disk undergoes a low-level format, the index markers, sector headers and sector trailers are written. With magnetic surfaces, a large amount of redundancy (or repetition) is often used to ensure that as the magnetism deteriorates the control information is still available. As the data sections are frequently updated this is not as important for them. When the information has been written, each sector is checked for integrity. It is almost impossible to produce a perfect surface and some parts may not record data correctly, so information is written to each block and read back. If a block is found to be faulty then its sector header is marked as such and that block will never be used by the disk controller unit. Some disk controller units require that the known bad blocks be input to them when the disk unit is installed, but modern controllers can detect them and, invisibly, ignore them – the user just sees a disk with slightly fewer blocks than normal. The low-level format can be performed afresh later in the disk's life and new bad blocks are then caught in this way.

During the disk's life blocks are written potentially many times. The error checking information in the trailer is used to detect errors here. When a block is written, a CRC value is calculated from it and placed in the trailer. When it is later read back, the CRC is calculated again and checked against the expected value in the trailer, and if they are different, then some action must be taken. It may be the case that some transient occurrence caused a spurious error in reading or it could be that that section of the surface has become permanently corrupt. The disk controller will usually read the block again in case it was a transient occurrence. After several unsuccessful attempts the block will be assumed to have become permanently corrupt and the read will have failed. Most disk controllers would then mark the sector header for that block as bad in the same way that this is done during the low-level format. It is, of course, too late as far as the user is concerned and the data in that block has then been lost.

5.6.2 Track seeking

Track seeking involves moving the head to the required track. This is done in two stages. Firstly the head is moved to a calculated position based on dead reckoning and a track found. Tracks have spacing between them which is neutral and so the head will *hunt* to position itself exactly over an area of activity. The track is identified by reading the next available sector header. From this information the unit can calculate how many tracks it has to move to find the required one. A separate positioning unit is used here which is extremely accurate but which is only capable of producing small movements. As mentioned in the earlier section on disk formats, a 'sensible' computer system will try to ensure that successive accesses to a disk will occur on the same track when possible. A disk file is recorded as a sequence of blocks and is usually read back in the same order. If it can be arranged that successive blocks are on the same track, then there will be less overhead of track seeking. The disk controller always maintains a record of which track it is currently operating upon and, if the next request for a block is for the same track, then the procedure of seeking is simply skipped.

In magnetic drives the head is positioned in a variety of ways depending upon the type and age of the device. Either a servo motor or a stepper motor can be used to move the head between tracks. This is typical in heavy mechanisms. If the head mountings are light then a *voice coil* can be used. The coil is similar to that which performs the movement of the cone in an audio loudspeaker. The coil is moved to the correct track and then kept there by continuously monitoring the reading of the track and adjusting the coil control accordingly.

5.6.3 Sector location

Once the required track has been found then the second process starts – locating the required sector. This is a relatively straightforward process and the controlling unit will simply wait for the correct sector header. The time taken waiting is called the latency, and can be minimised in certain cases, as previously described, by suitable choices of interleaving.

► 5.7 Magnetic Tape

Magnetic tape consists of a thin plastic tape with a magnetic coating, which is usually ferric oxide. The tape is held on reels which are either separate for reel-to-reel tape or enclosed in a cartridge. The reels are then mounted on a tape deck or, in the case of a cartridge, placed in a tape drive for use.

Magnetic tape is one of the oldest forms of storage. It is relatively cheap and has a high storage capacity. The drawback is that, compared to disks, it is slow. The transfer rate can be impressive but the major drawback is searching for the required section of tape. A disk is known as a *random access* device because different blocks on the disk can be selected almost instantaneously. With a tape, it can take a considerable amount of time to search for a block as the tape is inherently a *serial access* device. A tape can be several hundred metres long and searching from one end to the other can take several seconds even on the fastest of tape mechanisms. Thus, for use as a general storage device, magnetic tape is inconvenient at best. Magnetic tape is much more suited to tasks which are themselves serial in their storage requirements and for which data is simply written to or read from the tape from the start to the finish with little stopping along the way. This type of tape access is known as *streaming* as opposed to the *stop-start* form of access if the tape is used in a more general fashion. Tape streaming is almost exclusively used in modern systems. The main purpose of magnetic tape nowadays is twofold. Principally it is used for taking backup security copies of the information stored on disks. In the event of a disk failure or the accidental deletion of information stored on a disk, the copy on tape can be retrieved. The second common use of magnetic tape is to transport information from one system to another. Standards in tape recording are well defined, making tape particularly well suited to this second purpose.

There are four commonly used physical formats of tape. These are the older *reel-to-reel tapes* and the three common tape formats stored in cartridges which are *quarter-inch cartridge (QIC), 8 mm video tape* and *digital audio tape (DAT)*. The first two were designed specifically for computer use. The last two were designed for the entertainment business and have been adapted for use in computing. In both the latter two cases, tapes of a high standard are produced specifically for use with computers but the tape drives used for reading and writing them are much the same as their video and music counterparts. Another example of this technology migration is CD-ROM which is discussed in a later section. 8 mm video tape, when used in computing, is often alternatively referred to by its proprietary name of *Exabyte*.

The forms of the tapes vary considerably. Typical reel-to-reel tape is half an inch wide, about 200 µm thick and has a magnetic coating with a thickness of about 100 µm. At the other extreme, DAT is 4 mm wide, only 13 µm thick and the coating has a thickness of 3 µm. DAT is so thin that it is translucent.

Magnetic tapes are read and written by moving them over a read or write head. Often the head is a combined read/write head. Some systems employ a read head immediately following the write head which continuously checks what has been written. The head itself is fixed in position and accesses the tape as it passes over it. High data rates are then achieved by moving the tape rapidly. With video tape and DAT however, a helical scan mechanism is employed where the tape wraps around a cylindrical head which is spinning and the tape passes over the head at a leisurely rate. Problems to be addressed in tape systems include keeping the tape physically at right angles to the head (skew), allowing for stretch in the tape over time, and *print through* where data recorded on the tape can affect the tape wrapped above or below it on the reel. The four common types of magnetic tape are now described in more detail.

5.7.1 Reel-to-reel tape

Reel-to-reel tape is the oldest form of magnetic tape still in use and, despite its relative bulkiness, rarely achieves the same order of storage capacity as the other three cartridge varieties. There are two typical reel-to-reel tape drives in use. These are for stop-start access, when individual blocks of information are read/written, and streaming when several sequential blocks are read/written at a time. These drives are illustrated in Figure 5.20.

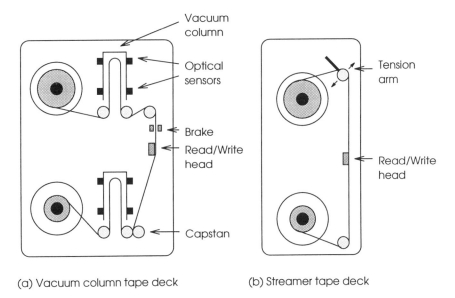

(a) Vacuum column tape deck   (b) Streamer tape deck

Figure 5.20 *Reel-to-reel tape drives*

In order to achieve an acceptable data transfer rate, the tape must be moved quickly over the head(s). In a stop-start application a block of information is accessed and then the tape must be stopped before it overshoots the next block. A reel-to-reel tape may be many hundred metres long and so a full reel is quite heavy. The inertial constraints imposed by such sharp accelerations and decelerations are addressed by keeping a buffer of slack tape between the reels and the head(s). One method of achieving this is shown in Figure 5.20(a) were the slack tape is held in vacuum columns. The tape is actually moved by a capstan drive and halted by a brake which clamps the tape. The reels can now slightly lag the initial startup up of the capstan and the stopping imposed by the brake as long as sufficient tape is kept within the vacuum columns. The columns are monitored by optical sensors to keep the length of slack constant.

Older tape drives achieve the same effect by employing a series of tension arms with several loops of tape over them, but such drives are awkward to load. As explained earlier, it is now rare to use magnetic tape in a largely stop-start manner. Tape streaming is much more common and this employs a simpler and cheaper tape drive of the form illustrated in Figure 5.20(b). With tape streaming the application typically reads or writes many blocks before stopping. This is certainly the case when, for example, taking a backup copy of a magnetic disk, where each file is copied in turn to the tape. With a tape streaming drive, the tape is stopped and started relatively slowly and there is little inertial problem. However, when the tape stops, it will still overshoot the next section, and the tape then needs to be rewound back to the correct position. This overhead is slight if the tape is stopped rarely, as is the case with a streaming application. With this method, the tape is controlled entirely through the two reels – there is no separate capstan or brake. The slight inertial problems that inevitably occur with such a method are smoothed out by a small tension arm which dynamically adjusts the slack of tape between the reels.

Both systems can also employ a fast forward/reverse mode when the tape is moved at the highest possible speed by the two reels (in the case of the stop-start deck the capstan is disengaged). In this way, the tape can be moved quickly near to a distant block with a *dead reckoning* algorithm. The block is then searched for using the normal speed.

Data is stored in a series of tracks which run parallel to the tape. Older varieties of tape deck store 9 tracks across the width although now 18 or more are common. The tracks can either be read in parallel or serially. To read them in parallel requires the use of multiple read/write heads which simultaneously read all or some of the tracks. Serial access employs a single head which reads one track at a time. This head is physically moved from track to track. With nine tracks, it is usual to store an 8-bit character across the tape. The ninth track is used to store the parity of the character. This is a similar format to that used on the old media of paper tape in which eight holes punched across the tape represent binary 1s and the absence of a hole represents a binary 0.

Serial recording stores information as a series of bits along the track as opposed to across the tracks. It largely eliminates the main problem with parallel recording on a tape, where the tape must be aligned exactly at right angles to the heads in order to keep each track in synchronization. When a track is recorded, rather than rewinding the tape before moving on to the next track, alternate tracks are recorded in opposite directions. Because of the resulting *snake-like* pattern, this method is known as *serpentine recording*.

The recording codes employed are NRZI, MNRZI and PE. The NRZI code has the problem that it is not self-clocking, as was explained earlier. It can be used successfully, however, with parallel recording if at least one of the tracks is holding parity information and the convention is to use odd parity. With odd parity, it is guaranteed that at least one track will be a 1 and so a flux reversal is always available for synchronization under one of the heads. With serial recording, NRZI is not sufficient, and one of the other codes must be employed.

Data is stored on tape, like disks, in a series of self-contained blocks. The format of a block is similar to that on a magnetic disk and one typical format is shown in Figure 5.21. The tape ends are marked with special *Beginning of tape (BOT)* and *End of tape (EOT)* characters. This is to allow blank leaders and trailers on the tape to ease the task of loading the tape onto the reels and so that the tape is not completely wound off a reel. If such markers are not correctly read then the tape will unwind from a reel. With reel-to-reel tape this is an irritating inconvenience. With the cartridge systems described later the tape is not easily accessible to be fastened back onto the reel, and so such an event is normally fatal. The cartridge tapes therefore employ more rigorous techniques, which have physical markers near the ends of the tape. Some reel-to-reel tape systems also employ physical BOT and EOT markers.

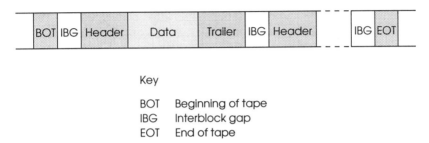

Key

BOT   Beginning of tape
IBG   Interblock gap
EOT   End of tape

Figure 5.21 *Magnetic tape block format*

Between the markers is a series of blocks and these are the unit of transfer. Like magnetic disk blocks, they start with a header which contains the block's identification and type and end with a trailer which contains error checking information. Unlike disks however, the tape is not preformatted with block headers – they are written with the data. The error checking information is usually of the form of a *cyclic redundancy check (CRC)*. Cyclic redundancy checks are employed in many computing applications and, especially, in data communications, and are described in more detail in Chapter 8.

Between each block is an *interblock gap* which is simply a short length of blank tape. On reel-to-reel tape this gap is about half an inch long and serves three purposes. Firstly, there must be time for the tape deck to assimilate the block and check it for errors before moving on to the next block. Because of the gap, it is not necessary to stop the tape while this is happening. Secondly, with wear, tapes can stretch and/or shrink slightly. If a block is to be re-written and the tape has shrunk then there would not be space to rewrite the block. The interblock gap gives sufficient breathing space to overcome this problem. This is only important for stop-start working because, with streaming, each block is always written/re-written as part of a sequence, and earlier blocks are not revisited in a discrete manner. Thirdly and finally, the interblock gap can be sensed by the heads even when the tape is moving in fast forward or fast reverse. A count of the gaps can be used in the dead reckoning procedure mentioned earlier in order to reach a distant block. Because of the self-clocking recording code used within each block, there will never be a sequence inside the block which looks like an interblock gap.

Reel-to-reel tapes are becoming less common, but they are still used by many organizations who have a large amount of data existing in that format. The following cartridge formats are in much more common use due to their convenience and their greater storage capacities.

5.7.2 Tape cartridges

Early domestic audio tape recorders employed reel-to-reel mechanisms and were replaced by audio cassettes largely for convenience – they are easier to load and distribute. In the same way, computer tapes are packaged into cartridges or cassettes which contain the tape and its two reels. While the audio cassette was used for storage in early home computer systems, more sophisticated tape cartridges are now used.

There are three common packages in use. The first is normally the format meant when simply referring to a tape cartridge or *data cartridge* and is described in this subsection. The other two are described separately in their own subsections. All three employ separate read heads which read data back from the tape immediately after it has been written, in order to check quickly for write errors. The quarter-inch cartridge is read and written in the normal way on tracks parallel to the tape. There exist well established standards for this tape. The other two write many short tracks diagonally across the tape. They employ a helical scan head. They are slightly more susceptible to less than clean atmospheres and, while they do have established standards, these are newer and not universally adopted. Helical scan methods are also more prone to error and so the two tape systems using them have sophisticated error correcting algorithms built into the drive units which are similar to those described for optical media in later sections.

The data cartridge is known as the *quarter-inch cartridge (QIC)* and is shown in Figure 5.22. There are two common sized cartridges – the 5¼ inch and 3½ inch size but both operate in the same manner. The length of tape varies in the same way that magnetic disk sizes vary but typical lengths are 200 to 1000 feet. The tape is a quarter of an inch wide. The tape is driven by a single capstan at the front and in the middle of the cartridge. Also along the front are a hinged door, opened by the cartridge drive to gain access to the tape, an angled mirror used to detect the end of tape and a write protect slot operated by turning a knob.

The drive belt is rubber and forms a *T-shape* around its three capstan wheels and between the two tape reels. Although the tape appears in this illustration to be in contact with the drive capstan, it is not. It passes underneath the drive capstan. As the capstan is turned, the belt moves around the drive capstan and the two capstans at the back of the cartridge. The drive belt is in contact with the tape for approximately half the circumference of each tape reel, and this is how the tape is driven. This arrangement is cunningly simple, but most effective, and automatically ensures linear tape speed regardless of the amount of tape on each reel.

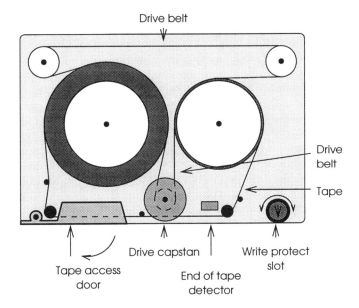

Figure 5.22 *Data cartridge (QIC)*

In the cartridge drive, the hinged door is swung open to gain access to the tape for the read/write head. The drive also reads two sensors. The write protect slot is controlled by a knob which, when turned, reveals a hole. When the hole is detected the tape may be written to. The second sensor detects the ends of the tape. Behind the tape is a mirror angled at 45°. Near each end of the tape are two small holes, one above the other. Light is shone from above the cartridge and is reflected by the mirror at the tape. The holes pass this light through where it can then be detected.

There are many different standards agreed for QIC drives. These are set by the Quarter-Inch Cartridge Drive Standards, Inc. which is an international trade association. They set standards for different recording codes and track densities. They also specify interface standards and other standards for drive heads, etc. The two most common standards found with drives on small computers are *QIC-40* and *QIC-80*. Their names come from the fact that, with the original length of tape employed, they can store 40 MB and 80 MB of data respectively. Both standards employ MFM coding and utilize the existing device controllers for floppy disk drives. They are both also aimed at the smaller mini-cartridge. A summary of some of the QIC standards for drives and recording codes is given in Table 5.4. Several of these standards have been adopted by ANSI. The quoted capacity is for a typical tape length, and the same standard can be used for higher capacities with longer tapes. Some of the standards specify recording codes and others, additionally, specify a particular interface. The available capacities cover a wide range, with transfer rates being typically between 200 and 600 kbps.

Table 5.4 *Some QIC drive and recording code standards*

Standard	Tracks	Code	Density kbits/inch	Capacity MB
QIC-24	9	GCR	8	60
QIC-40	20	MFM	10	40
QIC-80	28	MFM	14.7	80
QIC-120	15	GCR	10	125
QIC-128	32	GCR	20	128
QIC-150	18	GCR	10	250
QIC-525	26	GCR	16	525
QIC-1000	30	GCR	36	1010
QIC-2GB	42	GCR	40.6	2000
QIC-5GB	44	RLL 1,7	50	5000
QIC-5010*	144	RLL 1,7	40.6	13 000

* QIC-5010 was originally named QIC-10GB

The QIC data cartridge standards shown in Table 5.4 are a representative sample of a much larger number of QIC standards, and show the range of capacities up to several GB. Unlike reel-to-reel tape, the magnetic recording codes employed are often the same as those used on magnetic disks, in order to provide a high capacity.

5.7.3 8 mm video tape (Exabyte)

8 mm video tape was designed for video camera recorders. However, the same medium can also be used to store data in a computer system, and a special drive exists which interfaces to a computer, designed by the company Exabyte after whom the system is often called. A high grade of video tape is made especially for computer storage. The tape itself is shown in Figure 5.23.

The tape is held on two reels which themselves are held by small metal flexible bars. A slider is used to uncover a hole in the bottom of the cartridge to allow/forbid writing to the tape. When loaded in its drive, the door is swung open to gain access to the tape. The door is protected from accidental opening when outside the drive by a sliding catch, as shown in Figure 5.23(b). This tape and the following DAT form employ a helical scan method of reading and writing, as illustrated in Figure 5.24.

To achieve high data rates, the tape can be moved past the head at a high speed. With the helical scan method, the tape actually moves quite slowly – of the order of an inch a second – but the head spins at around 2000 rpm. The tape is wrapped around the spinning head as shown in

Write protect slider

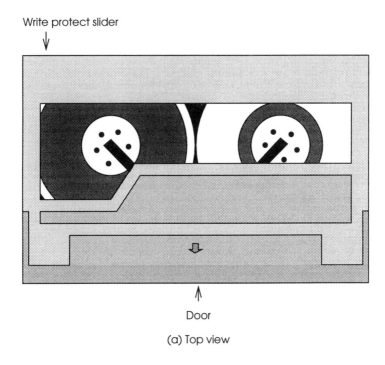

Door

(a) Top view

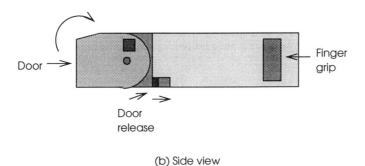

Door

Door
release

Finger
grip

(b) Side view

Figure 5.23 *8 mm video tape – actual size*

Figure 5.24(a). The tape passes in a skew such that the reading/writing head scans it at a small diagonal angle of around 5°, writing short diagonal tracks as shown in Figure 5.24(b). The tape is in contact with the head for 220° so that one of two or more heads on the spinning unit is always in

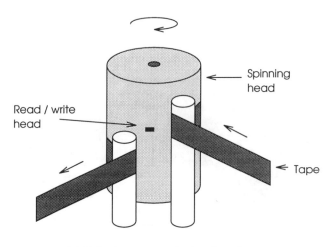

Spinning head

Read / write head

Tape

(a) Helical scan round rotary head

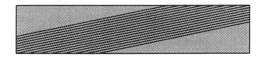

(b) Diagonal tracks

Figure 5.24 *Helical scan*

contact with it. The Exabyte standard has been adopted by the standards authority ISO. There are two main standards giving capacities of 2 to 5 GB, but these sizes are increased by compression techniques. Transfer rates are of the order of 250 to 500 kbps.

5.7.4 Digital audio tape

Digital audio tape (DAT) is a medium adapted from the music industry, where its ability to record sound digitally has been welcomed as a natural partner to the digital compact disc. Physically, it is the smallest tape cartridge being only 73 mm × 54 mm × 10.5 mm. It is shown in Figure 5.25. DAT is often referred to as 4 mm tape although it is actually 3.81 mm wide. The enclosing cartridge is a complicated device which has been designed to ensure that the tape and its mechanism are well protected.

Like video tape, DAT is protected by a swivel door. The tape hubs are not even accessible until the cartridge is in its drive mechanism. The hubs are held static by the two small plastic lugs shown in Figure 5.25(a), with the door being at the bottom of that figure. Figure 5.25(b) shows the

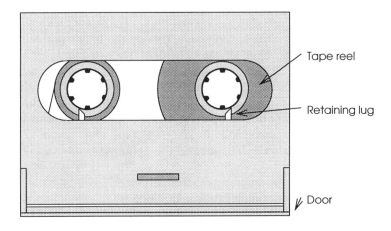

(a) Top view

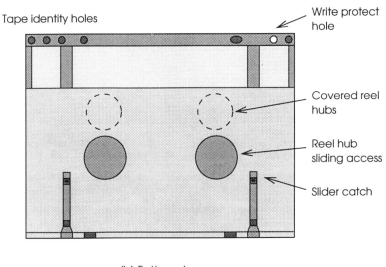

(b) Bottom view

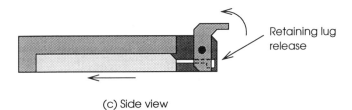

(c) Side view

Figure 5.25 *DAT tape cartridge – actual size*

underside of the DAT cartridge. At the top right is a small white circle which is the write protect hole, and which is opened and closed by a slider on the back of the cartridge not shown here. There are other holes there which identify the format of the tape. Also on the underside, a large area can slide towards the back of the cartridge. This is slid aside when the DAT is in its drive. When slid to the back position, it is retained by two spring loaded catches and the reel hubs are exposed. When the slider is in this position the door can move. The DAT unit then opens the door as shown in Figure 5.25(c). The opening of the door pulls on a slider which is connected to the plastic lugs holding the tape reels static. The drive mechanism then loads the tape around the spinning head unit. The main difference with the helical scan mechanism used for DAT is that the tape is only in contact with the spinning mechanism for 90°, which means that the threading of the tape is simpler than with video tape.

Unlike video tape, and because of this small contact angle, DAT can be put into fast forward or reverse without needing to detach it from the heads. The mechanism is shown in Figure 5.26.

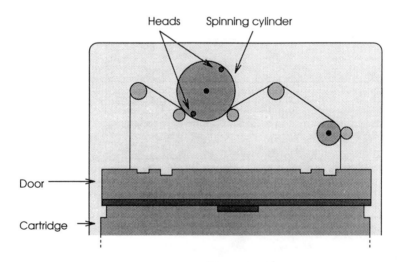

Figure 5.26 *DAT drive mechanism*

DAT has two main standards which are adopted by the standards authority ANSI. The first is *digital data storage (DDS)* and is the normal streaming approach. There is also the *data/DAT standard* which is slower but allows the stop-start approach found in some reel-to-reel drives. Capacities of DAT are typically 2 GB but newer recording techniques combined with compression can achieve up to 5 GB. Transfer rates range from 180 kbps up to several times that figure.

▶ 5.8 Optical Storage

The storage devices discussed so far store data using a magnetic form. Optical storage, like magnetic storage, is permanent in that it retains its information when the power is removed but differs in that it codes data as variations on an optical surface. These variations affect how light, usually in the form of a laser beam, is reflected. The surface is typically perfectly reflecting while the variations, in the form of small bumps or pits, are not. The amount of light directly reflected back from these bumps or pits is less than that reflected back from the smooth surface and this gives a means of binary storage. Although the information is read optically, it is not always recorded in a purely optical manner, since the permanent bumps in a compact disc (CD) are pressed on to the surface during production. In some other media, a laser beam is used to record variations on a surface, but it is the heat of the beam rather than its light intensity which is used. Laser beams can be focused to detect variations which are extremely tightly packed and so, for the same surface area, optical storage can give a much higher capacity than magnetic storage. The disadvantages are that most optical storage systems are not re-writable and data transfer rates are slower than with magnetic disks.

Optical storage is employed on disks and, less commonly, on tape. There are three common forms of optical disk storage. First is the read-only disk of which the most common form is the *compact disc read-only memory (CD-ROM)*. Information is recorded onto the disk during manufacture. Such disks can hold large amounts of information – typically over 600 MB – and are useful both for distributing data to customers and for keeping large read-only databases, such as dictionaries, on-line.

The second variety permits reading and writing but information, once written, cannot be altered. The common form is known as *write once read many (WORM)*. WORM disks can be used like magnetic disks – when information is to be changed the old version is simply ignored and a new part of the disk surface assigned. The effective size of the disk therefore diminishes with time and, eventually, it must be replaced.

The third variety allows reading and re-writing and is used in exactly the same manner as magnetic disk. There are few such common devices and most rely on various optical properties of a surface being altered by different forms of laser light. A medium which is commonly found that appears to be in this category is the *magneto-optical (MO)* disk which, as its name suggests, actually uses a combination of magnetic and optical technologies and is described under that heading in a later section.

The mechanism of optical reading is illustrated in Figure 5.27(a). A laser is a highly directional light source and can be focused on to a very small area with great accuracy. The laser light is first focused by a lens into a cylindrical beam which passes through a *beam splitter*. In Figure 5.27(a) the beam splitter is a half-silvered mirror which lets half the light pass through and reflects the remaining half. After the beam splitter, the remaining light is focused by the objective lens on to the small area of the surface to be read. The amount of light reflected back from the surface depends on the state of the surface being examined, and the beam splitter reflects half of this on to a light sensor.

Half-silvered mirrors are inefficient because much light is wasted. Only half of the original laser beam makes its way to the surface – the other half has been reflected to the left of Figure 5.27(a) and wasted. The reflected light is then split by the mirror and half is reflected to the sensor – one quarter of the original strength. The other half of the reflected light passes through in the direction of the laser source. These wasted rays are not shown in Figure 5.27(a) for clarity. A smaller and cheaper laser can be used if a more sophisticated beam splitter is employed. One such splitter is shown in Figure 5.27(b).

In this system the laser light is polarized so that all light waves are in the same plane. In Figure 5.27(b) the laser source light is polarized in the plane of the page. The prism beam splitter allows light which is polarized parallel to its own plane to pass through unaffected. Light which is polarized at 90° to that plane is totally reflected. Light polarized at an angle between these two is partially reflected and partially transmitted. The source laser beam then passes completely through the prism on its way to the surface. It then passes through a *quarter-wave plate* which shifts the angle of polarization by 45°. The reflected light from the surface passes through the quarter-wave plate a second time which shifts the light polarization by a further 45° before the light reaches the prism. The laser is now polarized at 90° to its original plane and the prism totally reflects it to the sensor.

▶ 5.9 Optical Recording Codes

Optical storage employs similar coding principles to those used with magnetic storage and for the same reasons. RLL coding is common, as it is efficient in terms of space, and is self-clocking. The main difference between optical and magnetic recording codes is that optical recording requires a much larger degree of error detection and correction. The medium is susceptible to corruption by any particles which obstruct or deflect the laser beam and the very high densities achievable with laser technology push the technical limits to their extremes.

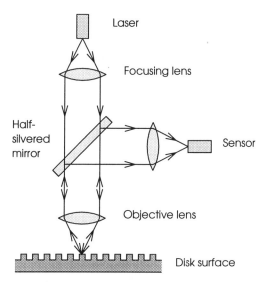

(a) Half-silvered mirror
beam splitter

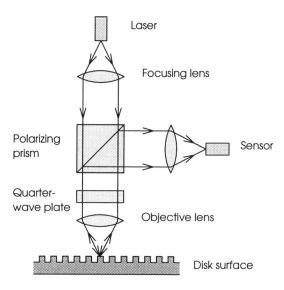

(b) Prism beam splitter

Figure 5.27 *Reading data with a laser beam*

Optical coding therefore includes much more redundancy error information than is normally used with magnetic media. There are two principal areas of concern. Firstly a read error must be detected and secondly, if possible, the error must be corrected by using the additional redundant information coded into the data. There are many error detection and correction techniques and some are described in Chapter 8 in the context of data communications, which is another field where the control of erroneous information is paramount.

The simplest error detection technique is *parity checking*. Here groups of bits are augmented with a parity bit which is set to either a 1 or a 0 so that the total number of bits in the group which are 1s is either an even number or an odd number. Whether the group contains an even or an odd number of 1s is known as its parity. When the information is written the parity bit is calculated and stored alongside it. When the information is read, the parity bit is re-calculated and compared with that stored. If one of the bits in the group (including the parity bit) has been altered then the parity will have changed and an error flagged. This system will not detect an error involving two bits however, as such a double error would result in the original parity being restored, and would therefore go unnoticed.

By adding more parity bits, more complex errors can be detected, but at the expense of more error detection information being stored. At the extreme, the data could be duplicated and both copies compared when read. Error detection is therefore a compromise between effectiveness and space, and many techniques have been used such as variations on the simple parity method described, and others such as Hamming codes.

Unfortunately, these techniques described so far detect an error but cannot all pinpoint the exact position of the error. Even if the data is duplicated it is not possible to know which of the copies is correct and, indeed, both may be corrupt.

A feature which can be exploited is that most errors are so-called *burst errors*. That is, the errors are infrequent but, when they occur they affect a relatively large amount of data. This is typical of the occasional imperfection on a compact disc, or a smudge on a tape. Imagine a system based on using many parity bits or on Hamming codes. This relies on the data being packaged into units each having its own redundancy error detection and correction information. The amount of redundancy dictates how much of the data can be corrupt, but still recovered. With a burst error, most units will be read perfectly, while some will be heavily corrupted and, probably, unrecoverable. In this situation it may be better if the units are not stored one after another but, instead, they are interleaved.

For example, assume that each unit is 32 bits long including the redundancy information. If a burst error affects, say, 100 consecutive bits then three or four of these units would be degraded beyond repair, while the rest would be read correctly if they were stored one after another. They could, alternatively be interleaved. One way to do this would be to group these 32-bit units into groups of 100. This group as a whole is then stored by storing the first bit of each of the 100 units then the second bit of each and so on until the thirty second and last bit of each is stored. A burst error will now affect many individual units, but only a small part of each is corrupted, and so they can be recovered.

One commonly used error detection and correction technique is the *Reed Solomon code*. It is a very sophisticated coding method which is very effective and relatively space efficient. Its method involves interleaving automatically. This code assigns many different codings of different parts of the data such that the same data can be restored in several ways. The code ensures that burst errors affect only one or two of these codings and, in effect, a voting system is applied to decide the final data. More detail on such codings is found in the further reading section.

▶ 5.10 CD-ROM Optical Disks

The CD-ROM optical disk is taken directly from the audio industry compact disc (CD). Digital audio is recorded using a standard which samples the analogue music data at a rate of 44.1 kHz and each sample is 16 bits long – two bytes. This requires a digital data transfer rate of $44\,100 \times 2$ bytes/second which equates to 88 200 bytes/second. In fact, the music is recorded in stereo, which requires two independent tracks, and so the overall digital data transfer rate required is 176 400 bytes/second. This is the standard transfer rate for compact discs. Compact discs have a capacity of the order of 600 MB.

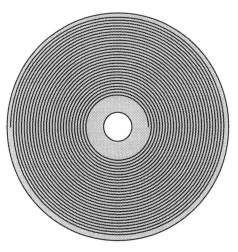

Figure 5.28 *Spiral track on a CD-ROM*

Recording digital data on optical disks requires a large degree of error protection and, hence, of redundancy. Because the integrity of the information needs to be more strict in a computer system, using a CD-ROM for computer storage requires even more error protection, and this reduces the effective data transfer rate for a CD-ROM to 150 kB/second. This rate is rather slow in the context of computer storage and so some CD-ROM drives spin the disk at faster speeds. Currently there exist double, treble and quadruple speed drives, with the latter able to achieve a data transfer rate of 600 kB/second.

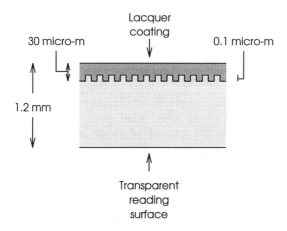

Figure 5.29 *A section through a CD-ROM*

A CD-ROM, like a magnetic disk, codes its data along tracks. A magnetic disk has many circular concentric tracks but a CD-ROM, like a vinyl record, has a single spiral track as shown in Figure 5.28. Another difference between the CD-ROM and the magnetic disk arises in dealing with the different length of track near the middle of the disk compared to an outer track. Here, a track in the context of a CD-ROM, is one complete revolution's worth of the spiral.

Magnetic disks, and some other optical disks, spin at a constant speed. This is described as a *constant angular velocity (CAV)*. The surface moves under the head at a faster linear rate on outer tracks than on inner tracks. On magnetic disks this is compensated for either by recording at a lower data density in outer tracks or using zoning. A CD-ROM uses *constant linear velocity (CLV)* whereby the total length of the spiral track is scanned at the same rate. To achieve this, the disk spins at a slower angular rate when outer sections of the track are being scanned, and speeds up proportionately as the laser beam moves towards the centre. This increases the capacity of the disk by about 50% but, the time taken to adjust speeds when moving from one section of the disk to another significantly increases the latency involved. While this is of little concern for an audio

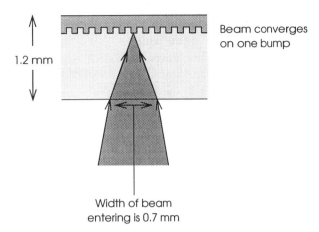

Figure 5.30 *Converging laser beam through a CD-ROM*

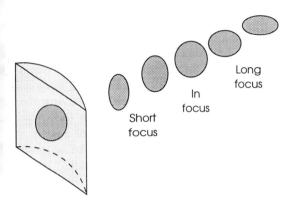

Figure 5.32 *Cylindrical lens to detect focus*

left and right sensors. When the beam is in focus they are the
f they differ, then the amount by which they differ is used to
ice coil that adjusts the objective lens.

ck following

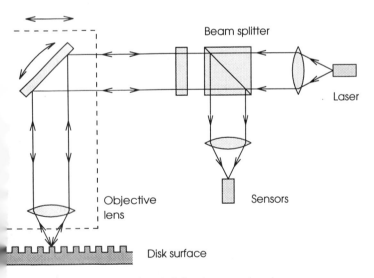

Figure 5.33 *Laser track following mechanism*

nd adjustment needed is tracking. Tracking is typically per-
y two mechanisms as shown in Figure 5.33. In order to save
laser and sensor mechanism are rotated through 90° and a mirror

compact disc, it is readily apparent in a computer system when many random accesses to different parts of the disk may occur.

Physically, a CD-ROM has a diameter of 120 mm and a thickness of
1.2 mm. The inner recording surface is coated with aluminium and is
highly reflective. Information is recorded by placing small bumps along
the track, which then reflect less light. Each bump is only around 0.1 μm
and the track separation is about 1.6 μm. Across a radius of the disk, the
spiral track passes over 20 000 times, and the total length of the spiral track
is 5.7 km.

A section of the disk surface is shown in Figure 5.29. This figure has
not been drawn in relative scale because the thickness of the recording surface and its lacquered backing are only one fortieth of the overall thickness. The aluminium surface is protected on its back side with a thin layer
of lacquer. The reading side is covered by a much thicker opaque plastic
material, and it is through this that the surface is read. The lacquered side
is considered as the top of the disk and is often printed with the disk's title
and contents. The disk is then read from underneath. In fact, a CD-ROM
is placed in the top of its drive and the laser and associated equipment are
underneath it. For a CD-ROM therefore, Figure 5.27 is upside down.

An important feature of a compact disc and, hence, a CD-ROM is that
it is removable and therefore resilient to a relatively rough handling environment. The lacquer side of the disk is only 30 μm thick and if it is significantly damaged then this will change some of the recorded bumps –
some solvents can penetrate the lacquered side. The recording surface is
unlikely to be damaged physically from the reading side but scratches and
particles can obscure the beam. It is largely for this reason that so much
error protection is built into the coding of any information recorded on
such a disk.

The laser beam itself is focused so that it converges to a point smaller than a bump size of 0.1 µm. This small area would easily be blocked by contaminating particles on the reading side. To compensate for this, the beam passes through almost the entire width of the disk before reaching the recording surface itself. As illustrated in Figure 5.30, the converging beam, at 0.7 mm, is still relatively wide when it enters the opaque reading side. It would require more than small contaminants to block the beam completely. Note also that, because of the different refractive indices of the plastic and air, the beam converges more quickly in the plastic.

▶ 5.11 WORM Optical Disk

The write once read many (WORM) optical disk consists of a thin sheet of metal sandwiched between two pieces of transparent material. One form uses tellurium between two pieces of glass. The metal recording surface starts life clear, and information is written to it by burning small pits into the surface with a high intensity laser beam. It is read in the same way as a CD-ROM but using a much lower intensity laser beam than that used for writing. The writing process can use the same mechanism as the reading process as shown in Figure 5.27. When writing, the power of the laser is increased and its heat burns a pit in the surface.

Because the WORM disk can be written to only once, the file control systems used need to be different to those used with magnetic disks. In the latter a directory of files is located at a fixed place on the magnetic disk, and the disk operating system accesses this directory to find the location of a particular file on the disk. The directory is continuously updated as file transactions occur. This updating cannot occur on a WORM disk. One approach is to hold the directory of the WORM disk on a separate magnetic disk, but the more common approach is to keep the directory on the WORM disk itself. If a directory entry is altered it is deactivated, and a new directory entry is put elsewhere on the disk. Similarly, files are changed by copying the new file into an unused part of the disk. (More economically, just those sections of the file that have changed might be allocated new space.)

WORM disks, unlike magnetic disks, are written to only once and are not re-usable, so with use they fill to capacity. This makes them well-suited to archiving applications. The write once property means that all earlier versions of a file remain stored, thus facilitating audit trails when the history of, say, engineering drawing modifications or financial transactions need to be traced. The write once property can be seen as a positive virtue in the latter case, as providing a deterrent to computer fraud.

▶ 5.12 Optical Positioning

There are two aspects to the positio optically. Firstly, the beam must ma pits or bumps on the surface. Disks the beam must continuously re-focus objective lens. Secondly the beam track pitch on a CD-ROM is only of smaller than the physical tolerances facturing the centre hole. In addition are subject to vibrations and shocks.

5.12.1 Focus control

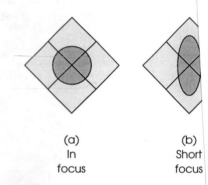

(a)   (b)
In   Short
focus   focus

Figure 5.31 *Four-segment sensor f*

The laser beam shown in Figure 5.27 is by adjusting the distance of the objective tion of the lens is controlled by a voice c to adjust the moving head on a hard needed are extremely small. In order t focus, two more additions are required. four separate sensors arranged in a dia 5.31. Secondly, a cylindrical lens is place splitter and the sensor array. This is show

The effect of this lens is to alter the sh such that, when in focus, it appears as a c the beam is out of focus the image is ellip in the horizontal or vertical plane will de short focused or long focused. This is sho of the top and bottom sensors is summed

sum of the
same, and
drive the v

5.12.2 Tr

Mirror

The sec
formed
space, th

is introduced to reflect the beam through 90° towards the objective lens and the disk surface. This mirror and the objective lens together form a carriage which can be moved across tracks. This is the prime mechanism for track following. A finer adjustment can also be provided by tilting the mirror slightly. When reading a track, due to the eccentricity, the carriage and/or mirror is constantly adjusted to keep the beam exactly over the track. One method of sensing the track is to use two additional laser beams focused on either side of the main beam. These will normally hit the gap between tracks and therefore always be totally reflected back. Should the track deviate slightly then one of the side beams will encounter the track and be only partially reflected. The difference in strength between the reflected two side beams can be used to control the carriage and mirror. Alternatively a single beam is used as before and the strengths of its left and right hand components measured. If it is on track then the left and right hand sides will encounter bumps or pits equally. If the beam is slightly offset then one side of the beam will be more directed over the smooth intertrack gap, and so will have a higher reflected component.

▶ 5.13 Optical Tapes

In principle, any of the optical disk mechanisms can be applied to tape. In practice very few are. Optical tape drives exist which operate in a similar manner to DAT, in that the tape is scanned at an angle to its directional travel. A common approach is to scan tracks across the tape and to employ many lasers to read/write tracks simultaneously. Positional servo information is often written separately along the length of the tape and read by a separate laser. Sections of the servo information are also written at a very low rate so that the information can be read while the tape is put into fast forward/reverse.

Currently optical tape drives are rare and expensive but the potential capacities of optical tape are enormous, with several thousand gigabytes on a single tape being common.

▶ 5.14 Combined Magnetic and Optical Recording

Two other forms of storage media are worth describing, which are hybrid forms of magnetic and optical storage. The first is the *magneto-optical (MO)* disk which, while read and written by a laser beam, stores the information magnetically. The second is commonly called the *floptical disk* and is a normal magnetic floppy disk, but with track servo information that is read optically.

5.14.1 *Magneto-optical disks*

Magneto-optical (MO) disks are operated in a similar fashion to WORM disks. A laser beam is used to alter the surface for writing and also for reading. Unlike a WORM disk however, information written can also be erased because it is stored and interpreted magnetically in the same way as on a magnetic disk. The equivalent of the reading/writing head is a laser beam, which is driven in the same way as on a normal optical disk.

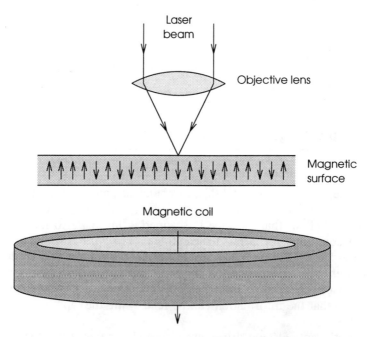

Figure 5.34 *Magneto-optical (MO) disk*

Underneath the disk is a magnetic coil as shown in Figure 5.34. Initially the disk is magnetized in a north (upward) direction and the coil is set with a south (downward) magnetic field direction. The magnetic material at normal temperatures will retain its direction. To write a section of the surface with a southerly direction the laser beam is briefly pulsed at a high intensity and the selected area of the surface momentarily heats up. All magnetic materials share the property that at above a certain temperature, known as their *Curie temperature,* their magnetic coercivity becomes zero. The area is now affected by the magnetic coil and takes on its direction. The surface then cools to below its Curie temperature and retains its new direction. The area can be re-written by repeating the process after reversing the field direction of the magnetic coil.

In order to read the surface, advantage is taken of the *Kerr effect* (sometimes known as the *Faraday effect)*. This effect changes the angle of polarization of light reflected from a magnetic surface depending upon the direction of magnetization. This small angle change is then measured by the laser sensor.

Magneto-optical disks are made from materials which have the magnetic properties that are most suited to taking advantage of the above two effects. Such materials are expensive, and most corrode in contact with air, and so are sandwiched between two plates of glass or plastic. These disks can be removable but often are manufactured as fixed disk drive units.

5.14.2 Floptical disks

A floptical disk is a normal magnetic floppy disk which has optically sensed track servo information written on it. This servo track information is read optically in a similar manner to the track following methods described above for optical disks, and this allows a much higher degree of accuracy than a standard floppy disk read/write head can achieve, as well as a very high track density. The magnetic read/write head is guided by the optical system but otherwise performs in the normal manner. These drives can also read ordinary floppy disks, simply by not using the laser, and the magnetic read/write head then operates in the standard floppy disk manner. Floptical disks have capacities of the order of 20 MB but, like magneto-optical disks, have so far not effectively secured a viable position in the market.

▶ 5.15 Disk and Tape Controllers and Interfaces

Disk and tape drives are connected to the computer system through a controller. The controller then performs read and write operations as instructed by the CPU. For example, commands are issued by the CPU to the controller which ask for particular sector(s) of a track to be read. Other tasks performed by the controller include formatting a disk with sector and track headers. One controller may have several disk and/or tape drives connected to it, or at the other extreme, some systems employ a separate controller for each physical drive. This relationship is illustrated in Figure 5.35.

Any number of controllers might be connected to a computer system and each may control many drives. Data is communicated between drives

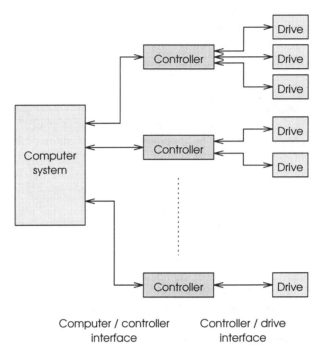

Computer / controller   Controller / drive
interface   interface

Figure 5.35 *Connection of disks and tapes through a controller*

and the computer system via the controller(s) in minimum sized units of blocks. The connection between the controller and the computer system is governed by a machine specific accepted interface as is, separately, the connection between controller and drive(s). The interface between the computer system and the controller is in two parts – both bidirectional.

The first part concerns communication between the computer and the controller to establish data transfers and to interrogate the controller's and drives' status. The second part is the path taken by the data between the computer system and the selected drive. Physically these two parts can use the same cabling or be quite separate. Two common approaches exist here. Using the first of these, the transfer takes place under program control and the CPU may accept data in the form of a block from the controller and place it in memory. It will receive the block in fixed size units of one or more bytes at a time. A second approach is to use *direct memory access (DMA)* where the controller bypasses the CPU and connects directly to the computer system's memory. This arrangement is shown in Figure 5.36.

In addition to disk and tape controllers, DMA is often used by communications networks and other peripheral devices which require high speed transfer of a large amount of data. It is most sensibly used when data transfers are in large units and where, sending each piece of information

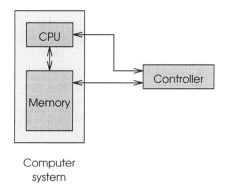

Computer
system

Figure 5.36 *Direct memory access (DMA)*

through the CPU will slow down the CPU to an intolerable level. Depending upon the particular architecture of the computer system, one of these two approaches will be faster.

With the DMA approach, the memory is connected to both the CPU and the devices which use DMA through an arbitrating circuit, which is not shown in Figure 5.36. Only one transfer can occur at a time, and if both the CPU and a DMA channel require the memory, only one will be granted access and the others will be made to wait. Because the controller is passing information to/from a drive as the disk or tape is moving, it must have priority over the CPU when transferring information to/from the memory, or data may be lost. If the CPU requires memory at the same time, then it will be suspended from operation.

With the program controlled approach, the CPU is directly involved with the transfer and must perform the transfers of data to/from memory itself. On the face of it it would seem that DMA should be more efficient because the CPU can be dealing with another task simultaneously, being suspended from time to time when it requires access to memory during a DMA transfer. However, with many modern architectures the CPU can transfer the information much faster than the DMA channel and, although it has to perform the transfer itself, this can be faster overall.

5.15.1 Controllers

A controller connects the computer system to tape and disk drives. Controllers can be physically separate from the drive(s) as shown in Figure 5.35 or they can be incorporated directly into a drive mechanism. In the latter case a separate controller is needed for each drive.

A controller receives information from the computer system such as 'read a block'. The block, in the case of a disk, will be identified by surface, track and sector numbers. The CPU will also include the memory location for the transfer if DMA is used. The controller has direct control of the movement of the surface and of the read/write heads. It will select the correct head, move it to the required track and continuously read the data from the track until the desired sector arrives, when it will start transferring data. The controller will also have to perform the coding between the binary sequences of 0s and 1s required by the CPU and the coding used on the drive – RLL for example. This function can alternatively be performed by the drive itself.

A controller will usually contain some memory allowing it to store the data in an intermediate buffer, so that the synchronization of the transfer can be eased. More sophisticated disk controllers buffer up whole tracks at a time even if only one sector of that track is asked for. This is in anticipation of future requests being likely to be for the same track. Some controllers include a large buffer and a sophisticated algorithm to provide a *disk cache* as described in the next section. Due to the sophistication of the controller it is usually a small dedicated computer system itself with its own CPU.

5.15.2 Controller interfaces

A controller has two interfaces. There is one between it and the computer system and the other between it and its attached drive(s). These interfaces and the three devices – computer, controller and drive – are illustrated in Figure 5.35. All three components can be made by different manufacturers and so specified interfaces must be agreed for the arrangement to function at all. A controller manufacturer then has to design controllers for each combination of computer system and drives. Fortunately, there are agreed connections both to computer systems and to drives and they are not too numerous. Additionally, as mentioned in the previous subsection, many drives now incorporate their own controller, and so that the interface can easily be customized specially by the manufacturer.

Most older tape systems used proprietary interfaces specially designed by each computer manufacturer for their own systems. The tape cartridge systems have specific interface standards such as those described in the sections concerning magnetic tape. These include the QIC standards, the Exabyte standards and the DAT standards. With optical devices, either a proprietary system is used or, more commonly, a universal system such as the *small computer system interface (SCSI)* is employed. SCSI is described later.

Older magnetic disk drives defined several interfaces between drive and controller, of which the most common is the ST-506 interface which is named after one of the Seagate manufacturer's drives. A modified version of this interface is the ST-412 whose name has the same origin. These interfaces are specified for drives coded either using MFM or RLL coding. Another common interface requires that the drive perform the MFM or

RLL coding and is the *extended small device interface (ESDI)*. These interfaces are mainly aimed at small personal computers, and larger systems use interfaces such as the ANSI adopted standard SMD interface.

These interfaces specify electrical and physical connections in addition to the functional features. The interface specification includes data transfer rates and ranges of size of disk drives.

Increasingly the complex system of combinations of interfaces is being resolved by employing a further universal interface such as SCSI. SCSI defines the interface to the drive in a high level functional manner, which permits it to be useful for virtually all possible drive units. In fact SCSI can be used for many computer peripherals including tapes, network connections and optical devices. A similar system aimed at larger computer systems is the IPI interface. There also exists a faster and more functional enhanced version called SCSI-2. These standards address the computer to controller interface by inserting themselves between the two. A SCSI controller is made with an interface for a particular computer system. To this can be attached any drives or other units which adhere to the SCSI standard. This scheme is illustrated in Figure 5.37

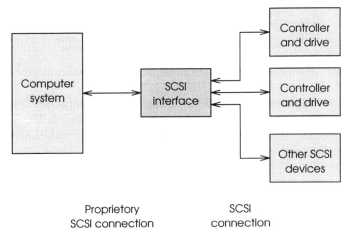

Proprietary   SCSI
SCSI connection   connection

Figure 5.37 *Use of an interface standard such as SCSI*

Normally the SCSI interface forms a separate component, and connects to disk drives which have their own controllers and a SCSI interface, but some drives include a SCSI to computer system on the drive itself.

An interface designed specifically for the IBM-PC personal computers is the *integrated drive electronics (IDE)*. Like SCSI, the controller for this resides on the drive and accepts commands at a high functional level. This interface is specifically designed for magnetic disk drives and is specific to the PC range of computers. The computer to IDE controller interface is built into the architecture of the PC system and no separate physical interface logic is required. Despite this, IDE cards exist which provide either a simple physical connection or, more usefully, can connect to many drives and may include a disk cache such as described earlier and in the next section. They are usually called controller cards, as are SCSI interface cards, but this should not be confused with the drive controller which is now on the drive itself.

The disk controllers which connect to SCSI, IDE and other interfaces are often themselves quite sophisticated. They often look after the reallocation of bad blocks automatically, so that the disk always appears to have contiguous blocks. This translation between logical and physical blocks is performed by the disk controller. IDE controllers provide an interface in terms of surfaces, tracks and sectors, but this may be different from the physical reality. This permits disks of all configurations to be used with computer systems which expect certain limitations on, for example, track density. A disk which has four surfaces and a high track density may appear to the computer system as having, say, sixteen surfaces and a correspondingly lower number of tracks on each. The mapping between the virtual disk of sixteen surfaces to the real one of four surfaces is performed by the controller.

To summarize, there exist specific controller interfaces for disk and tape drives. These include ST-506, ST-412 and ESDI in the context of magnetic disk drives. These connect to drives at the low level of control and control matters right down to head positioning. The magnetic disk drives are typically referred to by their coding method – MFM or RLL. Controllers are now more commonly integrated with the drive but the unit is usually still just referred to as a drive. The interface between the controller and the drive may well be one such as ST-412. Such disk drives are then referred to by the computer/control interface – IDE or SCSI – because, although the drive still uses MFM or RLL coding, this detail is hidden from this interface. IDE and SCSI make no reference to magnetic coding techniques.

▶ 5.16 Performance Enhancers

Backing store provides a large amount of permanent storage space which can be accessed relatively quickly. Backing store typically holds information in fixed sized units called blocks and one role of a computer system's operating system is to provide a file-store using these blocks. Earlier sections have explained how, by making sensible choices for the ordering of the blocks which make up a file, speed of access can considerably be improved. Other techniques can improve access either by speeding it further and/or reducing the space required. These techniques can be employed by the operating system or by the hardware itself.

Speed enhancement is commonly made by the use of a *cache*. A cache is a region of fast transient memory which sits between the backing store and the host computer. A similar notion is to employ a *RAM drive* which is an area of main memory that, under the control of a suitable program, mimics the features of a small disk drive, but with a very fast access time. Compression techniques are used to allow files to be stored on backing store in less space. Finally the two aspects of *archiving* will be described. One is to keep backup copies of information on a slower but larger medium such as tape. The other is to encode a group of, usually related, files into one file, called a library file or an archive. Neither aspect of archiving is strictly hardware related but they are included for completeness.

5.16.1 Caches

A backing store cache is a smaller but faster storage device which sits between the computer system and the main backing store. The principle of caching is not restricted to backing stores. For example, most computer memories consist of *dynamic RAM (DRAM),* which has a relatively slow access rate compared to modern computer processors, and a small memory cache of the more expensive but faster *static RAM (SRAM)* is inserted between the processor and the main memory. Caching is illustrated by Figure 5.38.

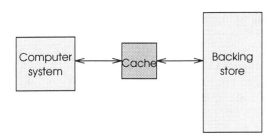

Figure 5.38 *Principle of caching*

The cache used with backing store may form part of the controller for the backing store which maintains its own region of memory and therefore operates totally transparently to the main computer system. Alternatively, it may be implemented by the operating system, which sets aside a region of the system's main memory for the cache, and implements the caching algorithm itself.

Caching works on the principle that access to the store is not entirely random and that at any point in time a small number of blocks are being regularly accessed. A cache is either a read cache a write cache or a read/write cache which is simply both of the first two combined.

A read cache is the most commonly used and, at its simplest, it retains a copy of each block as it is read from the backing store. When the cache is full the oldest copies are replaced. Whenever the computer system requests a block the cache is searched first and, if a copy of the block is present, it is sent to the computer system without the backing store being involved. Because the cache is much faster than the backing store then, if many blocks required are already in the cache, backing store access is considerably enhanced. The cache typically uses dynamic RAM which is the usual component of the main memory, and has access speeds of around 60 to 80 nanoseconds. It loses its contents when the power is removed and so the first few disk accesses will necessarily be directly to the backing store.

Sophisticated caching algorithms may also anticipate future disk read requests and, when directed to read a block, may also read a few blocks ahead into the cache on the assumption that a file has been placed in contiguous blocks.

Up to a point, the larger the cache, the better will be the performance. As more blocks are kept in the cache so the chances of finding one there improve. The improvement is not linear and, depending on the application, an optimum size is reached beyond which little extra performance is noticed. The reason for this is that at any one time only certain files from the backing store are regularly in use – perhaps only a very small percentage of the total backing store. If all the blocks required over the next few minutes are in the cache then the cache is large enough and making it larger would not improve performance. A typical cache size is of the order of one or more megabytes for a personal computer, and correspondingly larger for a computer system that has many simultaneous, and therefore diverse, activities.

A write cache comes in two forms. The simpler form is known as a *write through cache* and keeps a copy in the cache of each block written to backing store. The only advantage to this occurs if the written block is likely to be read back in the near future and, in many applications, this is quite common. The second form is known as a *write deferred cache* which also keeps copies in the cache but delays the writing to the backing store for a short time. Whenever a block is written to backing store it is instead actually written to the cache which is much faster. Later, when the computer is idle, the block is written to the backing store. If a block is written again before it has left the cache, then this new copy simply overwrites the one in the cache.

When a group of blocks is to be written to backing store they are ordered in such a way as to make the the access most efficient. For example, all blocks which lie on the same track of a disk would be sent together and in the correct sector order. This is much more efficient than sending discrete and random write requests to the backing store. There is, however, a serious problem with a deferred write cache and that is, if power is lost while the cache is still holding blocks then they will never reach the backing store and so will be lost. The consequences of this vary, depending upon what the block(s) represent. A block of a user's data file lost could just mean that the file is a slightly earlier version and this might be of little inconvenience, especially as a write cache would normally only buffer up blocks for a maximum time – typically a few seconds. If the block belonged to a disk directory then the consequences could be more serious. Some sophisticated caches are able to recognize whether a block should be cached or not and so the problem is lessened. A computer system may also employ a protected power supply with a backup which, in the event of power loss, takes over for at least the time required to empty the cache. Nevertheless many people are wary of deferred write caches and choose not to use them.

A read/write cache is simply a combination of the above two. It may employ two different fixed size regions of memory for the read cache and for the write cache or a single larger memory which serves for both on demand. Then, at peak reading times, more of this memory is given over to the read cache while, at times of large writing activity, the write cache would be given a larger share.

5.16.2 *RAM drives*

A RAM drive is an area of fast (temporary) memory which stores information in the same way as a disk drive. Usually it is an area of main memory (RAM) which is controlled by a special program. This program provides an interface to the computer which mimics, say, a disk drive that is very fast but relatively small. In principle, a RAM drive is very similar to caching as described above except that it operates on whole files rather than parts of them. The RAM drive will loose its contents when power is turned off and so must be loaded up with selected files when the system is started. The user will then store copies of the most frequently needed files on to the RAM drive and access them from there instead of the normal backing store. Some RAM drive and cache programs are combined providing both facilities by using a single area of memory for both a RAM drive and a cache. The sizes allocated to the two are adjusted dynamically depending on how much of the RAM drive is currently needed.

5.16.3 *Compression*

Compression attempts to re-code data in such a manner that less space is required on the backing store. Some disk and tape units have compression algorithms built in and so operate transparently. Many tape cartridges are actually advertised as having a capacity which assumes a degree of compression. As with the previous techniques, compression is also commonly performed by a program which, like a cache, operates at the interface between the computer system and the backing store. Clearly, when the data is retrieved from the backing store it must be uncompressed to its original form.

There exist two distinct techniques for compression. The first takes advantage of the fact that in any file certain bytes or sequences of bytes occur more frequently than others, and it can be performed by a program or built into the hardware of a disk or tape unit. The second uses the fact that, because files are stored as a sequence of fixed sized units, the last unit in each file has unused space. In effect it joins files together into one large file therefore wasting space in one unit only. This form depends upon intimate knowledge of the operating system in use, and so is exclusively performed by software. Programs which use this second technique will usually also combine it with the first technique to achieve high rates of compression. A typical achievement is to halve the space required on average, and such programs are commonly known as *disk doublers*.

Compression algorithms are commonly built into most cartridge tape drives – QIC, video and DAT. The capacity of many such drives and tapes is quoted at that value after compression, which assumes a value of 50%. Compression on magnetic disks is rarely automatically built in, as the disk is a fixed size and has a structure which must be known. On the other hand, a tape streamer is seen as a sequence of blocks of any arbitrary length. If the data is easily compressed then the tape simply appears to be longer. If the compression scheme is not successful then the tape appears to be shorter.

The first technique exploits the inherent redundancy that exists in most files. As a simple example, many text files consist largely of the 26 lower case alphabetic characters but each character is normally stored in a byte, which can potentially encode 256 characters. The file could be recoded by assigning 26 short codes to the common characters a–z and using the usual code for the rest. Only 5 bits would be needed for each of the short codes instead of 8. There is, however, an overhead penalty of keeping track of which data is short or long code. There are a variety of coding algorithms used with varying degrees of sophistication. All rely on a mapping scheme or a data dictionary, which changes the coding from a series of individual bytes into an equivalent shorter form. One such algorithm is called Huffman coding and is described in Chapter 8. These algorithms look for either common sequences of data or repetition of a value. Common sequences are stored in a dictionary and the numeric dictionary entry is substituted. Repetition of a character such as a sequence of the character code 0 in a binary program file can be detected and then replaced with a count of the length of the sequence and one copy of the character involved.

A data dictionary is illustrated by Figure 5.39. The dictionary can be fixed, and therefore the same for every file or it can be built up specially and optimized for each file. A fixed dictionary will not perform as well as a customized one, but a copy of each customized dictionary has to be stored alongside each coded file and, for short files, this could result in overall expansion instead of compression. There are also two kinds of

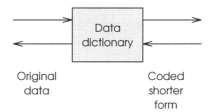

Figure 5.39 *Data dictionary for compression*

format for the coded form. It can be fixed size where each group of, say, 12 bits represents a character, word or phrase. Alternatively the coding could be variable length where, for example, very common codes occupy only a few bits and rarer codes are longer. A data dictionary employing a fixed length 12-bit code would have 4096 (2^{12}) entries. Each byte and sequence of bytes is looked up in the dictionary and the corresponding 12-bit entry code substituted. To take account of all possibilities, 256 of the 4096 entries would represent the original 256 bytes for cases where a byte is not part of a common sequence. Typical dictionary entries would include common words and phrases, and common word prefixes and suffixes. A customized dictionary can be created by first scanning the file or built up as the file is read and coded. The second approach lends itself more readily to automatic coding done by hardware, as information is sent to and from backing store.

Several algorithms are also available as programs which the user invokes manually on individual files. This is normally done to files which are not needed for some time or prior to transporting them to another system.

A file is stored as a series of blocks and so, on average, the last block will only be half full. With a block size of 512 bytes, that is an average 256 bytes of space unused for each file stored. The space unused is, in practice, much more because most operating systems group blocks into *clusters* and use this cluster as the minimum unit of storage. A cluster is a group of consecutive blocks. Cluster sizes are typically between 4 and 32. The reasoning behind allocating in such large units is twofold. Firstly consecutive blocks can be read/written in sequence more quickly than the same number of blocks scattered around the disk or tape. Secondly, it can be more convenient to the operating system to keep track of a smaller number of clusters on a large storage device. Some systems allocate cluster sizes proportionate to the total capacity of a disk drive so that each drive has the same number of clusters and can be handled by the same algorithms. When a file system consists of many small files each occupying (part of) one cluster then little advantage is gained by upgrading to a larger disk if such a system is in force.

Programs which perform compression can exploit this fact. A common practice is for the compression program to store all files in one large file and maintain a list of the original files' names, their starting position in this large file, and their length. Like the cache and data dictionary, this program interfaces between the computer system and backing store so that the user does not notice this transformation.

5.16.4 Archiving

Archiving is mentioned here briefly for completeness. There are two common meanings to the term archiving when used in the context of backing stores. First, stores such as magnetic hard disks are usually archived or *backed up*, in order to keep a copy should the original copy be lost or become inaccessible due to disk failure. This form of archiving is also known as *backing up* and typically consists of regularly copying files from the disk to a removable medium such as floppy disk or, more commonly, magnetic tape. Utility programs exist to make this task more convenient, allowing the user to select which type of file to back up, and to detect which files have changed – and need to be backed up again – since the last time the disk was archived.

The second meaning of the term archiving refers to taking a copy of a group of files and converting them into a single *library file*. In this way a complete hierarchy of subdirectories and files can be coded into a single file. This is a convenient way of copying a file structure from one place to another. Clearly there also needs to be a decoding program which recovers the original files from the file archive. This form of archiving will often include file compression in order to make the resulting archive as small as possible. A utility package may consist of many files – source files, programs and documentation – and can more easily be distributed or stored in a repository of software in an archive form. An example of archiving programs are the set of *zip* programs, which are used by many computer sites which retain copies of many software utilities and provide a service similar to a lending library, except that the users obviously take their own permanent copy of the package rather than borrow it.

As with the zip programs, these two forms of archiving are sometimes combined – a whole file-store structure or a substructure is archived into one compressed archive file, which is then saved on to magnetic tape as a security backup.

▶ **5.17 Further Reading**

Tanenbaum AS, *Operating Systems – design and implementation,* Prentice Hall, 1987

Watkinson J, *The Art of Digital Audio,* Focal Press, 1988

Reed IS and Solomon G, *Polynomial codes over certain finite fields,* Journal of the Society of Industrial Applications of Mathematics, 1960, Vol. 8, No. 2, pages 300–304

6

Analogue Signal Input–Output

▶ 6.1 Introduction

Analogue signals are continually variable in amplitude. This contrasts with the digital representation of quantities inside a computer where the finite number of bits to a word means that only discrete values of amplitude can be represented. Hence if analogue signals are to be passed to or from a digital computer, some kind of signal converter is required, as shown conceptually in Figure 6.1. The terms *data acquisition* or *data conversion* are applied to the process on the analogue input side, and *data distribution* on the output side.

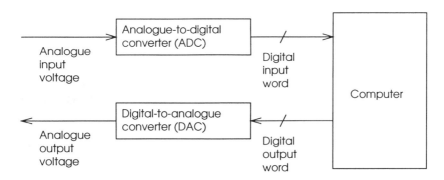

Figure 6.1 *Converters are needed for analogue signal I/O*

An analogue signal from the 'real world' outside a computer is shown in Figure 6.2. It is part of a speech waveform. A second example is shown in Figure 6.3, which is from a thermocouple used for temperature measurement. These examples illustrate the wide range of signal amplitude and time scales that are encountered.

Digital processing of analogue signals by computer offers several advantages including accuracy, flexibility, repeatability, and ability to perform complex operations. An exhaustive list of applications would be very long. Moreover, as hardware costs of computers continue to fall such a list would continue to lengthen. Current applications include: speech analysis, process control, artificial speech, simulators, sonar, computer-controlled

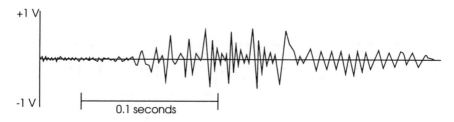

Figure 6.2 *Analogue signals, part of a speech waveform*

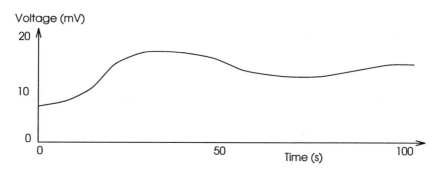

Figure 6.3 *Analogue signals, thermocouple signal*

experiments, seismography, automatic control systems, automatic test equipment, pollution monitoring and analysis, spectral analysis, vibration and noise analysis, automatic tracking systems, graph plotting X-Y recorders, instrumentation, transducer signal analysis.

Mini- and microcomputers are usually used for these applications, with mainframes being reserved for applications which require greater processing power, and where the costs are justified.

One consequence of using a computer is that data can only be input at discrete points in time. Hence only sampled values of an analogue signal can be taken, as is shown in Figure 6.4, and not the true signal itself. An obvious requirement is that the signal should not change significantly between samples, otherwise information is lost, and a high enough sample rate must be used. The upper limit of processing rate for a small computer is of the order of 10^5 samples per second. However, higher sampling rates can be handled if the data is stored in memory and not processed in real time.

Likewise, the computer can only output data at discrete points in time and so, for example, the reconstituted form of the analogue signal in Figure 6.4 would now appear as shown in Figure 6.5. The horizontal portions of the waveform occur while the next update of output amplitude is

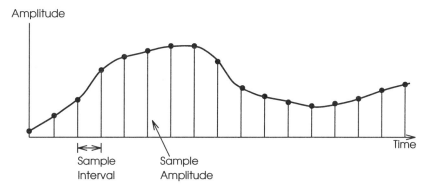

Figure 6.4 *Sampled analogue signal*

awaited. In many cases the staircase effect is not noticeable because the analogue signal is slowly varying, or because the steps are smoothed out by the inertia of the load (as for example when the signal drives a deflection-type meter). Alternatively a smoothing filter can be attached to the output of the converter. The optimum response is that of an interpolating filter, details of which can be found in texts on signal processing.

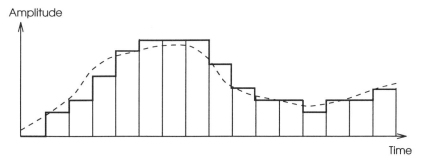

Figure 6.5 *Reconstituted analogue signal from samples*

A second consequence of using a computer follows, as was mentioned earlier, because data are represented by words having a finite number of bits. A three-bit data word can assume any of 2^3 (that is 8) different codes: 000, 001, 010, ... 110, 111. Each code is made to correspond to a fixed level of analogue signal amplitude, and the levels are usually chosen to be equi-spaced. This means that a sampled value of analogue signal is given a code which has the nearest corresponding fixed level, and the signal in Figure 6.4 now appears as shown in Figure 6.6. This process of assigning the nearest fixed level to a sample is called *quantization* and gives rise to a *quantization error* because the exact value of the original signal cannot be recovered. Quantization errors can have magnitudes up to half the spacing between quantization levels. It is important therefore to choose a sufficient number of data word bits so that uncertainty due to quantization error is kept to an acceptable amount.

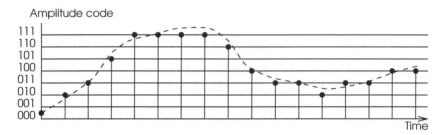

Figure 6.6 *Quantization of sample amplitudes*

Figure 6.7 shows a block diagram of a typical form of multi-channel analogue I/O system. The hearts of the input and output sides are the *analogue-to-digital converter (ADC)* and the *digital-to-analogue converter (DAC)*. The *sample/hold (S/H)* holds the signal sample constant for the ADC. The amplifier is used to condition the analogue signals, which may be small and differential, to take advantage of the full-scale range of the ADC. The *multiplexer (MUX)* enables several analogue channels to be input.

The construction and operation of these blocks are described in the following sections after first dealing with basic features of converters and aliasing errors. Subsequent sections then go on to show the various ways these blocks may be connected to form a complete analogue I/O peripheral unit.

▶ 6.2 Basic Features of Converters

6.2.1 Binary Coding

Binary codes, more properly called natural binary codes, are usually used for unipolar analogue signals. Unipolar signals do not change sign: they are always positive or always negative. Positive polarities are often adopted. Using this coding the output voltage from an n-bit DAC is given by

$$V_{out} = FSR \left(\frac{B_{n-1}}{2} + \ldots + \frac{B_2}{2^{n-2}} + \frac{B_1}{2^{n-1}} + \frac{B_0}{2^n} \right) \tag{6.1}$$

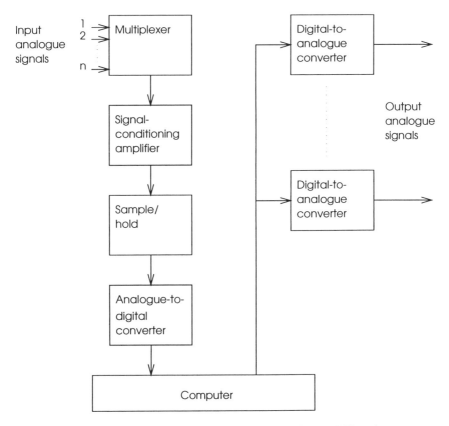

Figure 6.7 *Typical form of multi-channel analogue I/O system*

where the bits B_{n-1} to B_0 that make up the *n*-bit data word can each take on a value 1 or 0, and *FSR* is the full-scale range of the output voltage. Note that in this equation the bits contribute *weights* to V_{out} which decrease by factors of two going from B_{n-1}, the most significant bit (*MSB*), to B_0, the least significant bit (*LSB*). Table 6.1 for *n*=3 illustrates how these weights build up values for V_{out} for different code words. Hence V_{out} may assume values in the range zero to *FSR*, or more exactly zero to $FSR\,(\,1 - 1/8\,)$. In general, then, the highest value of V_{out} is $FSR\,(\,1 - 1/2^n\,)$, which is 1 *LSB* less than *FSR*.

The smallest increment of voltage that can be obtained is called the *resolution* and corresponds to the weight assigned to the *LSB*. Resolution is usually expressed relative to *FSR*, and therefore has a value of $1/2^n$. The data word lengths encountered in practice in nearly all converters used with computers fall in the range 8 bits to 16 bits. The resolutions obtained are shown in Table 6.2.

Values for *n* of 8, 10, or 12 bits give resolutions which are adequate for

Table 6.1 *Binary coding*

B₂ (MSB)	Code B₁	B₀ (LSB)	Binary fraction	V_out (by Eq. 6.1)
0	0	0	0.000	FSR (0+0+0) = 0
0	0	1	0.001	FSR (0+0+⅛) = ⅛ FSR
0	1	0	0.010	FSR (0+¼+0) = ²⁄₈ FSR
0	1	1	0.011	FSR (0+¼+⅛) = ³⁄₈ FSR
1	0	0	0.100	FSR (½+0+0) = ⁴⁄₈ FSR
1	0	1	0.101	FSR (½+0+⅛) = ⁵⁄₈ FSR
1	1	0	0.110	FSR (½+¼+0) = ⁶⁄₈ FSR
1	1	1	0.111	FSR (½+¼+⅛) = ⁷⁄₈ FSR

Table 6.2 *Resolutions*

No. of bits (n)	Resolution Fraction	%(approx.)
8	1/256	0.4
9	1/512	0.2
10	1/1024	0.1
11	1/2048	0.05
12	1/4096	0.024
13	1/8192	0.012
14	1/16 384	0.006
15	1/32 768	0.003
16	1/65 536	0.0015

many applications. For higher numbers of bits, both the costs and difficulty of handling signals so as to preserve accuracy increase rapidly.

For analogue-to-digital conversion using natural binary coding, the task of the converter is to find that binary code which corresponds most closely to the analogue input signal and amplitude. That is, B_{n-1} to B_0 are generated so as to satisfy the equation

$$FSR \left(\frac{B_{n-1}}{2} + \ldots + \frac{B_2}{2^{n-2}} + \frac{B_1}{2^{n-1}} + \frac{B_0}{2^n} \right) = V_{IN} + V_{QE} \tag{6.2}$$

The 'slack' variable V_{QE}, which is the *quantization error,* is included because the lefthand side of this expression assumes discrete values, whereas V_{IN} may assume any value in the continuous range of the converter. Since the resolution is 1 *LSB,* the nearest discrete value of the lefthand side to V_{IN} in this equation is never further than $\frac{1}{2}LSB$, and so:

$$\left| V_{QE} \right| \le \frac{1}{2} \times 2^{-n} FSR \text{ volts} \tag{6.3}$$

Typical *FSR* voltages for ADCs or DACs are 5 V and 10 V. A value of 10.24 V is sometimes used because it equals $(10\,\text{mV}) \times 2^{10}$ and the binary weights are then convenient multiples of 10 mV.

6.2.2 Converter Transfer Functions and Error Types

The converter transfer functions, that is Eqn 6.1 and Eqn 6.2, are shown graphically in Figure 6.8. The plot for the DAC is a series of dots because there is a unique voltage level for each discrete binary code. On the other hand, for the ADC a band of voltages up to $\frac{1}{2}LSB$ on either side of a quantization level has the same binary code, which gives rise to the 'staircase', as shown.

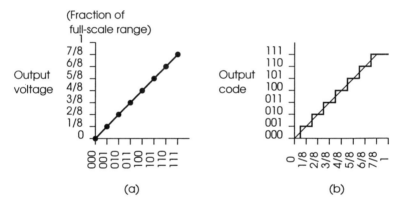

Figure 6.8 *Transfer function: (a) DAC; (b) ADC*

In practice, component imperfections within the converter cause deviations from the ideal transfer function, some of which can be adjusted for by the user and others not. In most applications precision is important and manufacturers' specifications are therefore of interest. Explanations of the terms more commonly used in specifications now follow.

(a) *Offset error.* In a DAC this occurs where the lowest binary input code (all bits 0) produces a non-zero output voltage. For an ADC, conversely, an offset error occurs if the mid-step analogue voltage which produces the lowest binary output code occurs at a non-zero value (see Figure 6.9). In practice an ADC offset error is more easily determined by adjusting the amplitude of a test input voltage until the transition 0...0 to 0...1 occurs. Ideally this should be at $\frac{1}{2}LSB$, any deviation from this is the offset error.

In many converters an adjustment facility is provided to nullify offset errors. Accurate adjustment is not easy and requires good test equipment. Fortunately, it is often not necessary, especially in low-resolution converters, where manufacturing tolerances guarantee offset errors which are not significant.

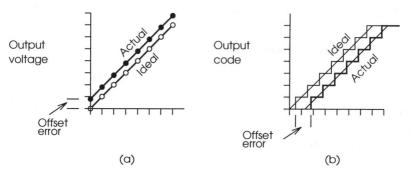

Figure 6.9 *Offset errors: (a) DAC; (b) ADC*

(b) *Scale-factor error* or *gain error*. This occurs when the full-scale range differs from the ideal value (see Figure 6.10). Again adjustment facilities are usually provided and should be used after offset errors have been corrected.

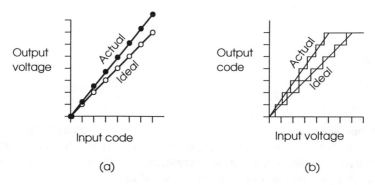

Figure 6.10 *Scale errors: (a) DAC; (b) ADC*

(c) *Linearity* or *non-linearity*. This refers to the maximum deviation of the actual converter transfer function from the best straight line that can be drawn through all points. It is computationally more convenient to take a straight line between the two end points, which gives a more conservative measure of linearity. See Figure 6.11. A typical figure for linearity is $\pm^{1}/_{2}LSB$.

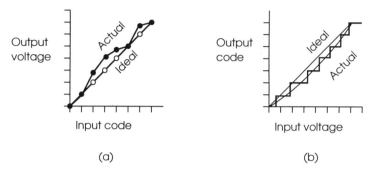

Figure 6.11 *Linearity errors: (a) DAC; (b) ADC*

(d) *Differential non-linearity.* This is a measure of the deviation of individual steps from the ideal size of 1 *LSB*. For example a maximum differential non-linearity of ¼ *LSB* means that step sizes for the converter lie in the range ¾ *LSB* to 1¼ *LSB*. When differential non-linearity is specified then linearity, as defined in (c) above, is sometimes called *integral linearity* to distinguish it from differential non-linearity.

(e) *Monotonicity.* A converter has a monotonic response (see Figure 6.12) if none of the steps over the whole range is negative. Monotonicity is guaranteed if the differential non-linearity is less than or equal to 1 *LSB*.

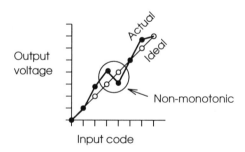

Figure 6.12 *Monotonicity error*

(f) *Missing codes* – see Figure 6.13. This occurs in an ADC only, where one or more of the codes are missed out as the input voltage is varied over the whole range. As is shown in later sections some types of ADC use a DAC internally, and where this DAC is non-monotonic then as a detailed analysis shows, missing codes can occur. Missing codes can also be caused by internal electrical noise.

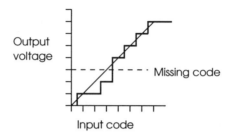

Figure 6.13 *Missing code in ADC*

(g) *Absolute accuracy.* This is the difference between the actual analogue voltage that corresponds to any code, compared to the theoretical value of this voltage. When the converter is an ADC the measurement is done at the horizontal mid-point of a step. Usually the maximum difference is specified and the measurement includes errors from all sources except quantization uncertainty.

(h) *Relative accuracy.* This is similar to absolute accuracy, but the difference is now taken between the numerical value of code expressed as a binary fraction, and the corresponding analogue voltage expressed as a fraction of the *FSR*. This measurement does not include scale-factor errors, which can usually be nullified by the user.

Errors are often expressed as fractions of an *LSB*, percentage of *FSR*, or parts per million relative to full-scale range.

In many applications an overall accuracy comparable to the resolution is desirable. However, this need not always be the case. For example, if a DAC is used to generate a small number of voltages for an experiment, say 1, 2, 3, ..., 9 V (using an *FSR* of 10 V), then only four bits of resolution are needed, but an accuracy corresponding to twelve bits may be required. Conversely for X- and Y-deflection DACs used to generate video display graphics images, a medium accuracy is acceptable, but a higher resolution may be desirable to ensure that the lines displayed have a smooth, rather than a stepped, appearance.

6.2.3 Bipolar Codes and Conversion

The unipolar coding as discussed so far is inadequate for bipolar signals, such as Figure 6.2. Several coding schemes are in use to represent bipolar quantities, and three of the more common ones are illustrated in Table 6.3. The *FSR*, which spans both positive and negative quantities, is taken to be 16 V for this example.

Table 6.3 *Bipolar coding*

Voltage	Offset binary	Two's complement	Sign magnitude
+7	1111	0111	0111
+6	1110	0110	0110
+5	1101	0101	0101
+4	1100	0100	0100
+3	1011	0011	0011
+2	1010	0010	0010
+1	1001	0001	0001
0	1000	0000	0000 or 1000
-1	0111	1111	1001
-2	0110	1110	1010
-3	0101	1101	1011
-4	0100	1100	1100
-5	0011	1011	1101
-6	0010	1010	1110
-7	0001	1001	1111
-8	0000	1000	N/A

From Table 6.3 it is easy to deduce that if a unipolar scheme of range 0 to +*V* volts is converted to a bipolar scheme of range -*V* volts to +*V* volts, then the magnitude of one *LSB* in volts will be doubled, unless an extra bit of resolution is used in the converter.

In practice bipolar converters are usually obtained using simple modifications to unipolar converters. Figure 6.14 shows schematically how this can be done for DACs. Circuit details are given later in this chapter. For ADCs, similar steps to those in Figure 6.14 can be used, but in reverse order. Alternatively, for those ADCs which use a DAC internally, a bipolar DAC will produce a bipolar ADC. Many commercial analogue I/O systems allow the user to select either a unipolar or one of several bipolar coding schemes.

▶ 6.3 Aliasing Errors and Bandwidth Limited Signals

Intuitively, it is obvious that to preserve information during the sampling of an analogue signal, samples have to be taken at a sufficiently high rate that important features of the signal are not missed. From Shannon's *sampling theorem* it is known that provided samples are taken more than twice as often as the highest frequency contained in the signal, then there is no loss of information due to the sampling process and it is possible

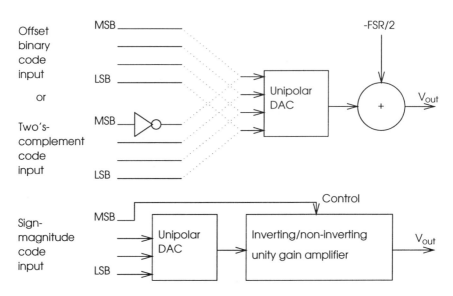

Figure 6.14 *Bipolar DAC's are obtained by modifying unipolar DAC's*

unambiguously to reconstruct the signal from the samples.

It might be tempting to go on from this and conclude that if a signal contains higher-frequency components of no interest (such as noise) then it does not matter if a sampling rate less than twice these frequencies is used since information about these components is lost. However, this would be a wrong conclusion and in fact these components are translated in frequency and contaminate the wanted signal. This can be seen from the example in Figure 6.15. The unwanted component is presumed to be a 9 kHz sine wave on a zero-frequency component which is presumed to be a wanted component. This composite waveform is sampled at 10^4 samples/s, which is less than twice the unwanted signal frequency. It can be seen that the resulting samples are indistinguishable from those obtained from a low-frequency 1 kHz sine wave sitting on the same zero-frequency component. After taking samples there is no way of knowing if this 1 kHz is genuine or not. The original sample has therefore taken on a new guise and this effect is called *aliasing*. These aliased components add on to the wanted components, thus constituting an error.

To avoid these errors the signal has to be *bandwidthlimited* so that it does not contain components with frequencies greater than half the sampling rate. Fortunately many signals are naturally bandwidth limited because they originate from physical phenomena which have mechanical inertia (as in many transducer signals) and the sampling rate can be chosen to avoid problems. Alternatively, a low-pass filter may be inserted in the signal path to cut out the higher-frequency components.

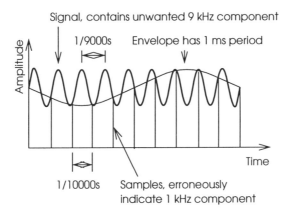

Figure 6.15 *Aliasing error*

Aliasing error contributions are generally negligible if the relative magnitude of the residual unwanted components is less than the overall accuracy required of the analogue input channel. A full mathematical analysis of this topic can be found in texts on signal processing and communications theory.

▶ 6.4 Digital-to-Analogue Converters (DACs)

6.4.1 The Weighted-Resistor Method

Converters operating according with a natural binary code must function so that an input number causes an output voltage according to Eqn 6.1. The righthand side of this equation is the sum of binary weighted terms $\frac{1}{2}B_{n-1}$, $\frac{1}{4}B_{n-2}$, $\frac{1}{8}B_{n-3}$, ..., and a conceptual way to realise this is shown in Figure 6.16. Each of the current generators produces zero or the value shown, depending on the state of the corresponding data bit. The output current is the sum of the currents:

$$I_{out} = I\left(\frac{B_3}{2} + \frac{B_2}{4} + \frac{B_1}{8} + \frac{B_0}{16}\right) \tag{6.4}$$

and is of the same form as Eqn 6.1.

In the arrangement shown in Figure 6.17 the function of the current generator has been replaced by a resistor in series with a switch, connected to an accurate reference voltage source. The switch is closed when the corresponding data bit is 1. The high-gain operational amplifier, and

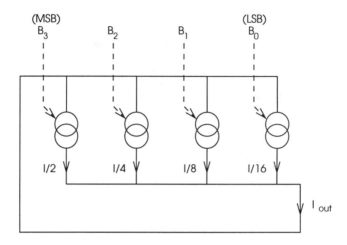

Figure 6.16 *DAC using current generators*

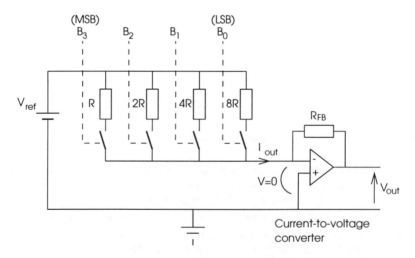

Figure 6.17 *Weighted-resistor DAC*

feedback resistor, R_{FB}, are added so as to act as a current-to-voltage converter. In most applications a voltage output is preferred.

This is an example of a negative-feedback (NFB) circuit, and one property is that the voltage at the input terminals of an operational amplifier is
approximately zero provided the amplifier approaches the ideal. This
property can be seen from the defining relationship $V_{out} = AV$. That is,
$V = (1/A)V_{out}$, so taking a typical value for V_{out} of 10 V maximum, and
A=100 000, V has a maximum value of $100\,\mu V$, which is very small

compared with other voltages around the circuit. Also, operational amplifiers have high input impedances, and therefore, to a first approximation, the terminal input currents can be assumed to be zero.

That is, for any ideal operational amplifier in an NFB circuit

$$V = 0 \tag{6.5}$$

$$I = 0 \tag{6.6}$$

These conditions enable us to analyze operational amplifier circuits. For Figure 6.17, all of I_{out} must pass through R_{FB} because of Eqn 6.6 above, and causes a voltage drop across R_{FB} which can be equated to the voltage difference between its ends: $I_{out}R_{FB} = V - V_{out}$. Substituting Eqn 6.5 gives

$$V_{out} = -I_{out}R_{FB} \tag{6.7}$$

Further, because of Eqn 6.5, when any switch is closed the full voltage V_{ref} appears across the resistor, consequently the current sum is given by

$$I_{out} = V_{ref}\left(\frac{B_3}{R} + \frac{B_2}{2R} + \frac{B_1}{4R} + \frac{B_0}{8R}\right) \tag{6.8}$$

Combining Eqn 6.7 and Eqn 6.8,

$$V_{out} = \left(-V_{ref}\frac{2R_{FB}}{R}\right)\left(\frac{B_3}{R} + \frac{B_2}{2R} + \frac{B_1}{4R} + \frac{B_0}{8R}\right) \tag{6.9}$$

This is of the form required, with a full-scale range of $-V_{ref}(2R_{FB}/R)$. To obtain a positive value of *FSR* a negative reference voltage is used. In practice the reference voltage is obtained using the breakdown voltage of a *zener diode,* or by using a so-called *band-gap reference* which is based on the logarithmic voltage–current relationship of a semiconductor PN junction, wherein a doubling of current produces a known and stable increase in voltage. The requirement of V_{ref} is stability rather than accuracy, since any resulting scale-factor error is easily compensated by adjusting R_{FB}.

Electronic switches are used in practice, and are described in the next section.

Although the circuit in Figure 6.17 will work, it suffers from a number of disadvantages. The principal one is the high range of resistor values required: R to 2^nR. Even for a modest resolution of eight bits a range of R to 256R is required. It is difficult to manufacture such wide ranges to have adequately matched temperature coefficients and ageing properties when using preferred fabrication techniques such as thin-film, or monolithic-integrated circuits. In practice, then, this technique is limited to DACs with up to four or five bits of accuracy.

6.4.2 R-2R Ladder Method

Difficulties in obtaining a wide range of resistor values, as required for the weighted-resistor method are overcome by using an *R-2R ladder,* shown in Figure 6.18, because resistor values are now confined to a two-to-one range. Most practical DAC circuits are based on the R-2R ladder.

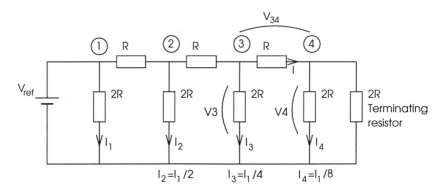

Figure 6.18 *R-2R ladder*

One of the useful properties of the ladder is that a reference voltage applied at one end causes the currents I_3 to I_0 to take on values in a decreasing binary weighted sequence. This can be seen by first considering the right-most current I_0. By Ohm's law, the voltage at node 4 is $V_0 = (2R)I_0$. Also the current I must split equally down the two identical (2R) resistors, and so $I = 2I_0$. From this $V_{34} = RI = R(2I_0)$ and because $V_3 = V_{34} + V_4$; $V_3 = R(I_0) + (2R)I_0 = (4R)I_0$. Substituting this result for V_3 in $I_3 = V_3(2R)$ for the current down the next element in the ladder gives $I_1 = 2I_0$. This argument can also be applied to the next stage of the ladder to give $I_2 = 2I_1$, and once more, $I_3 = 2I_2$.

Combining these relationships we obtain the binary weighted sequence shown at the bottom of Figure 6.18. This leads directly to the R-2R ladder DAC circuit shown in Figure 6.19 where the weighted resistors of Figure 6.17 have been replaced by the R-2R ladder. The switches serve to route each binary weighted current down to the zero-volt line or into the current-to-voltage converter. Using the results above, we obtain

$$V_{out} = \left(-V_{ref}\,\frac{R_{FB}}{R}\right)\left(\frac{B_3}{2} + \frac{B_2}{4} + \frac{B_1}{8} + \frac{B_0}{16}\right) \qquad (6.10)$$

This is of the form required, with a full-scale range of $-V_{ref}(2R_{FB}/R)$ volts. This scheme can easily be extended to higher resolutions, provided suitably accurate resistors are available.

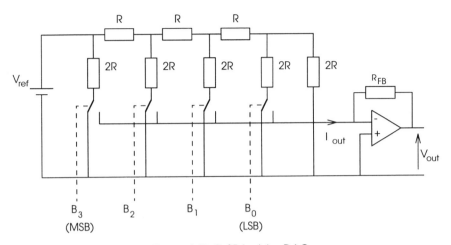

Figure 6.19 *R-2R ladder DAC*

Speed requirements dictate that electronic switches are used and the principle of operation of the *field effect transistor (FET)* switch is shown in Figure 6.20(a). The terminal characteristics, Figure 6.20(b), indicate that for V_{GS} positive the FET acts as a low resistance (typically $r_{on} = 100\,\Omega$), whereas for V_{GS} negative the FET is switched off and a negligibly small leakage current flows. The action of the two-position switch is summarised in Table 6.4.

The finite value of r_{on} increases the effective values of the (2R) resistors which can affect the binary-weighting property. This effect can be minimized by choosing the ladder resistances to be high (say $10\,k\Omega$ or more) and also trimming down the (2R) resistors by an equal amount to r_{on}.

Fabrication techniques vary, but typically the FET switches, and associated drive circuitry, are made as an integrated-circuit chip, and the passive R-2R ladder is made in thin-film form on a separate substrate. Both chips are mounted in the same encapsulation. At least one manufacturer is able to put the thin film R-2R circuit directly on the surface of the active-device IC chip.

Various other DAC circuits are also used in practice, based on the binary-weighting property of R-2R ladders.

6.4.3 Bipolar Output Voltages

As can be seen from Figure 6.14, to convert a unipolar DAC to provide offset binary-coded bipolar output, the output voltage must be offset negatively by $\frac{1}{2}FSR$. This operation is particularly simple when a current-to-voltage converter is used at the DAC output; see Figure 6.21. Here R_{OS} is

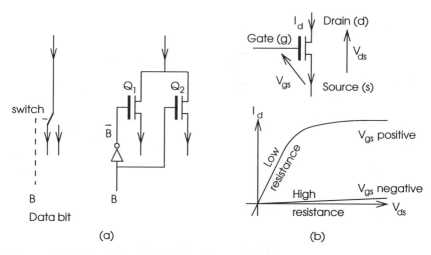

Figure 6.20 *FET switch for R-2R ladder DAC; (a) principle, (b) FET terminal characteristics*

Table 6.4 *Action of a two-position switch*

Control B	Q_1	Q_2	Result obtained
1 (positive)	OFF	ON	current passed to volt/current convertor
0 (negative)	ON	OFF	current passed to zero-volt line

chosen so that an offset current equivalent to $\frac{1}{2}FSR$ is subtracted from the output current of the unipolar converter before conversion to the output voltage.

Two's-complement coding may be achieved by simply complementing the MSB of the input data word before it is applied to the offset-binary DAC just described.

Sign-magnitude coded data conversion requires that the analogue output signal be inverted, or not, under control of the MSB of the data word. Figure 6.22 shows one way to do this. With the MSB at a '0', corresponding to positive V_{out}, the switch is down and the ladder output current is connected to the input of A_2, which with R_3 acts as a normal current-to-voltage converter. With the MSB at '1', the switch is up and the current is applied to the current-to-voltage converter, R_1 and A_1. However, in this connection R_2, R_3 and A_2 behave as a voltage-inverting amplifier with unity gain, and so the polarity of V_{out} is reversed. Although the sign-magnitude DAC requires another operational amplifier, one point in its favour is that one fewer bit resolution is required for the unipolar DAC.

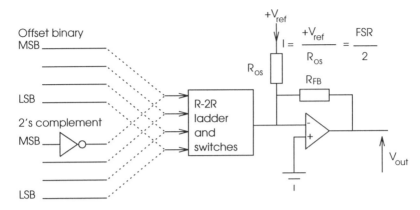

Figure 6.21 *Bipolar operation (offset binary and twos-complement codes) of the R-2R DAC*

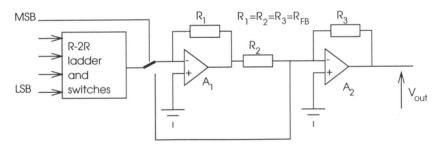

Figure 6.22 *Bipolar operation (sign-magnitude) of the R-2R DAC*

6.4.4 Performance Limitations

Static imperfections arise when all voltage and current transients have settled down, and are principally those outlined in Section 6.2.2. *Offset errors* can be nullified by adding a small adjustable current to the input of the current-to-voltage converter, in a similar way to the ½ *FSR* offset mechanism in Figure 6.21. *Scale-factor errors* may be nullified by adjusting the feedback resistor R_{FB} in the current-to-voltage converter. Other errors, such as non-linearity, etc., are usually under the control of the manufacturer.

Other static performance parameters of interest are the error temperature coefficients, since an error nullified at one temperature will return to some degree at another operating temperature of the circuit.

The principal dynamic performance parameter of interest is the *settling time*. When the input data code to the DAC is changed it takes a finite time for the circuit to settle down and provide the new output value. Worst-case settling time occurs during the transition from the most negative output level to the most positive output level, or vice versa. The settling time is defined under these worst-case conditions as the time taken for the output to settle to the steady-state value to within some specified band of error (see Figure 6.23). Often this band of error is taken to be $\pm\frac{1}{2}\,LSB$. It follows therefore that the higher resolution DACs, because of narrower error-bands, tend to have longer settling times. For example, a low-resolution 8-bit converter has a typical settling time of 1 µs , whereas 50 µs is a typical figure for a 16-bit DAC.

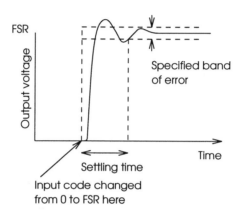

Figure 6.23 *Settling time of a DAC*

Another dynamic effect is known as a *glitch*. This occurs because of small differences in the closure times of the switches in the DAC. These differences can effectively cause the DAC to be activated by several intermediate codes as the input code is changed from one to another. For example, suppose the original code to the DAC is $\frac{1}{2}\,FSR$ (1000), and is changed to a code which is 1 *LSB* less (0111), and assume that the *MSB* is a little slower to change than the other bits. Then the sequence is

1000 original code
1111 intermediate code (B_2, B_1, B_0 have changed, but not B_3)
0111 B_3 changes to give final code.

The intermediate code in fact corresponds to *FSR* and a large spike, or glitch, may appear at the output (see Figure 6.24). Fortunately the settling time of the DAC smooths out these effects to some extent and glitches are usually of importance only in high-speed DACs. When necessary a sample hold can be used as a *deglitcher,* see Section 6.6.

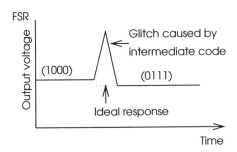

Figure 6.24 *Example of a glitch in a DAC*

▶ 6.5 Analogue-to-Digital Converters (ADCs)

6.5.1 Introduction

An *ADC* outputs a binary code representing a voltage as near as possible to the applied analogue input voltage. Many techniques to do this are known. For maximum speed *flash conversion* is used, a good compromise on speed and accuracy is given by the *successive approximation* method, and accurate but slow conversions may be obtained from the *dual-slope* method.

6.5.2 Flash Converters

Very high conversion rates are possible with a flash converter; 8-bit accuracy at several hundred million conversions per second is available from off-the-shelf devices. A rather brute-force approach is used whereby the input signal is compared with all possible subdivisions of the reference voltage at the same time, see Figure 6.25.

The reference voltage, V_{ref}, is divided in a resistor chain to give 1 *LSB* steps apart from the two ends when a $\frac{1}{2} LSB$ interval is generated. Thus, the reference input to the bottom comparator is $\frac{1}{2} LSB$, to the second $1\frac{1}{2} LSB$, etc. An input of zero results in no comparator switching; an input of between $\frac{1}{2} LSB$ and $1\frac{1}{2} LSB$ causes the lowest comparator to switch; between $1\frac{1}{2} LSB$ and $2\frac{1}{2} LSB$ the lowest two comparators will switch and so on until a full-scale input causes all comparators to switch. This running code is converted to produce a binary output.

Clearly, the number of comparators grows rapidly. An *n*-bit converter uses 2^n comparators which, in practice, means that this technique is limited to 8 or 9 bits.

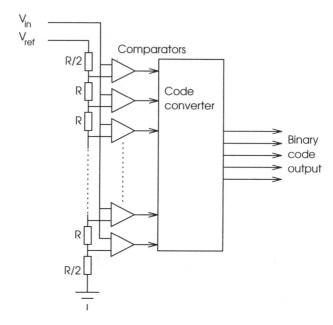

Figure 6.25 *Flash converter*

6.5.3 Successive Approximation Converters

As can be seen from Figure 6.26 this comprises three main parts:

(i) A *digital-to-analogue converter (DAC)*.

(ii) A *comparator*. This compares the incoming analogue voltage, V_{in}, with the output of the DAC, V_{dac}, and outputs a logic 1 if V_{in} is greater than V_{dac}; otherwise logic 0 is output.

(iii) A *successive-approximation register (SAR)*. This includes necessary logic to use the comparator output so as to find the binary code such that the DAC output is closest to V_{in}. This binary code is then the required output code of the ADC.

The method is reminiscent of a chemist's scales, in which ever-decreasing weights are tried in the balance pan and left in, or taken out, according to which way the scales are tipped. Consider a simple example using a 4-bit DAC with FSR of 16 V. The binary weights corresponding to B_3, B_2, B_1 and B_0 are 8, 4, 2, and 1 V respectively. Suppose the input voltage to be converted is 6.8 V. The timing diagram is shown in Figure 6.27 and the sequence is as follows.

Period T0: The arrival of the 'start' command resets all bits to zero and sets the status signal to 'busy' to indicate that conversion is in progress. Subsequent events are synchronized with the clock.

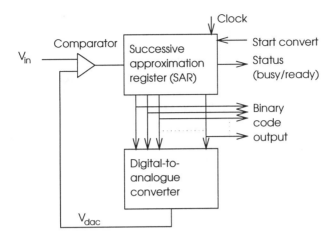

Figure 6.26 *Successive approximation ADC*

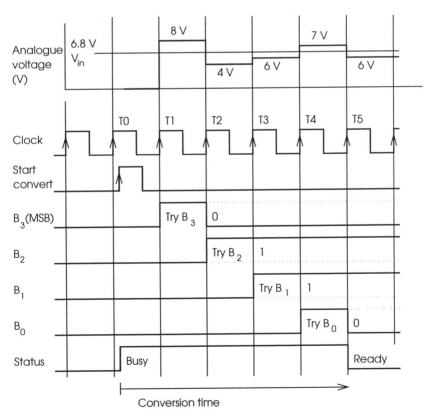

Figure 6.27 *Timing of the successive approximation ADC*

Period T1: The most significant bit, B_3, is tried. The DAC input is 1000, so $V_{dac}=8$ V. This is greater than V_{in} and the comparator output is 0 which results in the SAR resetting B_3. We now know that in the final result B_3 will be 0.

Period T2: Bit B_2 is tried. The DAC input is 0100, so $V_{dac}=4$ V. This is less than V_{in} and the comparator output is 1 which results in the SAR retaining B_2. We now know that in the final result B_2 will be 1.

Period T3: Bit B_1 is tried. The DAC input is 0110, so $V_{dac}=6$ V. This is less than V_{in} and the comparator output is 1 which results in the SAR retaining B_1. We now know that in the final result B_1 will be 1.

Period T4: The least significant bit, B_0, is tried. The DAC input is 0111, so $V_{dac}=7$ V. This is greater than V_{in} and the comparator output is 0 which results in the SAR resetting B_0. We now know that in the final result B_0 will be 0. The status signal is reset to 'ready' to indicate that conversion is complete.

For this example the output code corresponds to 0110=6 V, whereas the nearest code to $V_{in}=6.8$ V in fact corresponds to 0111=7 V. A close examination of this strategy shows that the result will always be the code producing a DAC output just less than V_{in}. It is seen that even if the DAC is ideal, an ideal ADC transfer function does not result, and an offset error of $1/2\, LSB$ is present. This effect occurs in all types of ADC which use a DAC in a feedback connection and is corrected simply by subtracting a $1/2\, LSB$ offset to the DAC output. The extension of the above for 8 bits and more, as used in practice, is obvious. Also, minor variations in the above timings may be encountered.

6.5.4 Dual-ramp, Integrating Converters

Illustrated in Figure 6.28, this method is widely used in digital voltmeters and panel meters, but is also used for analogue input to computers. The method indirectly converts a voltage to a function of time, and then converts this function to a digital number, using a counter.

The operation of the integrator is as follows. Eqn 6.5 and Eqn 6.6 once again apply at the input to the operational amplifier, and so

$$I_1 = \frac{V_1}{R} \tag{6.11}$$

This current must also flow through the capacitor, which is therefore related to the rate of change of capacitor voltage by

$$I_1 = C\frac{dV_c}{dt} \tag{6.12}$$

But V_c also equals the difference in voltages at the ends of the capacitor:

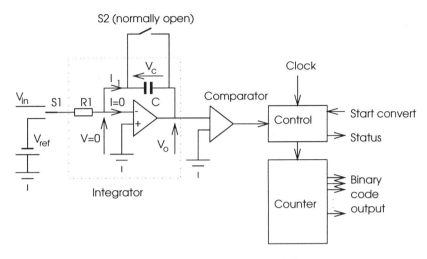

Figure 6.28 *Dual-ramp ADC*

$V_c = V - V_o$; and since $V = 0$ (from Eqn 6.5), $V_o = -V_c$. Combining this with Eqn 6.11 and Eqn 6.12 gives $V_1 = -RC(dV_o/dt)$. Hence

$$V_o = -\left(\frac{1}{CR}\right)\int V_i \, dt \qquad (6.13)$$

That is, the output of this circuit is proportional to the time integral of the applied voltage V_1.

Passing now to the operation of the converter, the sequence begins with the arrival of the 'start 'command, as shown in the timing diagram of Figure 6.29. Switch S1 is momentarily closed to discharge the capacitor and reset the integrator output to 0 volts. At the same time
(i) the counter is set running,
(ii) S1 is switched to the input voltage V_{in} (assumed here to be positive unipolar), and
(iii) the status signal is set to 'busy' to indicate that conversion is in progress.

V_{in} causes the integrator to produce a negative going ramp, the slope of which is proportional to V_{in}.

After a fixed period of time, T, as determined by the counter reaching a predetermined value, the switch S1 is turned to the negative reference voltage, $-V_{ref}$. At the point of changeover the integrator output has a value proportional to V_{in}; or to be more exact, proportional to the average of V_{in} over the interval T. At this time, the counter is reset and again set running in order to determine how long it takes to return the integrator output to zero.

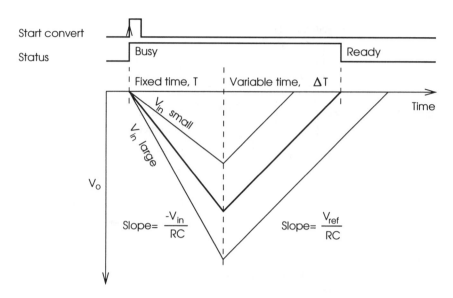

Figure 6.29 *Timing diagram of the dual-ramp ADC*

The integrator now produces a positive-going ramp, with constant slope equal to $(1/CR)V_{ref}$. After a period of time ΔT, the integrator output reaches 0 volts. This condition is detected by the comparator, which signals the counter to stop. It then holds a count which is a measure of the time ΔT. The status signal is reset to 'ready' to indicate that conversion is complete.

As is now shown the counter contains a digital number corresponding to the analogue input voltage, V_{in}. At the end of period T the output of the integrator is given by

$$V_o(T) = \left(-\frac{1}{CR}\right)\int_0^T V_{in}\,dt = \left(-\frac{T}{CR}\right)\frac{1}{T}\int_0^T V_{in}\,dt = \left(-\frac{T}{CR}\right)\overline{V_{in}} \qquad (6.14)$$

where $\overline{V_{in}}$ denotes the average value of V_{in}. The voltage $V_o(T)$ is reduced to zero over time ΔT. The ratio defines the slope of this portion of the integrator output:

$$\frac{-V_o(T)}{\Delta T} = \left(\frac{1}{CR}\right)V_{ref} \qquad (6.15)$$

Combining Eqn 6.14 and Eqn 6.15 to eliminate $V_o(T)$ gives

$$Counter\ contents\ (\Delta T) = T\,\frac{\overline{V_{in}}}{V_{ref}} \qquad (6.16)$$

The count representing T is chosen to be the full-scale of the counter, and then the final counter output conveniently equals $\overline{V_{in}}$ as a proportion of V_{ref}.

This type of converter has two useful properties. Firstly, the accuracy of the conversion, as can be seen from Eqn 6.16, does not depend on the accuracy of the passive components C, R or the clock frequency. Stable components and an accurate V_{ref} ensure good accuracy of the converter at a modest cost. Secondly, the average value of V_{in} is converted. This means that fluctuations in the signal over the period T are averaged out. A common type of unwanted fluctuation is that due to 50 Hz (or 60 Hz in some countries) mains supply. Even a small amount of fluctuation can be troublesome when converter accuracies of 8 bits up to 16 bits are required. By choosing T to be equal to an integral number of periods of the mains supply the average value of any interference voltage in the signal is zero and its effect is therefore eliminated.

6.5.5 Other ADC Methods

The three methods described so far are probably the most commonly used for analogue input to computers, but not exclusively so. For example in the counter-method the *SAR* in Figure 6.26 is replaced by a simple up-counter which produces a staircase waveform for V_{dac}. When V_{dac} exceeds V_{in} the counter is stopped and then contains the digital number required for output. Although simple, the conversion time is much greater than for the successive-approximations method, and is not suitable for high-performance applications. A further variation is to use an up-down counter in place of the *SAR*.

Variations on the dual-ramp are used (for example, 'quad-slope') which improve on the performance of the dual-ramp by minimizing small errors due to integrator drift, etc.

6.5.6 Bipolar Input Signals

Digital conversion of bipolar analogue signals in ADCs using an internal DAC, as in the successive-approximation method, is most easily achieved by using a bipolar DAC. This is not applicable to the dual-ramp type of ADC since an internal DAC is not used. In this case the methods used to produce a bipolar DAC can be used in reverse. Offset binary coding is obtained by subtraction of $\frac{1}{2}FSR$ voltage, from V_{in}. The MSB is then complemented if a two's-complement output code is required. For sign-magnitude conversion, the analogue signal is first passed through an 'absolute value' circuit. This circuit converts any negative voltage to a positive one of the same magnitude, and can be arranged to give a logic signal to indicate the original polarity of the signal.

6.5.7 Performance Limitations

Accuracy and other static parameters of the successive-approximations type of ADC obviously cannot be better than those of the internal DAC. In fact the parameters will be slightly worse because of the offset errors in the comparator. This is caused because the changeover of the comparator output in practice does not occur exactly when the two inputs are equal. Overall offset and scale-factor errors can be nullified, however, by adjustments to the internal DAC.

Offset errors in the dual-ramp converter can be corrected by adding a small voltage to V_{in}. Scale-factor errors can be nullified by trimming V_{ref}.

The dynamic performance parameter of interest is the conversion time. For an n-bit successive-approximation ADC this is equal to slightly more than n clock periods, as can be seen from Figure 6.27. To avoid dynamic errors introduced by the DAC, the clock period must not be less than the settling time of the DAC. This means that the increase of conversion time of the ADC accelerates with n because the settling time of the DAC also increases with n. Even so, conversion times are fast enough for most applications, being typically in the range $25\,\mu s$ down to $1\,\mu s$ or less.

The conversion time of the dual-ramp method is considerably longer than for a successive-approximations converter because of the long counting sequences. Typical conversion times are in the range $10\,ms$ (low-resolution ADC) to $200\,ms$ (high-resolution ADC). However, for slowly varying analogue signals these times are adequate and the advantages of economy and mains-frequency rejection favour the choice of this method.

▶ 6.6 Sample/Hold (S/H) circuits

6.6.1 Introduction

A *sample/hold (S/H)* circuit is used to overcome a problem that can arise with an ADC. In many types of ADC, such as successive approximations, if the input voltage changes during the conversion process, an erroneous digital output can result. To achieve a conversion uncertainty of less than $\pm^{1}/_{2}\,LSB$, then the voltage must change by less than this amount over the time it takes to do a conversion, t_{con}. Assuming the signal is smoothly varying then this places a restriction on the gradient of the signal of

$$\left| \frac{dV_{IN}}{dt} \right| \le 2^{-n} FSR \, \frac{1}{t_{con}} \qquad (6.17)$$

For example, taking typical figures of $t_{con} = 10\,\mu s$, FSR=10 V, $n=8$, then

dV_{IN}/dt must be less than 2000 V/s. This may not appear too restrictive at first glance. However, suppose the signal is a sine wave of maximum amplitude: $V_{IN}=\frac{1}{2}(FSR)\sin(2\pi ft)$. Then simple calculus shows that the greatest rate of change occurs as V_{IN} passes through the origin, and is given by

$$\frac{dV_{IN}}{dt} = \pi f(FSR) \qquad (6.18)$$

Using the above figures in this equation shows that a signal frequency, f, in excess of about 120 Hz will give rise to problems. This figure is quite low, especially when compared with the maximum sample rate of the converter of $1/t_{con}$, that is 100 000 samples per second.

Greater signal speeds can be used if the signal is sampled and held constant while digital conversion takes place. The sample/hold circuit performs this function, and the basic idea is shown in Figure 6.30. With the control at 'sample' the switch is closed and the capacitor C quickly assumes a voltage equal to V_{IN}. When the control is changed to *hold,* the switch is opened and the capacitor which is across the output terminals holds its voltage constant until the next sample is taken. During the *hold* period the ADC is able to perform a conversion on an unchanging voltage, and the code produced is that of the input voltage at the instant of the *sample* to *hold* transition. In practice the 'start convert' command to the ADC is first taken to the *sample/hold* control, and then passed on to the ADC, possibly after a small time delay to allow the sample to be taken.

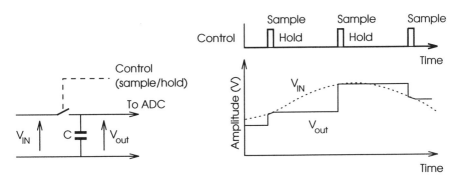

Figure 6.30 *Principle of operation of a sample/hold circuit*

Another use of a S/H circuit is as a *de-glitcher* on the output of a DAC. As mentioned in Section 6.4.4, unwanted glitches can occur at the output of a DAC when the input code is updated. Here the glitches are removed by sampling the DAC output in the middle part of one clock period and holding this value past the glitch until the middle of part of the next period. The high speeds involved call for very careful circuit design, and the de-glitcher is often incorporated by the manufacturer within the DAC module.

6.6.2 Practical S/H Circuit

Attaching buffers with unity voltage gain to the basic circuit in Figure 6.30 gives the circuit shown in Figure 6.31(a). Each operational amplifier has its output connected to one of its input terminals. From Eqn 6.5 the voltage between the input terminals of the operational amplifier are constrained to be zero by negative feedback. Hence the output voltage of a buffer is equal to its input voltage, that is, it has unity voltage gain. Unity buffers are used because they are able to deliver a load current while drawing a negligible current at the buffer input. The buffer A_1 provides a high charging current to C when a sample is taken. Without this buffer the current would be taken from the signal source and would probably cause a loading effect. Buffer A_2 conveys the 'hold' voltage on C to the output of the S/H, and protects C from unwanted discharge by load current flowing to the output terminals.

A further modification is shown in Figure 6.31(b), which is a popular configuration used in practice. Here the feedback signal to A_1 is now taken from the S/H output. With the switch closed in *sample* mode there is no basic difference in operation compared with Figure 6.31(a), since negative feedback ensures that in both circuits V_{IN}, V_{OUT} and the capacitor voltage are all the same. However, there is a practical advantage in the second circuit which is apparent when the switch is open, in the *hold* mode, and about to close to take a sample. If the previous sample voltage stored in C and the present value of V_{IN} are close in value, then in the circuit in Figure 6.31(a) the voltage across the open switch is not large and when the switch is closed a modest charging effort is applied to C. However, with S open in Figure 6.31(b) the operational amplifier A_1 is in the open-loop condition, and although the differential input to A_1 is small, it is amplified by a typical gain value of 100 000. The operational amplifier A_1 will saturate at its maximum positive or negative value (typically ±15 V) depending on the polarity of the differential input. Hence quite a large voltage exists across the open switch, so that when it is closed C is charged to the sample value at high speed.

6.6.3 Performance Limitations

Practical *S/H* circuits differ in small ways from the ideal shown in Figure 6.30. However, these differences contribute to the overall accuracy of the system and can be significant. The more important effects are shown in Figure 6.32 and are now discussed.

Acquisition time (typically 1–10 μs). This is the time taken from the start of the *sample* condition for the output voltage to equal the input voltage to within a specified band of error. A large component of acquisition time is due to the charging time of the capacitor. A low capacitor value

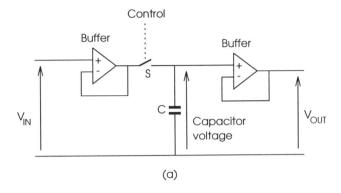

(a)

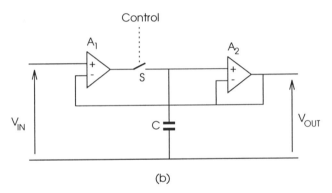

(b)

Figure 6.31 *Practical sample/hold circuits: (a) buffered input and output; (b) modification for faster sampling*

should therefore be used.

Aperture time (typically 10–200 ns). This is the time between the *hold* instruction being given and the actual time the switch is opened.

Aperture uncertainty or *jitter* (typically 2% to 10% of aperture time). Of itself aperture time is not very important, since if necessary the *hold* instruction can be advanced in time to compensate. However, aperture-time jitter, which is the fluctuation in aperture time from sample to sample, can be important. For a changing signal, uncertainty in sampling time is equivalent to uncertainty in sample amplitude. To ensure an amplitude uncertainty of less than ±½ *LSB*, the slope of the signal is restricted by the same relation as Eqn 6.17, but with t_{con} replaced by the aperture uncertainty, t_{AU}.

$$\left| \frac{dV_{IN}}{dt} \right| \leq (2^{-n})FSR \frac{1}{t_{AU}} \qquad (6.19)$$

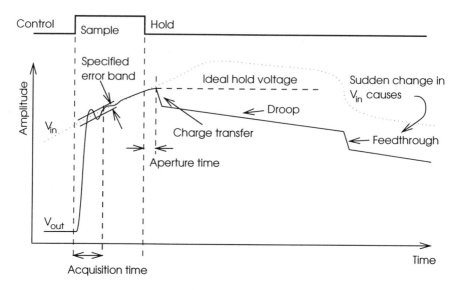

Figure 6.32 *Imperfections of a practical sample/hold (effects are exaggerated)*

As an example, suppose a *S/H* with a typical t_{AU} =20 ns feeds into the same *ADC* as in the example in Section 6.6.1. Then from Eqn 6.18 and Eqn 6.19 the maximum frequency of a full-size sine wave signal is about 60 kHz before jitter errors become significant. This figure is probably acceptable in this case, since it is consistent with the maximum *ADC* conversion rate of 100K samples/s (that is $1/t_{con}$).

Droop (typically 0.1–100 mV/s). Ideally the output voltage of the *S/H* in the *hold* condition should stay constant. However, in practice V_{OUT} drifts from this value with time. This is called droop and is caused by discharge of the *S/H* capacitor due to (a) leakage current of the open switch, (b) self-discharge of the capacitor through its own dielectric, and (c) input current to the buffer A_2. Droop is specified as the maximum rate of change of output voltage, and can be reduced by using a larger capacitor value. This conflicts with requirements to minimize acquisition time but an adequate compromise can usually be obtained.

Feed through and *charge transfer.* Feed through occurs during the *hold* condition when a change in input voltage causes a small unwanted change in output voltage even though the *S/H* switch is open. It is caused by stray coupling between the input and storage capacitor C. Charge transfer can also take place when the switch is opened and a small charge dumped in the storage capacitor causing an output voltage offset.

Both these effects contribute small errors and are significant only in high-accuracy analogue-input channels.

▶ 6.7 Signal Conditioning

6.7.1 Introduction

Best accuracy is obtained from the *S/H* and *ADC* if they are driven by signal amplitudes which approach the *FSR* (typically 10 V). In this way the offset errors and quantization errors are relatively small compared with the signal.

However, many signals have low amplitudes at source, so amplification is desirable. Moreover, when the signal source is some distance from the computer, the signal wire is susceptible to electrical interference. It is then necessary to use a second wire connected to ground at the signal source, as shown in Figure 6.33. The two wires are placed close together (preferably twisted together) and pick up essentially the same interference noise signal E_n.

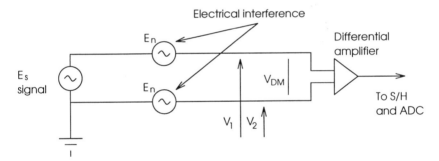

Figure 6.33 *Amplification of differential mode voltage eliminates effect of electrical interference*

Two frequently used terms are now defined.

Differential-mode voltage (V_{DM}). This is defined as $V_{DM} = V_1 - V_2$. Substituting for V_1 and V_2 using Figure 6.33, we obtain:

$$V_{DM} = (E_s + E_n) - (E_n) = E_s \qquad (6.20)$$

Note that the noise terms cancel, and V_{DM} equals the original signal source e.m.f.

Common-mode voltage (V_{CM}). This is defined as $V_{CM} = \frac{1}{2}(V_1 + V_2)$. Substituting for V_1 and V_2, we obtain:

$$V_{CM} = \frac{(E_s + E_n)}{2} + (E_n) = E_n + \frac{E_s}{2} \qquad (6.21)$$

For small signals it is seen that V_{CM} is dominated by the noise component.

Hence a differential-input type of amplifier is required which has the required differential mode gain, A_{DM}, to raise the differential mode voltage V_{DM}, to a level comparable with (but not greater than) the *FSR* of the *S/H* and *ADC*. The differential amplifier should have low common-mode gain, A_{CM}, (ideally zero) to common-mode voltage, V_{CM}, to avoid corruption due to electrical interference.

6.7.2 Instrumentation Amplifier

A differential-mode amplifier with the desirable characteristics of precise A_{DM}, small A_{CM}, low-signal input currents, and the ability to supply a sufficient output current to a load is known as an *instrumentation amplifier.*

An operational amplifier on its own meets all these requirements except one. That is that A_{DM} (typically 100 000) is imprecise and varies markedly with temperature, power-supply voltage, and from device to device. A more complicated circuit is necessary and a popular instrumentation amplifier circuit is shown in Figure 6.34. The first stage amplifies V_{DM}, while taking very little input current from the signal. The output of the first stage contains a common-mode component and the second stage eliminates the component while further amplifying the differential mode component. The full analysis is found in texts on operational amplifiers. The output voltage is given by the formula

$$V_o = A_{DM}V_{DM} = -\left(1 + 2\frac{R_2}{R_1}\right)\left(\frac{R_4}{R_3}\right)V_{DM} \qquad (6.22)$$

The negative sign indicates that the output is inverted with respect to V_{DM}. A non-inverted output is easily obtained by interchanging the amplifier input terminals.

Resistor values are chosen to give A_{DM} typically in the range 1 to 10 000. It is convenient to vary R_1 to set the required gain, since other resistors are in pairs which have to retain accurate matching. In many cases the instrumentation amplifier is supplied without R_1 to enable the user to set the required gain easily.

A programmable instrumentation amplifier is obtained by using digitally controlled electronic switches to connect different combinations of resistors inside the circuit module to achieve a range of discrete differential mode gains. Typically A_{DM} can be set at values in the range of 1 to 1024 in steps of 1. Although more expensive than fixed A_{DM} instrumentation amplifiers, programmable gain has the advantage of greater flexibility and the convenience of being able to change the gain under the control of the computer.

Complete instrumentation amplifiers are obtainable in one package giving excellent performance over a wide temperature range.

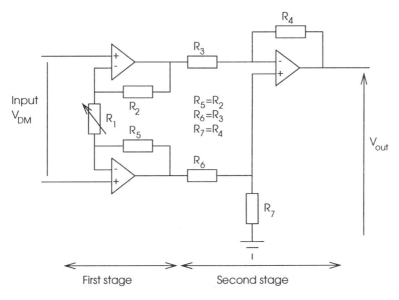

Figure 6.34 *Instrumentation amplifier*

6.7.3 Isolation Amplifier

Although the instrumentation amplifier eliminates the effect of V_{CM}, this common-mode voltage does have to stay within the working range of the circuit. Typically this range is ±10 V.

In some applications the V_{CM} component may be much higher than this. Other applications, notably in medical instrumentation, require, for safety reasons, very high isolation between the signal source (often a patient's body) and the main part of the instrumentation system. In these cases an *isolation amplifier* is used in place of the instrumentation amplifier.

The main approach in the isolation amplifier (see Figure 6.35), is to allow direct connection of the amplifier to the signal inputs, but other connections are via transformer coupling. One transformer supplies alternating current to the AC/DC converter which supplies DC power to the rest of the circuit. Since the output of the differential amplifier may contain zero frequency components, it is not possible to transfer directly via a transformer, and it is first converted to an alternating signal by the high-frequency modulator, as indicated. Outside the isolated area the demodulator recovers the amplifier output voltage. As an alternative to transformer coupling of the modulator output, optical couplers are popularly used.

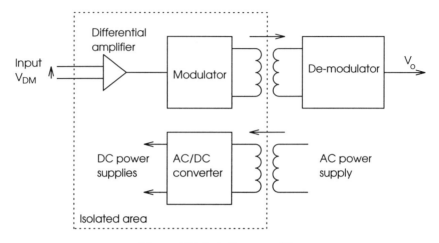

Figure 6.35 *Isolation amplifier*

Figure 6.36 *4–20 mA current loop*

6.7.4 4–20 mA Current Loop

Long connecting cables may result in unacceptable voltage drops causing errors in measurement. By converting an input signal into a current the effect of cable resistance can be eliminated. A widely used industrial scheme is to transmit a current of between 4 and 20 mA, where 4 mA indicates 'zero' for the input and 20 mA indicates a full-scale input. This is known as a *4–20 mA current loop* and, because two wires are used the device at the sensor end is called a *two-wire transmitter*. A representative set-up is shown in Figure 6.36, a resistor R_L is used to convert the current to a voltage output. Use of a twisted pair connection provides considerable immunity from interference, even over the long distances permitted by using a current rather than a voltage signal.

Typically, the minimum voltage at the transmitter is 12 V and up to 40 V may be supplied, thus the 24 V supply shown in Figure 6.36 could be replaced by a 40 V supply and up to 40 - 12 = 28 V dropped in the connecting leads. A minimum current of 4 mA allows the transmitter to draw up to this amount to power itself and any other signal conditioning amplifiers at the sensor.

An alternative range sometimes used is 0 to 20 mA but this is not common and does not allow for power for the transmitter to be supplied on the signal leads; a third wire is required.

6.7.5 Performance Limitations

Some of the principal parameters are:

Gain error (typically ±0.25%). This is the difference between the measured gain and that predicted by Eqn 6.22.

Non-linearity (typically ±0.002% to ±0.2%). Ideally the graph of V_o versus V_{DM} should be a straight line. Non-linearity is a measure of the maximum deviation of the actual graph from the best straight line. It is expressed as a percentage of full-scale output.

Voltage-offset. In practice the graph of V_o versus V_{DM} does not pass precisely through the origin. This means that the output voltage will contain a small unwanted offset voltage. The intercept of the line on the V_{DM} axis is called the voltage-offset. A typical value is 0.4 mV. This effect is not too troublesome since it can be nullified on most amplifiers. However, changes in temperature can cause offset voltage to return, and the voltage-offset temperature coefficient is of interest. Values for this are typically in the range 2 to 100 μV/°C.

Common-mode rejection ratio (CMRR) (typically 60 to 120 dB). This is the ratio of the differential mode gain to the unwanted common-mode gain, and is usually expressed in decibels,

$$CMRR = 20 \log_{10}(A_{DM}/A_{CM}) \ dB \qquad (6.23)$$

It is a measure of the ability of the amplifier to reject the unwanted V_{CM} while amplifying V_{DM}.

Full-power bandwidth. This is the maximum sine wave frequency at which the amplifier can supply a full output amplitude without significant distortion. Typical values are in the range of 10 kHz to 100 kHz, for instrumentation amplifiers. For the isolation amplifier, the use of modulators constrains the usable frequency range to typically 10 kHz or less.

▶ 6.8 Multiplexers and Multiple Analogue I/O Channels

6.8.1 Introduction

Consider the problem of inputting 64 analogue channels to a computer using the circuits described so far. A separate amplifier, S/H and ADC would be required for each channel. This would be a highly expensive solution to the problem.

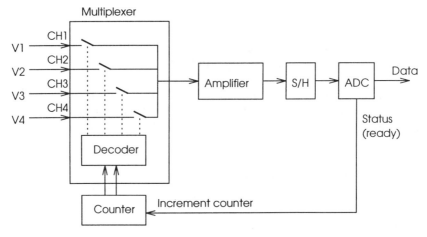

Figure 6.37 *Multiplexer (MUX) used for a four-channel analogue input system*

A *multiplexer (MUX)* allows a single amplifier, S/H and ADC to be 'time-shared' over several analogue channels, thus saving on costs. The operation of the MUX can be understood from the simple four-channel system shown in Figure 6.37. The associated waveforms are shown in Figure 6.38. Each channel is coupled to the output of the *MUX* via a digitally controlled electronic switch. Channel addresses are input to the decoder, which closes the appropriate switch for a sufficient period to allow the *S/H* and *ADC* to perform a data conversion. In the arrangement shown the channel addresses are generated in cyclic sequence by a counter. The counter is incremented to address the next channel by the ADC 'ready' condition which signifies that data conversion of the current channel is completed.

Channel addresses may also be provided by a register which may form part of the interface register set and thus able to be loaded by the computer. This allows channels to be accessed in any desired sequence, under software control.

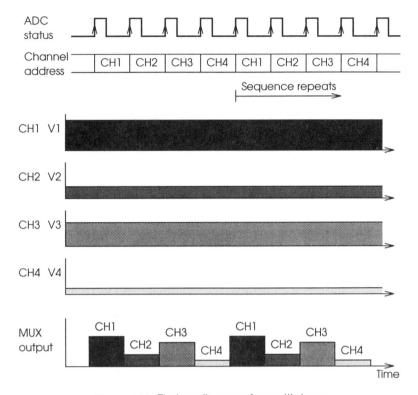

Figure 6.38 *Timing diagram for multiplexer*

6.8.2 Types of Multiplexer

Three types of multiplexer input connection are used:

Single-ended input: This is as shown for the MUX in Figure 6.37. A single-ended voltage requires one wire for connection, the zero-volts point of the signal being also that of the converter circuitry.

Differential input: Here each channel requires two wires, to overcome common-mode interference problems, as mentioned in Section 6.7.1. The MUX now has two output connections which pass to a differential amplifier, as shown in Figure 6.39.

Quasi-differential input: A differential signal contains a signal wire and a return wire. If a cluster of differential signals is exposed to interference, then under favourable conditions the return wires will contain the same interference signal, and can therefore be replaced by one return wire.

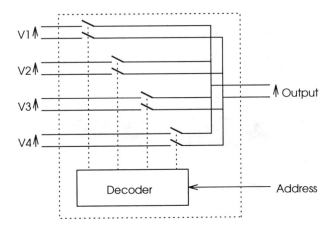

Figure 6.39 *Multiplexing of differential signals*

In a quasi-differential connection the signal wires are multiplexed to one terminal of a differential amplifier using a single-ended MUX, and the one return wire is taken directly to the other input terminal of the differential amplifier.

In practice, 8 to 16 switches are typically enclosed in one MUX module. To multiplex a greater number of channels, several MUX modules can be connected using the two-tier technique shown in Figure 6.40, which is sometimes called *sub-multiplexing*.

6.8.3 Multiple Analogue-input Channels

Connecting the MUX before the amplifier as shown in Figure 6.37 is most straightforward. However, conditions sometimes require the MUX to be placed at other points in the chain.

In many applications the signal amplitude levels vary from one channel to another. Consequently a fixed-gain signal-conditioning amplifier is unable to scale all channels. To overcome this a more expensive programmable-gain amplifier can be used. Alternatively the *MUX* can be put between the amplifier and *S/H*. This requires an amplifier per channel, which is not necessarily uneconomic since medium specification integrated-circuit instrumentation amplifiers are not very expensive. Where isolation amplifiers are needed it is also necessary to place the *MUX* after the amplifier to preserve the isolation of the signal.

In the arrangements considered this far, the channel samples are taken in sequence. Sometimes it is necessary to sample and convert all channel signals at the same point in time: for example, in measuring the simultaneous responses to a stimulus in an experiment. In these cases a *S/H* is used for each channel and the *MUX* is placed after the *S/Hs*. All channels are

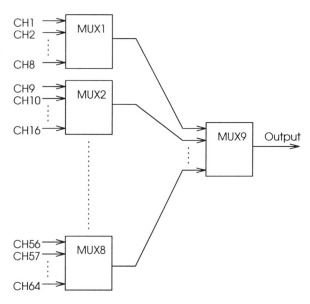

Figure 6.40 *Increasing the number of input channels by sub-multiplexing*

sampled at the same instant and then held while the *ADC* converts each channel voltage in turn.

Occasionally, a *MUX* may not be used at all. This can be the case where the number of channels is low and the costs and complications of the *MUX* are not warranted. This is especially so where conditions are favourable, and each channel requires only an *ADC* and not an *S/H* and amplifier. In other cases the sampling rate of each channel needs to be high and the conversion time of the *ADC* is not low enough to allow it to be time-shared, and hence one *ADC* is used per channel.

6.8.4 Multiple Analogue-output Channels

Use of a multiplexer in reverse to time-share one DAC over several output channels, is shown in Figure 6.41. It is often then called a *demultiplexer (DEMUX)*. The DEMUX provides an output to each channel for only one part of the channel sequence. When the MUX is serving other output channels the output on a channel falls to zero. A S/H is therefore usually required on each channel to hold up the voltage until replenished by the DEMUX on the next cycle.

Added costs incurred by the S/H make the advantages of using a DEMUX on analogue output less certain. In many applications, only a few analogue outputs may be needed, and one DAC per channel may then be preferred.

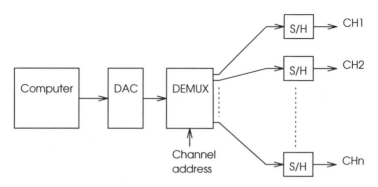

Figure 6.41 *Multiple output channels using a demultiplexer (DEMUX)*

▶ 6.9 Input Transducers

6.9.1 General

In this section we will briefly review some input devices known as transducers, which are used to measure quantities such as length, force, pressure or temperature depending upon the type, by converting input energy into an electrical (analogue) signal. The analogue signal can then be converted into a digital quantity for a computer system if required using an ADC. Hence transducers can be computer peripheral devices. Such peripheral devices find application in control applications.

Input transducers convert one form of energy, typically mechanical energy, thermal energy or electromagnetic radiation, into electrical energy. Transducers with a mechanical input are used to measure, for example, distance or rotation force or pressure. Transducers with thermal input are used to measure temperature. Transducers with radiation input are used, for example, to detect or measure visible light. Transducers can also be designed for electrical input, for example to convert from current to voltage.

Sensors are input devices which detect the presence of a form of energy or a change in the energy level or other physical stimulus. For example, light can be detected by a photodetector type of sensor. We shall consider sensors and transducers together as, normally, sensors are parts of transducers and are coupled to circuits to form complete transducers.

Only a short selection of the many possible transducers will be covered in this section, they could occupy a complete book by themselves!

6.9.2 Mechanical Input Transducers

Displacement transducers are used to measure a change in position. Relatively low-precision displacement transducers can use a resistive potentiometer, as shown in Figure 6.42. The movement of the wiper of the potentiometer produces a change of resistance between the wiper and each fixed terminal, and hence with the application of a constant voltage across the fixed terminals, a change in the wiper terminal voltage occurs. The potentiometer can be designed for linear movement of the wiper or rotational movement of the wiper. Accuracy can be about 0.1%. These forms of displacement transducers suffer from wear of the wiper and resistive track.

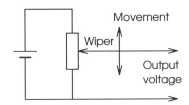

Figure 6.42 *Resistive displacement transducer*

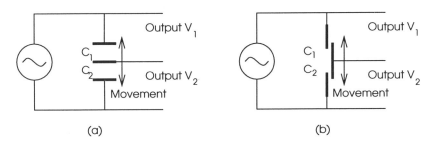

(a)   (b)

Figure 6.43 *Capacitive displacement transducers: (a) variable separation type; (b) variable area type*

Capacitive displacement transducers avoid wiper and track wear by using the movement of a plate of a capacitor to cause a change of capacitance which is directly related to the movement. Normally three plates are used to obtain a linear relationship or approximately linear relationship between the movement and the capacitance or measured signal. Two plates are fixed and one can move. The movement can alter the area of the movable plate exposed to the fixed plates, or alter the separation of the movable plate relative to the fixed plates depending upon the configuration, as shown in Figure 6.43.

The capacitance of a capacitor is given by:

$$C = \frac{\varepsilon a}{d} \qquad (6.24)$$

where ε is the permittivity constant $\times$ relative permittivity, a is the cross-sectional area and d the separation of the plates. For the configuration in Figure 6.43(a), we can derive the two capacitances as:

$$C_1 = \frac{\varepsilon a}{d + x} \quad \text{and} \quad C_2 = \frac{\varepsilon a}{d - x} \qquad (6.25)$$

where d is the separation of the movable plate and the two fixed plates in the central position, and x is the movement of the movable plate from the central position. The output voltages are given by:

$$V_1 = \frac{VC_2}{C_1 + C_2} \quad \text{and} \quad V_2 = \frac{VC_1}{C_1 + C_2} \qquad (6.26)$$

Hence by substitution we get the voltage difference between V_1 and V_2 directly proportional to the movement:

$$V_1 - V_2 = \frac{Vx}{d} \qquad (6.27)$$

with the permittivity and area eliminated.

As with many other transducers, a Wheatstone bridge circuit is often employed to measure the change in the parameters of a particular capacitive transducer. For the capacitive transducer C_1 and C_2 form two arms of the bridge, and the ratio C_2/C_1 is measured. This ratio is given by:

$$\frac{C_2}{C_1} = \frac{d - x}{d + x} = 1 + 2\frac{x}{d} \quad \text{for } d \gg x \qquad (6.28)$$

For the configuration shown in Figure 6.43(b), we have:

$$C_1 = \frac{\varepsilon w(l/2 + x)}{d} \quad \text{and} \quad C_2 = \frac{\varepsilon w(l/2 - x)}{d} \qquad (6.29)$$

where w is the width of each plate, $l/2$ is the length of the movable plate over each fixed plate in the central position and the gap between the fixed plates is sufficiently small to be neglected. Fringe effects are also neglected. Hence we have a capacitive ratio in a similar form to previously.

Inductive displacement transducers, as shown in Figure 6.44, typically employ a movable non-magnetic shaft with a ferromagnetic plunger within an inductor or transformer. Moving the shaft alters the output voltage measured. In the transducer shown in Figure 6.44(b), an alternating voltage is applied to one coil and a signal obtained from two coils wound in opposite directions on either side of the input coil, such that when the plunger is in the central position no output signal is measured. When the plunger is moved, the voltage induced in one coil increases and the voltage in the other coil decreases but adds to the change output voltage, to produce an output voltage.

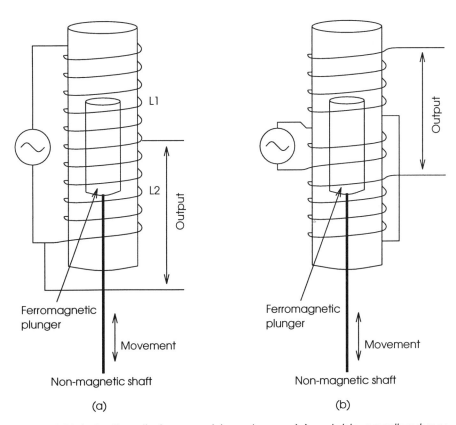

Figure 6.44 *Inductive displacement transducers: (a) variable coupling type; (b) linear variable differential transformer (LVDT)*

The *optical displacement transducer* shown in Figure 6.45 measures rotational movement of a disc by sensing markings on the disc. The markings on the disc have traditionally been in the form of a *Gray code* to limit errors at the change from one number to the next position. Alternatively, the markings can represent a single binary pattern of $010101\cdots$ and the markings counted as the disc is rotated.

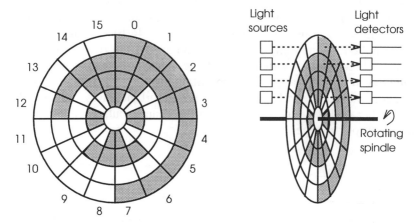

Figure 6.45 *Angular encoder: (a) markings; (b) shaft with sensors*

Optical displacement transducers can be used for linear movement, and in this case the markings can be in the form of a grating, that is, a large number of parallel finely spaced lines. Typically there are two sets of gratings, one on a movable member and one on an adjacent fixed member. As the movable grating passes over the fixed grating, light from a light source is transmitted through the gratings to a detector only when the two gratings are in line. Each occurrence of light passing through the gratings is counted.

Strain gauges. The principal element of a strain gauge consists of a material whose resistance changes when stretched or compresses (strained). The substrate of the gauge is typically about $10\,\text{mm} \times 10\,\text{mm}$. Displacements in the region of $50\,\mu\text{m}$ can be measured with appropriate circuitry. Strain gauges can be used to measure force by mounting the strain gauge with suitable adhesive on a cantilever beam as shown in Figure 6.46(b).

6.9.3 Thermal Transducers

Thermal transducers are used to measure changes in temperature. There are four major types: resistance, thermocouple, thermistor and semiconductor.

(a) *Resistance thermometers* measure the change in resistance of a wire when the temperature changes. Copper wire exhibits a nearly linear change but has a low resistivity making it difficult to use. Platinum is almost universally used although it is not quite as linear as copper. The ratio of resistance at a given temperature, R_t, to that at 0°C, R_0, is described by the equation:

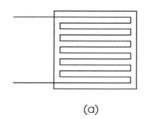

(a)

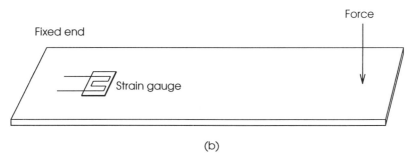

(b)

Figure 6.46 *Strain gauge: (a) typical pattern; (b) strain gauge mounted on cantilever beam*

$$\frac{R_t}{R_0} = 1 + At + Bt^2 \tag{6.30}$$

where A and B are determined by calibration. Standard devices have a resistance of $100\,\Omega$ at $0°C$ and $138.5\,\Omega$ at $100°C$. They are usable from $-200°C$ to $850°C$.

(b) *Thermocouples* use the fact that a temperature gradient along a wire results in a voltage gradient in that wire. In a closed circuit the total voltage is zero since the return wire experiences the same temperature gradients. If, however, the circuit is made from different materials, producing different voltage gradients, an overall voltage can be produced. The usual arrangement is shown in Figure 6.47; metal1 and metal2 are joined together at the measuring point and to extension leads, typically of copper, at two further junctions; these two junctions must be at the same temperature. The voltage produced depends not only on the temperature of the measuring junction but also on the temperature of the measuring device where another junction at a known temperature (the *cold-junction*) exists.

Different combinations of metal1 and metal2 produce different voltages, typically from 3 to $80\,\mu V/°C$. Table 6.5 lists some of the more common combinations; type K is by far the most common. As indicated, the output coefficients vary with temperature and follow a very complex relationship; a typical polynomial approximation has degree 8 or more!

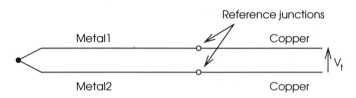

Figure 6.47 *Thermocouple*

Table 6.5 *Some standard thermocouples*

Type	Materials	Temp. range (°C)	Output μV/°C at 100°C	Comments
E	Nickel-Chromium Copper-Nickel	0 to 800	68	High output Output: 81 μV/°C at 500°C
K	Nickel-Chromium Nickel-Aluminium	0 to 1100	42	Very common
R	Platinum-13% Rhodium Platinum	0 to 1600	8	High temperature Output: 13 μV/°C at 1000°C
T	Copper Copper-Nickel	-185 to 300	46	Accurate at room temperature Used for food measurements

(c) *Thermistors* consist of a mixture of materials, such as nickel oxide, cobalt oxide and manganese oxide, whose overall resistance changes considerably with temperature, though the change may be far from linear. They are used only near room temperatures, typically in the range 0°C to 200°C. The resistance change may be as large as 1 kΩ/°C.

(d) *Semiconductor diodes,* when forward biased, exhibit a change in voltage drop of about -2 mV/°C (the voltage falls with increasing temperature). Integrated circuits containing measuring junctions and amplifiers can be produced such that accurate voltages are produced, typically 10 mV/°C with an accuracy of better than ±0.5°C.

7

Other Input and Output

▶ 7.1 Introduction

In Chapter 3 and Chapter 4 many of the more common input and output peripherals were described. This chapter describes some other devices which are not commonly considered to be with core peripherals. Such a distinction is clearly difficult to make and many of the peripherals addressed here could be said to be mainstream, but a line is drawn albeit, possibly arbitrarily.

Many of these devices attempt to make communication between the computer system and the human user more accessible. Methods of *reading* printed information are first reviewed. Next, communication via human speech is explored and, as there is much in common, the discussion moves on to the manipulation and storage of musical sounds in general. This chapter then concludes with a section on how several of the devices already mentioned can be used together to create virtual environments, which completely absorb the user in the fast developing world known as *virtual reality*.

▶ 7.2 Optical Mark and Character Recognition

7.2.1 Introduction

When large quantities of alpha-numeric data need to be processed, systematic procedures are usually adopted to input the data. The main steps are:
(i) collection of source data, often in the form of source documents (e.g. invoices from other organizations);
(ii) transcription of source data on to written or typed coding sheets or suitable forms;
(iii) keying in the data. Originally this was coded on to paper tape or cards but the approach now is to use a computer terminal for direct input;
(iv) correcting errors which originate in steps (ii) and (iii);
(v) correcting errors which subsequent processing reveals to have occurred at the generation of source data.
This can be a lengthy process. The computer can help by displaying pre-

stored forms for step (ii) or by having built-in editors for steps (iv) and (v). However, the keying of data, step (iii), remains a time consuming task.

Entering source data straight in to a computer is clearly a better method. *Optical mark reader (OMR)* and *optical character reader (OCR)* technology can be used to read original forms directly and produce suitable forms of computer data. The information that is read can be from three types of source:

(i) marks that are put in predefined areas of the document;

(ii) printed or typewritten characters;

(iii) hand-printed characters.

An OMR is used for the first type, whereas an OCR is used for the second and third types.

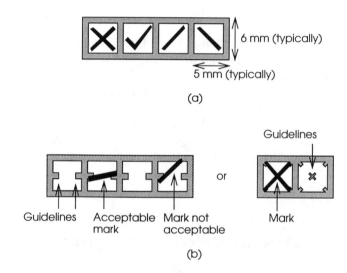

(a)

(b)

Figure 7.1 *Typical marks that may be used*

7.2.2 Types of Marks and Characters

(i) *Location* Readers are generally designed to read marks or characters that are positioned in a matrix formed by regularly spaced locations on each of several rows. This pattern is obtained automatically where a printer or typewriter is used. For hand-printed marks or characters, however, it is necessary to use pre-printed paper or cards on which the required locations are shown (usually as small rectangles).

Often a coloured ink (pink or pale blue) is used in pre-printing, and the reader is designed to be insensitive to this colour. This avoids the possibility that the mark location rectangle could be misread as a mark. Also the rectangles can be coloured in to improve the layout of the form, or can be printed with characters or short words to indicate the meaning of each mark.

(ii) *Marks* Optical mark readers detect the presence or absence of a mark placed in each permitted location. Some machines will read a wide variety of marks. Figure 7.1 shows some examples of these. Simpler machines require the mark to be made in a particular way, for example, as shown in Figure 7.1(b).

Generally, marks can be made using an ordinary pencil or pen.

(iii) *Printed or typed characters* Various machine-readable character sets, or fonts, are used. Two standards for these are *OCR-A* and *OCR-B*, shown in Figure 7.2 and Figure 7.3, respectively. The A font was the first to be produced and originated in the United States. The stylised appearance of some of the characters aids machine recognition. The B font, which originated in Europe, is less stylised and contains a wider range of characters. Both of these fonts are defined by the ISO committee.

In addition, quite a range of ordinary fonts can be recognized so that, as the technology improves, the use of OCR-A and OCR-B is diminishing.

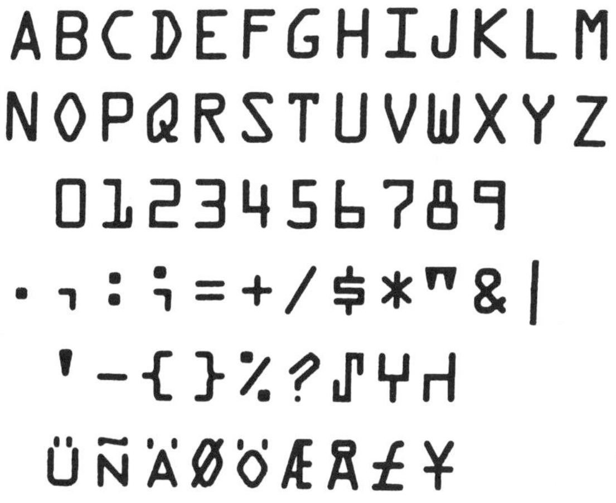

Figure 7.2 *OCR-A Characters*

(iv) *Hand-printed characters* Because of the differences in style between different people's handwriting, recognition of hand-printed characters is more difficult than with printed text. The task is made easier if the text is in block capitals at known locations; forms often carry boxes to guide the user.

Currently emerging software, designed for hand-held computers, is now able to recognise hand-written characters with good accuracy.

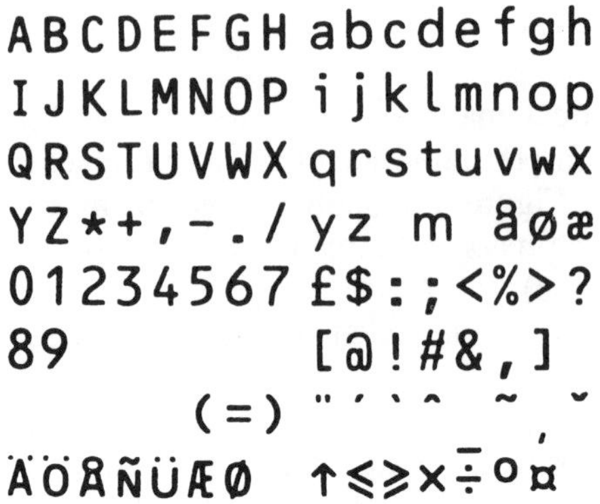

ABCDEFGH abcdefgh
IJKLMNOP ijklmnop
QRSTUVWX qrstuvwx
YZ*+,-./ yz m åøæ
01234567 £$:;<%>?
89 [@!#&,]
(=) " ´ ` ^ ~ ¸ ˇ
ÄÖÅÑÜÆØ ↑≤≥×÷°¤

Figure 7.3 *OCR-B Characters*

7.2.3 Document input

If standard forms are used with mark boxes in predefined locations it is possible to read the form with a simple device consisting of photo-cells at the locations of the boxes. This uses a line of sensors, and the form is passed across them by hand or with a motorised drive.

Improved flexibility can be obtained by using a general purpose scanner such as one of those described in Section 4.4.2. These are now relatively cheap and can accommodate a range of forms simply by changing the recognition software.

7.2.4 Recognition

Recognition can be thought of as being a three stage process: pre-processing, feature extraction and classification. There are several recognition techniques in use and these determine the exact function to be performed at each stage.

(i) *Pre-processing* This stage normalises the character before feature extraction. Operations that may be performed are: adjusting the brightness of the image, adjusting the width and height to a standard size, and centring the character. With hand-printed characters it may also be necessary to correct for character skew and rotation due to individual styles.

(ii) *Feature extraction* This stage identifies a set of characteristics or features in a character which allow it to be distinguished from other characters in the set. The features extracted depend on the recognition method being used. For stroke analysis the features are the various strokes which make up the character. The outline of the character is used for contour tracing, sometimes approximated by a closely fitting irregular polygon.

(iii) *Classification* This stage finally identifies the scanned character. A set of reference features, extracted for each member of the reference character set, is stored in the machine. The set of features extracted from the scanned character is then compared with each of the reference characters until a match is found, thus identifying the character. In practice, short cuts are taken in this comparison process.

Small distortions in the scanned character may cause the extracted features to differ from the ideal. The procedure then adopted is to find the closest, rather than an exact, match to a character in the reference set. This may lead to substitution errors if large distortions occur. If the match is not good it is often better to raise a reject condition than mis-classify a character.

▶ 7.3 Bar Codes

7.3.1 Introduction

Bar codes were first created for use in retail applications, in particular to assist with automating supermarket checkout counters. Nowadays they have many other applications in addition to this.

Any situation in which a machine readable identification is required may make use of a suitable bar code; there are dozens of codes for different applications. At its simplest the code consists of a series of black and white bars of varying widths used to encode data. Figure 7.4 shows a sample bar code from the back of this book which encodes that fact that the product is a book and includes its unique *International Standard Book Number (ISBN)*. There is also additional information in the form of a *check digit* which assists with the detection of erroneous data, i.e. an error in reading the code.

Figure 7.4 *Example bar code*

7.3.2 *Input Devices*

Reading the bar code involves determining the widths of the dark and light bars across the pattern. This can be achieved with a simple light source and photodetector if these are manually scanned. A solid-state laser source provides a bright source of illumination which is reflected back to a photocell via a focussing lens. Different reflectivities of the light and dark regions produce a varying output from the photocell. This may be a hand-held wand which is run over the surface of the product, a hand-held gun which is maintained a small distance away, or a fixed device using spinning mirrors to scan the product, as typically found at a supermarket checkout.

Elements of the bar code may be only fractions of a millimetre wide and the reader has to be able to focus to at least this resolution if a clean output is to be produced. Figure 7.5 shows the outputs from good and marginal scanners. The good scanner can focus to better than the distance between elements and can easily follow the changes of lightness. The poor scanner resolves only to the order of the element size resulting in reduced outputs which are much more difficult to analyze accurately.

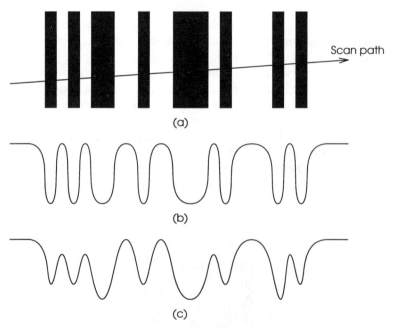

Figure 7.5 *Scanning a bar code: (a) the scan path; (b) output from a good resolution scanner; (c) output from a poor resolution scanner.*

Using line scan technologies such as the *charge coupled device (CCD)* sensor allows the construction of scanners with no moving parts which do not require a manual scan to be performed. Figure 7.6 shows a typical arrangement. Illumination is provided by one or more light sources, often by means of a *light emitting diode (LED)* array. An image of a line across the bar code is formed on the sensor by a lens, and is scanned electronically to give a time-varying signal which is then amplified and analyzed in the same way as for any other scanner.

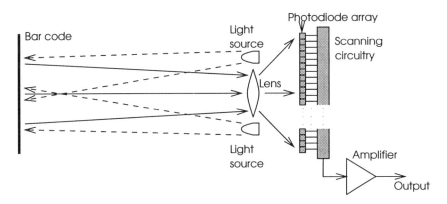

Figure 7.6 *CCD scanner arrangement*

7.3.3 Codes

Patterns used for the bar codes have not only to encode the data but also to be able to assist with detecting incorrectly scanned products. It is possible that the bar code may be only partly scanned, with a sweep that crosses a corner, or may be scanned in reverse, if the product happens to be upside-down.

First created in the United States of America in 1973 the *Universal Product Coding (UPC)* scheme allocated a unique number to each manufacturer who could then add a number that was specific to a product. Europe followed in 1977 with the *European Article Number (EAN)* scheme, designed to be compatible with the UPC scheme.

Numbers to be coded consist of a prefix (1 digit for UPC, 2 for EAN), manufacturer number (5 digits), item reference (5 digits) and check digit (1 digit). There are thus 12 digits in the UPC scheme, although only 10 of these are normally printed in human readable form (the prefix and check digit being hidden), and 13 digits in the EAN scheme (where all are normally printed in human readable form). The UPC prefix denotes the product category, 0 for grocery, 3 for pharmaceuticals, etc. The EAN scheme is encoded so that a UPC can be read and doing so gives prefixes from 00 to

09; these values are not used in Europe so there can be no confusion between UPC and EAN labelled products.

The example code shown in Figure 7.4 is an EAN code with prefix 97, manufacturer 80340, product 60658 and check digit 2. In fact the prefix 97 indicates a publication and the number should be parsed as 978, a book; 034060658, the ISBN; and 2, the check digit.

Codes used on either side of the centre line are different so that the direction of scan can be determined. To the right the codes have an even number of 1's, i.e. *even parity,* as shown in Table 7.1. Lefthand digits are encoded using 'Left Hand A', with *odd parity,* for UPC codes and a mixture of 'Left Hand A' and 'Left Hand B' for EAN. The choice of left-hand character types in the EAN scheme allows the coding of the 13th (actually the first!) digit by using Table 7.2.

Table 7.1 *UPC/EAN character set ('1' represents a dark band)*

Number	Left Hand A	Left Hand B	Right Hand
0	0001101	0100111	1110010
1	0011001	0110011	1100110
2	0010011	0011011	1101100
3	0111101	0100001	1000010
4	0100011	0011101	1011100
5	0110001	0111001	1001110
6	0101111	0000101	1010000
7	0111011	0010001	1000100
8	0110111	0001001	1001000
9	0001011	0010111	1110100

Table 7.2 *Code for the first prefix character in EAN13*

Number	Prefix 2	Data 1	Data 2	Data 3	Data 4	Data 5
0	A	A	A	A	A	A
1	A	A	B	A	B	B
2	A	A	B	B	A	B
3	A	A	B	B	B	A
4	A	B	A	A	B	B
5	A	B	B	A	A	B
6	A	B	B	B	A	A
7	A	B	A	B	A	B
8	A	B	A	B	B	A
9	A	B	B	A	B	A

The simple calculation with the first 11 (UPC) or 12 (EAN) digits used to generate a checksum is shown in Figure 7.7. This figure shows the EAN code used earlier – a UPC does not have the first digit but is otherwise the same. Indeed, the coding scheme used ensures that, when a UPC is read in Europe, it finds a first digit value of zero and this does not affect the calculation or checksum digit at all. On input the checksum is calculated and compared with that read in order to detect errors.

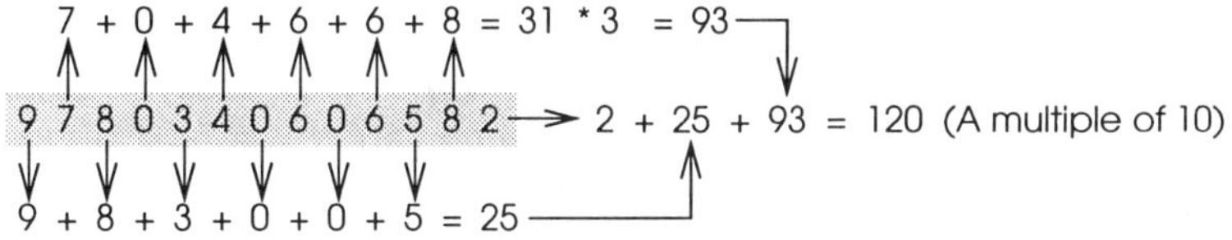

$$7 + 0 + 4 + 6 + 6 + 8 = 31 * 3 = 93$$

$$9\ 7\ 8\ 0\ 3\ 4\ 0\ 6\ 0\ 6\ 5\ 8\ 2 \rightarrow 2 + 25 + 93 = 120 \ \text{(A multiple of 10)}$$

$$9 + 8 + 3 + 0 + 0 + 5 = 25$$

Figure 7.7 *Checksum calculation*

Knowing the checksum value the whole code for this book can be determined as follows -
The first seven digits (9780340) are used to code the lefthand portion. The first digit (9) determines which coding to use for each of the remaining six digits:

7	8	0	3	4	0
lefthand	lefthand	lefthand	lefthand	lefthand	lefthand
A	B	B	A	B	A
0111011	0001001	0100111	0111101	0011101	0001101

The last six digits are used to code the righthand portion:

6	0	6	5	8	2
righthand	righthand	righthand	righthand	righthand	righthand
1010000	1110010	1010000	1001110	1001000	1101100

The final printed pattern consists of a lefthand edge marker (101), the lefthand portion shown above, a centre marker (01010), the righthand portion and a righthand edge marker (101). The patterns are placed adjacent to each other with no additional gaps – the codes chosen ensure suitable limits on the bars generated (there is no bar or gap more than four elements wide in the UPC/EAN code).

Only a fixed number of digits are permitted in the code described above. Other codes allow for more or fewer digits, alphabetic characters etc. Some codes are more compact than others and some even use a two-dimensional representation to pack in large amounts of information. A description of these is, unfortunately, beyond the scope of this book.

► 7.4 Magnetic Character Readers

7.4.1 Introduction

Magnetizable characters can be printed using ink loaded with iron oxide. The printed document can then be passed through the reading machine which first magnetizes the characters and then passes the document under a small coil. The magnetized characters induce a voltage in the coil, from which the character can be decoded.

The term *magnetic ink character reader (MICR)* is used to describe this device, as well as *magnetic character reader (MCR)*. A special printer is used to print the characters on documents.

This method has found widespread use in banks (for example, on cheques) because of its security and reliability. The method is secure because characters are not easily altered without the special printer. Reliability is obtained because dirty marks and other blemishes, which might cause errors in an optical character reader, are less likely to cause errors here because they are generally non-magnetic.

Reliability and simplicity of the recognition process is also enhanced by using stylized fonts. Two MICR fonts that are in widespread use are *E13B* and *CMC7*.

7.4.2 E13B font

This font originated in the United States of America and is now also used in Britain (see Figure 7.8). It includes the ten numerals and four special characters used to specify data fields, but no alphabetic characters. The special characters signify: 'dash', 'bank-branch', 'amount' and 'on us', respectively.

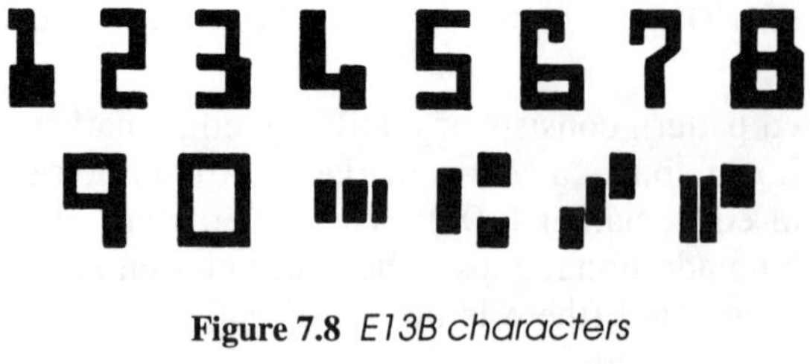

Figure 7.8 *E13B characters*

A thin vertical slice of each character is scanned, which produces a signal amplitude proportional to the quantity of magnetized ink in the slice, as shown in Figure 7.9. The signal is unique to each character, which can therefore be easily identified.

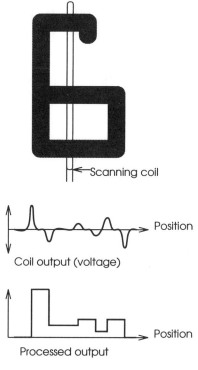

Figure 7.9 *Reading a character*

7.4.3 CMC7 font

This font, see Figure 7.10, is in widespread use in Europe. Numerals, special characters and letters are included. The coding principle differs from that of the E13B font, with each character being made up of seven vertical magnetic ink bars. The six spaces between the bars are binary valued: narrow (binary 0) and wide (binary 1). This creates a 6-bit code which allows a maximum of 64 possible characters to be represented. CMC7 uses 41 of these.

The magnetic character reader scans a thin vertical slice of the character, detecting voltges induced in a small coil of wire. After processing to produce a clean signal, the time between the bars is measured and from this the character can be decoded.

The method is therefore insensitive to the length of each bar, provided it is long enough to be detected. This allows pieces to be cut out of the bars so that they can be visually readable, as shown.

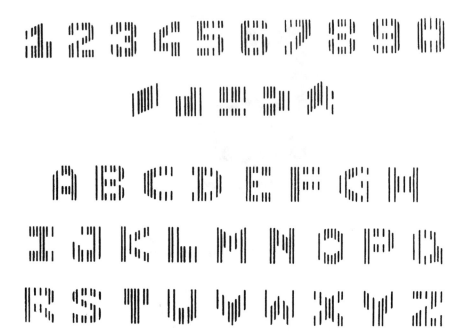

Figure 7.10 *The CMC7 magnetic character font*

▶ 7.5 Voice input

7.5.1 Speech Storage

Speech storage involves digitizing an analogue speech signal and then storing this data, possibly after using a compression technique. This process also has applications in speech synthesis, which is discussed in a later section. Direct applications of speech storage exist, and one such application is the facility to attach spoken messages to parts of a text document. This can be used, for example, by persons who do not have the time or skill to operate a keyboard, to specify changes and corrections to the document.

A microphone is used to sense the speech, and the analogue waveform produced is then digitized prior to input to a computer. This is achieved using an analogue-to-digital converter (ADC), as described in Chapter 6. The digitized samples can then be stored in the computer system. The original waveform can later be reproduced by putting the digital data sequence through a digital-to-analogue converter (DAC) and then subsequently sending the analogue output to an amplifier and loudspeaker.

For good quality, the waveform should be quantized to at least 8-bits resolution and sampled at at least 11 000 samples a second. The result is that even short utterances require a large amount of storage space.

A number of techniques can be used to reduce the amount of data. One way is called *companding*. Here the quantization levels in the ADC are distributed unevenly over the signal amplitude range. They are closely spaced at small amplitudes and allowed to be more widely spaced at high amplitudes. The effect is to keep the quantization error relative to the signal amplitude at acceptably low levels while, saving on the number of quantization levels. This then reduces the number of bits required for each sample.

A second approach is to use information from previous samples to help with the digitization of the present sample. An example is the *differential pulse code modulation (DPCM)* method. This relies on the property of analogue speech signals that sample amplitudes do not change rapidly from one sample to the next. Only the amplitude difference between the current sample and the previous is stored. Since these differences are usually small, they usually occupy less space than is the case when each sample is an absolute amplitude.

These techniques typically halve the space required to store speech but the space required is still large. The problem is even more acute when storing more detailed sound information such as music, where similar approaches are required. The storage and reproduction of music is discussed in a later section and was also discussed briefly in Chapter 5.

7.5.2 Speech Recognition

A *speech recognition* system accepts spoken input, identifies it and converts it to a standard code such as ASCII. Speech recognition has been the subject of research for many years, and some of the features of recognition are shown in Table 7.3.

The more complex features in the right hand column are difficult to achieve and are currently found only in the human listener. Those on the left, while more restrictive, do find applications and are available in commercial systems.

Figure 7.11 shows the system block diagram. The three main steps of preprocessing, feature analysis/extraction and classification are also found in optical character readers as described earlier. In fact, this framework applies to the general discipline of pattern recognition, of which speech recognition and OCR are examples.

Spoken sounds can be voiced or unvoiced. Voiced sounds originate from vibrations of the vocal cords and are periodic. Unvoiced sounds are obtained by the movement and control of air at certain points of the mouth (lips and teeth for example) and are not periodic. For example, the waveform shown in Chapter 6 is for the utterance *sham*. The unvoiced *sh*

Table 7.3 *Features of speech recognition*

Feature	Simple	Complex
Utterance	Isolated words	Continuous speech
Vocabulary	Limited	Very large
Number of speakers	One	Many
Training mode required	Yes	No

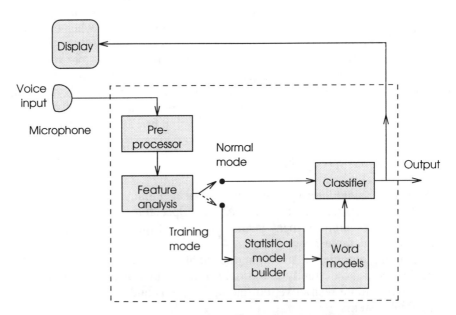

Figure 7.11 *Block diagram of a voice-input system*

and voiced *a* and *m* can clearly be seen. By changing the shape of the mouth and opening and closing the nasal cavity, the tonal quality (that is, the spectrum) of these sounds is altered sequentially in a wide variety of ways to create speech.

The word or short phrase to be recognized is spoken into the microphone. The signal produced is then pre-processed by shaping the frequency spectrum. The feature analysis stage computes sequences of *feature vectors* which characterize the utterance. Many different features such as *power spectrum coefficients* or *linear prediction coefficients* have been used, but *mel frequency cepstral coefficients (MFCC)* appear to give the best results. These feature vectors provide a pattern for the classifier.

Attempts to classify the pattern by comparing them with stored reference patterns (templates) have met with only limited success. This is because of the inherent variability of speech sounds. No word is ever pronounced twice in exactly the same way, even by the same person.

In order to accommodate this variability the recognizer is trained by the user speaking each word in the required vocabulary a number of times (usually between 3 and 10). From the feature vectors produced, a statistical model known as a *hidden Markov model (HMM)* is built for each word. When the system is used, the probabilities that each of the models has generated the unknown word is computed and the most likely word is chosen.

Typically a few tens to a few hundred words or phrases can be recognized. As the size of the vocabulary is increased, both the time taken to recognize an utterance and the incidence of errors increase.

Recognition reliabilities of 98% have been reported for larger vocabularies. Errors are practically eliminated by the use of a display which shows the chosen word, so that the errors can then be corrected manually or, more usually, by speaking a special word such as 'erase' and repeating the utterance. Achievement in this field is not limited by the hardware, but rather by our ability to write algorithms that can match the amazing human ability to understand speech delivered in many accents and intonations, and with much extraneous noise.

▶ 7.6 Voice Output – Speech Synthesis

Computers that talk have long been a part of science fiction, and commercial products that satisfy real applications are now viable. Speech synthesis differs from the reconstruction of stored speech in that there is the flexibility to output any desired speech utterance.

Speech can be synthesized by joining together segments of generated speech. Sentences are formed of words, and words can be formed by joining up *phonemes*. Phonemes play a similar role in speech to that played by letters in writing. The utterance 'sham', whose waveform is shown in Chapter 6, can be formed by the three phonemes /sh/, /a/ and /m/.

Speech synthesis methods vary in the size of segments used and the method of generating these segments. The three prominent methods are (i) recorded segment synthesis, (ii) formant synthesis and (iii) linear predictive coding (LPC).

In the first of these, segments of speech, such as words and short phrases, are uttered by a speaker, recorded, and stored as described in the previous section. A dictionary of words and phrases is then created and called upon to provide a sequence of stock words and phrases. This method is limited by the size of the dictionary, but it is cheap, and the output is readily recognized.

In formant synthesis, use is made of the resonances in the vocal tract. Sounds are caused by the vibration of the vocal cords (for example /O/) and by the fricative action of the controlled release of air by the lips, teeth and tongue (examples are /p/, /th/ and /t/ respectively). To produce the full range of phonetic sounds the movable parts of the mouth take up different shapes, forming cavities which resonate at different frequencies. These frequencies are termed *formant* frequencies.

Synthesis is achieved by constructing an electronic circuit model of this action, with signal generators to act as the vocal cords and fricatives, and adjustable filters to copy the action of the resonant cavities. By updating the parameters of the circuit model at a rate of typically once every 5–20 ms, acceptable quality speech can be synthesized. This entirely analogue approach is fast being replaced with equivalent digital techniques using digital signal processing (DSP) methods to the same end.

The linear predictive coding method has proved to be very successful and is widely used. The basis of this method is quite mathematical, but it can be thought of as a form of curve fitting. The parameters of a special function are found which closely predict the sequence of speech samples. Synthesis is achieved by evaluating the function, using these parameters. The parameters are updated every 10–20 ms to give acceptable speech quality. Again, storage requirements are low and the LPC method is well suited to low-cost digital implementation. Formant synthesis and LPC can be used to synthesize phonemes, words or longer segments of speech.

Synthesis at the phoneme level has the advantage that any message can be synthesized without the restrictions caused by using word dictionaries. However, the speech produced can sound robot-like and unnatural. The generation of speech is a complicated process. One reason for an unnatural sound is that phonemes can depend on adjacent phonemes. For example, the phoneme /k/ in 'kew' differs from that in 'kite' because when speaking /k/ the tongue anticipates the following vowel 'e' in one case and 'i' in the other. These effects are called *allophonic variations,* and they can be overcome to some extent by building extra rules into the synthesizer. Even so, the speech does not sound completely natural. Natural speakers utter the same word in different ways, with the tempo, pitch and emphasis all being altered, depending upon the desired meaning. These effects apply to the utterance as a whole and are called *prosodic features.* For most applications a degree of unnaturalness in the quality of speech generated can be accepted.

Speech synthesis products are manufactured as stand-alone units or as assemblies for incorporation in other units such as computer systems. Most units for general sound production, including music, incorporate features for speech synthesis/input and, sometimes, speech recognition. These soundcards are described in the next section.

Applications to automated speech are numerous. Instructions to machine operators can be given without the need for them to look away from the work to read a screen display. Alarms need not merely ring, but can say what the problem is. A remote plant can be monitored by telephone. Another application uses voice response systems which allow communication with a remote database which responds using speech synthesis. Typically the user has a touch-tone telephone, which is used even after connection in order to provide numerical input from the keys. The remote system responds accordingly in voice. These can be used for remote shopping, or for simple enquiries of a database, such as a bank balance or stock prices.

▶ 7.7 Sound Cards and Sound Sampling

In order to manipulate sounds, a computer system needs a way of inputting a sound, storing it and, possibly, modifying a stored copy and finally it must also be able to reproduce the sound. Being able to communicate sound information to other systems and devices is also useful, and certain standard musical sounds have associated codes such as the MIDI system. Storing sound in digital form is described in Chapter 5 in connection with compact disc devices. Speech storage has been covered in the previous sections and similar techniques are used for general sound storage. The collection of circuits associated with these tasks are often available in one unit which is usually referred to as a soundcard. The most common features of such a unit are:

DAC and ADC circuits	To sample and digitize analogue data and later reproduce analogue sound
Synthesiser/Sampler	To reproduce musical notes
MIDI interface	To communicate musical information
CD-ROM interface	To play sounds stored on the disk

These features are illustrated in Figure 7.12 and are now covered in turn.

7.7.1 Sound Sampling

Sound sampling is the process of digitizing the analogue waveform of a sound using an analogue-to-digital converter (ADC). The sound is represented by an analogue voltage which can be produced by a microphone. Speech sampling was described in earlier sections and the same principles

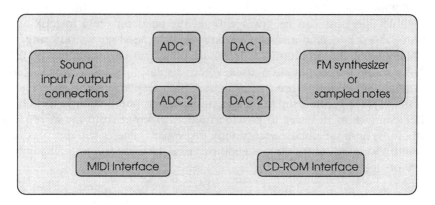

Figure 7.12 *Typical main features of a soundcard*

apply except that, in general, the samples must be more accurate and frequent.

A sample is a digital value representing the amplitude of the sound at a particular point in time. A sequence of samples, if sufficiently close together and sufficiently accurate, can faithfully record and be used to reproduce the sound.

The frequency range of human-audible sounds is from 20 Hz to about 20 000 Hz. To record accurately in this bandwidth the samples should be taken at twice that frequency – 40 000 times a second. The standard sampling rate used is actually 44.1 kHz and easily copes with this bandwidth. Some people advocate a wider bandwidth for high quality reproduction and *digital audio tape (DAT)* enables this by sampling at 48 kHz. There are other standard sampling rates which are lower and so compromise on their faithfulness but require less space to store the samples. The standard sampling rates available are 5.0125, 11.025, 22.05, 44.1 and 48k Hz.

The second feature of a sound sample is the quantization of the input sound amplitude. Again there are two common values – 8-bit and 16-bit. An 8-bit sample records an amplitude as one of 256 (2^8) possible values. This results in samples which, when reproduced, are noticeably different from the original. A 16-bit sample can accommodate 65 536 (2^{16}) different levels and is generally accepted as being sufficient for recording sounds which are 'perfectly' reproduced (within the limitations of the human ear).

Sound is quantized by using an analogue-to-digital converter (ADC) set at the required frequency and resolution. Music is often recorded in stereo and requires the independent processing of two sounds in parallel. The better soundcards include two DACs and two ADCs. These can be set to one or more of the above sampling frequencies and sample either at 8- or 16-bit quantization.

7.7.2 Music Production

Whereas any sound can be processed by sampling, music is often also stored and produced using other techniques which require less space. The most common feature is to include the sound production capabilities of a standard musical keyboard synthesiser. This electronic circuit can then be sent signals which are analogous to physically pressing and releasing the keys of a musical keyboard.

Most commercial musical keyboard synthesisers have a range of different *voices* that mimic other instruments. These instruments include most actual musical instruments such as piano, flute and violin and percussive instruments such as drums. Other 'instruments' which are some of the more common electronic sounds of earlier synthesisers are also reproduced. There are two common approaches to reproducing these voices. They can be synthetically produced by a combination of waveforms or a set of samples from the real instruments can be stored and called upon. It should be noted here that the word *sample* is normally used to mean one value of a wave's amplitude and many samples – typically 44 100 a second – constitute a note. Unfortunately the word sample is also used to mean a note which has been sampled. Here, the word note will be used for such a sample.

The synthesis approach itself has many methods associated with it. The purest sound is a simple sinusoidal wave and this is one of the building blocks of a synthesizer. A sinusoidal wave is shown in Figure 7.13(a). The production of this wave can be governed by a keyboard switch such that it sounds only when the key is depressed and constitutes one note. For a little more reality the amplitude of the wave is made to change as the note sounds and a common approach is to use an *ADSR envelope* as shown in Figure 7.13(b). This envelope governs the amplitude of the sinusoidal wave, and it has four phases – attack, decay, sustain and release. The initials of these phases give the envelope its name. Each of the four phases can have both their amplitudes and lengths altered to produce different effects. The attack phase starts when the key is pressed and governs how quickly the note starts. Many instruments have a very short attack phase – such as an organ. Some – such as a flute – have a longer attack phase. After the note has hit its maximum amplitude it may decay slightly to a sustained lower level. When the key is released, the note may take a short time to fade away and this is the effect governed by the release phase.

A sinusoidal wave by itself is too pure a sound and many waves can be combined and processed to produce sounds which are similar to actual instruments. The most common approach here is to use frequency modulation which is at the heart of *FM synthesis*. In brief, FM synthesis modulates the frequency of waves at a frequency which is the same as the wave itself or some multiple of that frequency. The resulting wave then has more sharply defined peaks and troughs and further processing through

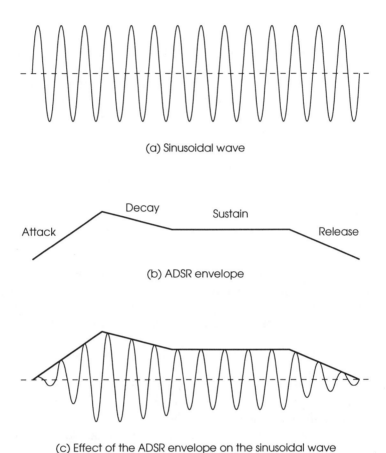

(a) Sinusoidal wave

(b) ADSR envelope

(c) Effect of the ADSR envelope on the sinusoidal wave

Figure 7.13 *Sinusoidal waves and ADSR envelopes*

possibly many stages of wave additions and more modulation can lead to some very realistic sounds.

Even FM synthesis cannot produce sounds which would fool a musician completely and so some synthesizers and, hence, soundcards use sampled notes of actual instruments stored on a chip.

It would take up too much space to store every note in an instrument's range. One note of an instrument is stored at a particular frequency of, say, 440 Hz which is middle A on a keyboard. Other notes are played by either stretching or squashing this note in order to change its fundamental frequency. Playing the note back at half the speed, for example, would produce a note one octave below (half the frequency). This change of playback rate is achieved by altering the speed at which the DAC recreates the note from its digital image. Some of the individual samples of the note can be dropped or repeated to augment this effect. When the note to be played is too far from the original note then the result can sound unrealistic. To overcome this, several notes of the instrument can be stored at various intervals and the one nearest to the required note is then used.

Synthesis and sampling can produce very good reproductions of different musical instruments. They can even play, for example, violin notes outside the range of an actual violin. Such notes on a soundcard are played by sending signals to the card which indicate which note is required from which voice and for how long. There are other signals which can be used which perform the other features which a normal music keyboard synthesizer is capable of. These include *pitch bend* which moves the pitch of the note slightly up or down.

Because this sort of communication is required for music synthesizers themselves a standard is required. By far the most commonly adopted such standard is the MIDI standard.

7.7.3 Musical Instrument Digital Interface (MIDI)

The MIDI standard was designed to allow music synthesizers to communicate with each other. A synthesizer can accept commands from another device which could be another synthesizer or a *sequencer* which controls many instruments at a time.

The MIDI standard specifies a 5 ma current loop serial connection as mentioned in Chapter 2. Information is transmitted as sequences of bytes at a speed of 31.25 kbps which, given a start and stop bit for each byte, permits a maximum transmission rate of 3125 bytes a second.

The standard specifies 5-pin connectors. Equipment such as controllers/sequencers (which may be computers) and instruments have three or more sockets as shown in Figure 7.14(a). These three connections are *OUT* for output of MIDI information, *IN* for receipt of MIDI information, and *THRU* which retransmits any MIDI information received at the IN connector.

A connecting cable has a 5-pin plug at each end and pins 4 and 5 are used for the current loop as shown in Figure 7.14(b). The centre pin (2) connects to the cable's screening shield so that the cable itself does not transmit (or receive) radio interference. This is connected to earth at the transmitting end only so that connected equipments do not have their chassis connected together. This is most important in a music stage or studio environment in order to avoid *earth loops* with their associated noise. This is also the reason that a current loop system is used rather than a more conventional voltage system such as RS232, which requires a common earth reference point.

The normal use of MIDI is to designate one piece of equipment as the controller, which then communicates with a slave instrument as shown in Figure 7.15(a). The controller can be a computer, or it could just be another MIDI equipped musical instrument.

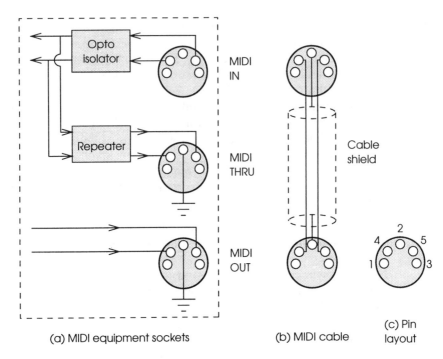

(a) MIDI equipment sockets   (b) MIDI cable   (c) Pin layout

Figure 7.14 *MIDI connections*

All events which occur on a MIDI instrument – key presses and changes in settings for example – are assigned MIDI codes which are transmitted. These codes are interpreted by the receiving instrument which, normally, will carry out the same function. In this way one music keyboard can be used to play itself and another slave keyboard simultaneously. Alternately, the MIDI codes which make up a piece of music can be transmitted from a computer to play an instrument remotely.

Most MIDI codes have an identifying channel number associated with them. There are 16 different channels possible. Several instruments can be connected to the controlling device by daisy chaining from each instrument's THRU socket to the next instrument. The signal from the main controller's OUT socket will only safely drive one slave although, in practice, several instruments can be connected. Information is retransmitted from the IN socket to the THRU socket and so a fresh full power signal is always available to each instrument. Such an arrangement is shown in Figure 7.15(b).

Each instrument can be set to respond to one of the 16 channels only. In this way, MIDI codes can be sent to a specific instrument using its channel identification code and the other instruments will ignore those codes. In

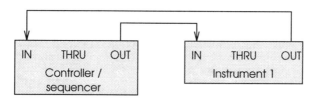

(a) Simple MIDI layout

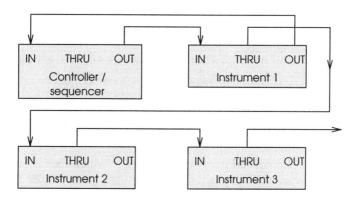

(b) Controlling several instruments

Figure 7.15 *Possible MIDI instrument layouts*

this way all the instruments can be controlled separately from the same cable.

MIDI codes (or messages as they are more usually called) are a sequence of one or more bytes. Each byte transmitted is either a control byte or a data byte. The first byte of a message is a control byte and this can be followed by some data bytes. The most significant bit of each byte designates whether that byte is a control byte or not – 1 for control, 0 for data. There are many control codes but only one or two of the more common ones will be mentioned here by way of example. Two messages are shown in Figure 7.16. The first message in Figure 7.16(a) is a clock signal which is sent 24 times for each crotchet or quarter note. This is received by all channels and is used to synchronize events such as drum beats. The second message in Figure 7.16(b) is three bytes long. This message turns on one note on one channel. The first byte is a control byte and so has a most significant bit of 1. The next three bits (001) indicate that it is a *note on* message and the least significant four bits give the channel number. Following are two data bytes. The first gives the note or key number in the

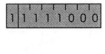

(a) Single byte message
(system clock)

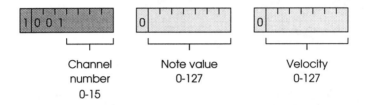

Channel   Note value   Velocity
number   0-127   0-127
0-15

(b) Three byte message - 1 control and 2 data
(note on)

Figure 7.16 *Some MIDI codes (messages)*

range 0 to 127. The second gives the velocity at which the key is pressed. Some keyboards are touch sensitive and will play notes louder if they are struck quickly.

Notes are turned back off using a similar message to the note on message. Because turning notes on and off are the most common messages a special dispensation is granted. In a sequence of note on (or note off) messages with no other message types, only the first control byte need be present. Following this are pairs of key and velocity data bytes. To reduce the traffic even further, the special velocity value of 0 in a note on message translates to a note off message for that key. Thus a sequence of note on/off messages requires only one control byte.

MIDI is used in computer systems with special software to provide sequencing of many instruments. A piece of multi-track music can be assembled on the computer and stored as MIDI messages. The piece can then be performed by sending these messages. Software exists to allow on-screen composition using standard musical notation and to turn this into MIDI messages that actually play the music.

Pre-recorded pieces of music exist simply to play, for example, the synthesizer on a soundcard using its MIDI interface. A typical MIDI tune requires of the order of 100–200 bytes per second while a sampled piece of music requires 88 200 bytes per second. The sample can, however, contain any sound information. The MIDI piece is restricted to the musical notes and voices of the synthesizer, although a wide range of high quality instruments is available.

▶ **7.8 Virtual Reality**

In Chapter 3 and Chapter 4 peripheral devices such as graphics screens and positional trackers were described. This chapter has also discussed the production of stereo sounds. The combination of these devices allows the user to experience what is now described as *virtual reality.* Many researchers and other users of these techniques prefer to use the phrase *virtual environments,* which more accurately describes most applications.

Virtual environments can be created by the use of fast graphics and, often, the interaction with the environment of various positional devices. There are different levels of sophistication in creating virtual environments. Systems exist which display a three-dimensional image that is shown on a screen using perspective projections. The user can alter the viewpoint by moving, say, a mouse and explore the three-dimensional world so produced. This sort of application allows someone to *see* how a yet to be constructed building would appear. It also allows the exploration of synthetic worlds which can only realistically exist as a computer simulation, such as displaying molecular structures and moving around them.

At a slightly more sophisticated level, *stereopsis* techniques are employed which offer slightly different viewpoints to each eye so that depth is more easily perceived. There are many ways of achieving this such as looking through special filtering spectacles at a single display. The display actually shows both intended images simultaneously but each image is only visible through its own filter. The best way of achieving stereopsis is to produce two separate images and then project them separately at each designated eye. See Chapter 3 for an example stereoscopic image. This is the method most commonly employed in the current extension of virtual reality – *total immersion virtual reality.*

Total immersion attempts to give the illusion of being bodily within the virtual environment. The field of view is completely taken over by the projected images and the viewpoint changes as the user's head moves. This is usually accompanied by a hand positional device such as one of the data gloves described in Chapter 4 and an image of the user's hand becomes part of the observed environment and interacts with it. Another novel feature is that more than one person can participate. Each user will see images of the other users as they interact in the same virtual environment.

There are many applications for these complex techniques. The common perception is that they exist solely for the entertainment industry, but other applications include simulating otherwise dangerous or expensive environments, as well as communicating at a distance. Pilots are trained in simulators which display images which occupy most of the user's field of vision, and which change in response to aircraft control inputs. People can practice tasks in potentially dangerous situations in the safety of its

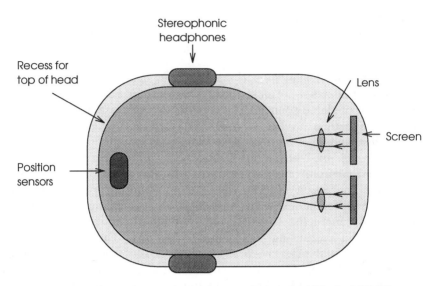

Figure 7.17 *Plan schematic view of a Head Mounted Display (HMD)*

simulation as a virtual environment. Students can learn by practising in a virtual environment using simulations which would be prohibitively expensive in their real form.

An application which combines the virtual environment and a real one involves *telepresence.* In this, the user is in a fully immersed virtual environment that accurately mirrors a real situation which is typically some distance away. At the real location is a robot device with sensors and the output of these sensors are relayed back to the user in the equivalent virtual environment. The user controls the robot by head and hand movements. This remote telepresence is used when the real environment is hazardous such as inspection and repair of the inside of a nuclear reactor.

Telepresence can also be used when it is impractical or inconvenient for someone to be at that real location. A person can *meet* and interact with other people through this virtual environment. The remote people are actually interacting with a robot controlled by the virtual environment user who sees the world as viewed by the robot. In principle, a team of experts from different parts of the world can meet together – albeit as a team of robots – to perform a complex group task. This could involve, for example, surgery although the techniques in this area are not yet sufficiently advanced to gain universal acceptance and approval.

The immersive virtual environment is provided by devices such as the data glove described in Chapter 4 and, more importantly, the *head mounted display (HMD).* The head mounted display is shown in schematic form in Figure 7.17. Whole body suits that detect the movement of all limbs are also becoming available.

The eyes are completely covered by the HMD unit. Each eye has its own imaging system which focusses on and enlarges a small display. The displays are commonly of the liquid crystal colour display variety. Some of the more expensive systems have very high resolution screens and enlarge them so that the whole normal field of view is covered. The displays are continuously updated as the user moves head position. The user may also move bodily about the environment but this is usually achieved by manipulating input devices rather than actually walking around.

The HMD contains positional trackers of the form described in Chapter 4 to detect movements of the head and alter the view accordingly. It is important that this can be achieved quickly as, otherwise, a mild form of dizziness and/or sickness can ensue. The HMD may also contain stereo headphones which permit more realism by including positionally accurate sound effects to be part of the environment. With telepresence, these are simply connected to two microphones on the remote robot and the images displayed are transmitted from two cameras. In other applications these sound and visual stimuli must be created.

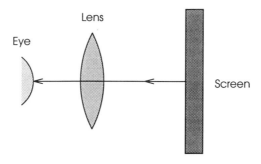

Figure 7.18 *Simple focussing system for a HMD*

The small screens used to display the images are seen through a lens system such as the simple example in Figure 7.18. The lens system has several functions. It enlarges the image so that it occupies a realistic field of view. By virtue of there being a separate system for each eye, it effectively ensures that each eye is only observing its correct image. The focussing system can also be used so that the eye is focussing at some distance away instead of at a screen only inches away.

The distance between the eye and the screen must be some minimum depending upon the sophistication of the optical system used. Longer paths can be achieved within the same short space using reflectors and two systems are shown in Figure 7.19. It is important that the HMD is light and not bulky otherwise its presence detracts from the experience of the environment. The systems shown in Figure 7.19 permit a minimal overhang of the HMD peak. The figures show mirror(s) but 90° prisms are often employed and provide a better image.

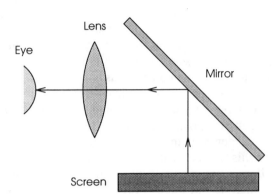

(a) One mirror to extend optical path

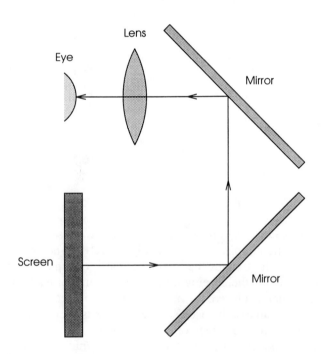

(b) Two mirrors for extended optical path

Figure 7.19 *Use of mirrors to increase the optical path*

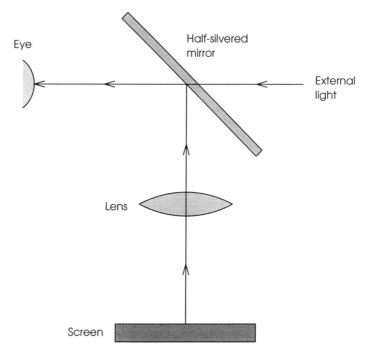

Figure 7.20 *Mixture of real and virtual environments*

Some applications call for the user to experience a mixture of a virtual environment and a real one. That is, the user sees the same scene as that without the HMD but with a virtual scene superimposed upon it. One common application is for an aircraft pilot to see the terrain normally, but with extra information also being projected through an HMD.

A system which achieves this is shown in Figure 7.20. This is similar to that in Figure 7.19(a). The mirror is replaced by a half-silvered mirror which reflects and transmits light thus allowing two sources to reach the eye. The real view is simply straight ahead. The virtual view is reflected from the side. In this case, the lens system is moved so that it is only involved in the virtual optical pathway.

Hardware for the provision of virtual environments is currently expensive. The main reason for this is that an extremely fast high quality graphical system has to be employed. Commercial systems exist which have screens with in excess of a million pixels and can update the image faster than the minimum 30 frames a second required for a totally convincing view. These systems rely on dedicated graphical specialist hardware and cost tens or hundreds of thousands of pounds. Less impressive systems are available which cost in the region of hundreds of pounds and, while they are not wholly convincing, they are adequate for most users to experience a form of virtual environment.

▶ 7.9 Further Reading

The Bar Code Book by Roger C Palmer, Helmers Publishing Inc.

8

Data Communications

▶ 8.1 Introduction

In Chapter 2 various ways of electrically connecting computers and peripheral devices were described so that data may be passed between them over quite short distances. When the distances are relatively long, other factors come into play, and these come within the subject of *data communications*. Two of these factors are the type of transmission path and the occurrence of errors in the transmission of data. The transmission path may require special circuitry (such as *modems* in the case of telephone lines) to send and receive data. Errors in data transmission occur typically due to circumstances directly related to the relatively long distances over which data is sent. Noise may be picked up in certain electrically hostile environments.

Another major concern of data communications is *networking,* that is the connecting together of several computers and peripheral devices. The peripheral devices are commonly terminals, workstations and printers. The computers may be used remotely. Computers may connect together to share their filestores and other resources. Such a network permits computing power and filestores to be distributed and shared amongst many users.

Such networks are common in a suite of offices where all the participating devices are sited locally. These are usually referred to as *local area networks* (LAN). Other networks may cover a wider geographical area. Examples include banking systems and ticket booking services. A business with many branches may have central computing facilities providing database facilities to all branches via a network. These networks are usually referred to as *wide area networks* (WAN).

In most countries the telecommunications facilities are administered by government departments or public corporations. In other countries this is carried out by private companies called *common carriers*. Collectively they are referred to as Post, Telegraph and Telephone administrations (PTT). Most PTTs are members of the Comité Consultatif International Téléphonique et Télégraphique (CCITT), which belongs to the International Telecommunications Union (ITU), itself an agency of the United Nations. The CCITT sets standards governing communications. These are not strictly standards but are recommendations since the PTTs are not obliged to follow them. In practice there is generally good conformity with the recommendations. Examples of CCITT recommendations are the V-series, which govern the use of the (analogue) telephone system for data communications, and the X-series which apply to digital networks. The standard V24 has already been mentioned in Chapter 2 and the X25 network standard is commonly referred to in the literature. Other standards bodies such as the international organisation for standardization (ISO), and the EIA (Electrical Industries Association), of the USA also play a large part in governing data communications. In the USA the EIA carries greater influence than in Europe, where the CCITT is more prevalent. However, EIA and CCITT standards are frequently similar or identical. A good example of this similarity is the pair RS232C and V24. The name ISO is not a (misspelled) acronym but the Greek prefix iso- meaning same.

Standards are important because they allow a degree of commonality among and between countries and they allow compatible systems to be constructed by different manufacturers.

▶ 8.2 Data Transmission

Data items can be coded either in digital or analogue form. The equipment used to transmit the data will send signals in either digital or analogue form depending upon the media and the drivers used for transmission and reception. The data therefore has to be encoded into the same form as the transmission media, in the most efficient format, in order to optimize the transmission media in use. Then digital or analogue data can be transmitted on digital or analogue signals. This gives four possibilities to consider. While this chapter is principally concerned with the transmission of digital data, for completeness, the transmission of analogue data will briefly be described.

Whether analogue or digital media are used, if the distance of transmission is sufficiently long, the signal will weaken and at some point it will be so weak that it cannot be received with acceptable accuracy. To avoid this, at regular points on the transmission line the signal is read and re-transmitted at full strength.

For digital signals the devices used are called *repeaters*. A repeater reads the digital (usually binary) signals before they have degraded so as to be indistinguishable and then retransmits the digital signals at the original strength. The repeater only needs to detect discrete values – usually only two. Any noise which has degraded the signal, if small, can be eliminated because all signal levels are resolved to the nearest discrete value. Repeaters then will always recover their original signal exactly.

For analogue signals the devices used are usually called *amplifiers*. An amplifier simply boosts the strength of the signal exactly as it is received. Because analogue signals have continuous values, any noise that has been introduced to the analogue signal cannot be distinguished from the original signal itself and is propagated throughout the transmission.

Instead of simply boosting the analogue signal, the date can be read and retransmitted on a newly generated carrier wave. This is particularly common with digital data. In this case the device is often referred to as a repeater.

The two types of transmissions, digital and analogue, are now looked at in more detail.

8.2.1 *Digital signals*

Digital signal transmission requires a physical connection between devices and so cannot be used with media such as radio or microwave links. The various methods of providing digital links between devices are described in Chapter 2. Digital signals take on a number of discrete values. The most commonly used media use a binary coding which only requires two values to be transmitted and received.

8.2.2 *Digital data transmitted in digital format*

When both the transmission media and the data are digital, the data can be transmitted without change. This is the usual method of transmitting data between a computer and nearby peripherals. The data is usually sent as a sequence of bytes over either a parallel or serial interface. The transmitting and receiving devices need to synchronize in order that the transfer can occur. A parallel interface will usually incorporate a control line which is used to synchronize the transfer. A serial interface requires that the two devices have clocks which are sufficiently close that, over the period of transmission of one byte, all bits are clocked in correctly. When data is transmitted as a sequence of many bits, and if one clock is slower than the other, the receiver and transmitter will eventually step out of synchronisation and bits may be read twice or lost. This problem is resolved by the receiving clock resetting itself each time a transition between a 0 and 1 occurs and so is rarely a problem if the data contains no long sequences of either 0s or 1s. Unfortunately this cannot be guaranteed and long sequences of one code would result in corruption of data as the receiver's clock drifts out of step by a time interval equal to the width of one bit. This problem is illustrated in Figure 8.1. In that figure, the receiver's clock is slightly slower than the transmitter's. Whenever the receiver receives a transition between 0 and 1, it resets its clock and this is shown by a dotted line to indicate where the receiver's clock would otherwise have triggered. When the sequence of ones or zeroes is sufficiently long, this resynchronisation is too late and one bit of information has been lost.

This problem can arise when storing data on backing store, as described in Chapter 5. The solution used there is to encode the digital

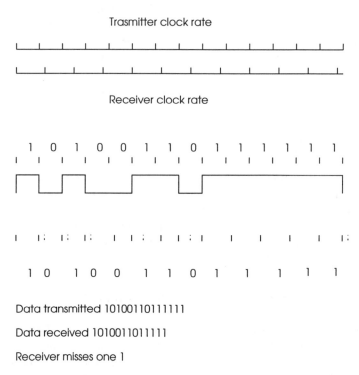

Figure 8.1 *Loss of synchronisation in digital transmission*

data into another form which cannot have long sequences of 0s or 1s no matter what the original data consists of. The same forms of coding are used in data communications – typically FM (frequency modulation) and MFM (modified frequency modulation) are found in such transmissions. The reader is referred to Chapter 5 for a discussion on these coding methods.

8.2.3 Analogue data transmitted in digital format

Analogue data such as speech and music is commonly stored in digital format and increasingly it is being transmitted using digital signals. The analogue data is first digitized as described in Chapter 6 and then treated in the same manner as above.

8.2.4 Analogue signals

Many fast transmission media such as microwave satellite links, radio and fibre optic cables can only use electromagnetic analogue signals. The most commonly used slower analogue medium is the public telephone system which was designed for voice transmission within a frequency range of approximately 300 to 3400 hertz.

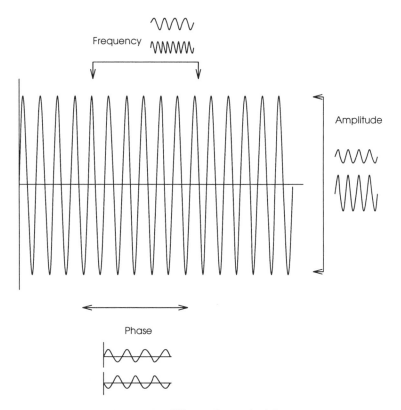

Figure 8.2 *Wave characteristics*

Whatever the media, the principles of transmission are the same. A *carrier* frequency is selected and transmitted. This carrier frequency is then modulated with the data. In order to describe the different forms that this modulation takes, it is necessary to review the characteristics of a wave. The wave used is typically a sine wave whose principal three characteristics are amplitude, frequency and phase as shown in Figure 8.2. The amplitude is the strength of the wave. Its frequency is the number of peaks each second. Its phase is a measure of where the wave cycle starts in relation to some reference point. Any one of these three or any combination of them may be modified in order to convey information. In order that these modulations can easily be detected and distinguished, they may occur at a frequency close to but lower than that of the carrier and this means that high frequency carriers such as electromagnetic waves can carry data at the highest rates. The rate at which the carrier is modulated is called the baud rate. The carrier wave without modulation will occupy a single frequency. Whatever modulation is used, the carrier wave will occupy a range of frequencies spread equally on either side of the fundamental frequency and of a width slightly greater than the chosen baud rate. The transmission media must therefore be capable of carrying reliably a range of frequencies. Its range is known as its *bandwidth* and is the upper limit of the baud rate that can be employed. As will be seen later, if the media's bandwidth is much wider than the required baud rate, two or more carrier frequencies can be used on the same medium, each carrying a different set of signals, as long as their spacings are sufficient to avoid overlap.

8.2.5 Digital data transmitted in analogue format

Digital data can be transmitted by modulating the carrier wave such that discrete values can be coded. Two different amplitudes or two different frequencies or two different phases can be employed as shown in Figure 8.3. These three methods of modulating an analogue carrier wave are also called *amplitude shift keying (ASK), frequency shift keying (FSK),* and *phase shift keying (PSK).*

Combinations of modulating more than one of the three characteristics can also be used in order to send more information at the same baud rate, and this is described in the later section on modems. In addition, more than two values could be transmitted, and this is another method of sending more information in the confines of the same baud rate, but at the expense of more sophisticated transmitting and receiving devices.

8.2.6 Analogue data transmitted in analogue format

The principle of transmitting analogue information on a carrier wave is the same as that for digital data. The most common use for this method is transmitting radio and television signals. The equivalent of the baud rate is the highest frequency required in the analogue data.

▶ 8.3 Multiplexing

An analogue signalling system has a particular bandwidth which is centred around a carrier frequency. A digital signalling system also has a bandwidth or baud rate. In both cases the available bandwidth can be used to provide several independent channels. This is achieved by *multiplexing.*

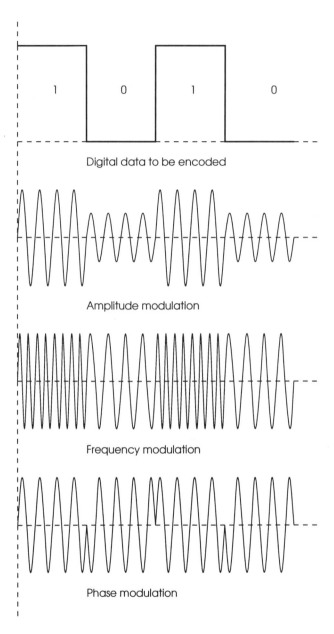

Figure 8.3 *Modulations of a carrier wave*

8.3.1 *Frequency division multiplexing*

Frequency division multiplexing (FDM) divides the available frequency range into bands. Each channel uses only the bandwidth in its allocated range and centred around its own carrier frequency. As long as there are no overlaps between bands, the signals will not interfere with each other. The receivers in turn must filter out all frequencies except those in the range of their selected bands. This is shown in Figure 8.4.

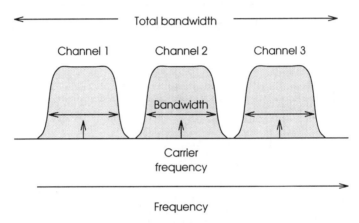

Figure 8.4 *Frequency division multiplexing (FDM)*

This form of multiplexing is most commonly encountered in broadcast radio transmissions, where the available spectrum is allocated to many stations, each of which only requires a bandwidth that is sufficient for speech and music.

8.3.2 *Time division multiplexing*

Time division multiplexing (TDM) allocates *time slots* to each of several channels and each channel is assigned the full bandwidth of the link for a short period of time as shown in Figure 8.5.

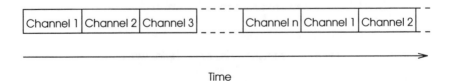

Time

Figure 8.5 *Time division multiplexing (TDM)*

Such a multiplexer contains a number of registers, one for each channel. Each register stores one character and is written to by the attached low speed device. The multiplexer scans these registers in sequence and transfers the contents serially on to the high speed link to form a continuous data stream. If no character is ready on a channel then a NUL character is sent instead.

At the receiving end of the link is a *demultiplexer.* This distributes each received character in turn to its corresponding low speed devices. For communications in both directions a multiplexer and a demultiplexer is required at each end of the link. These units are usually combined into one and, confusingly, they are then collectively referred to simply as a multiplexer. This arrangement is shown in Figure 8.6.

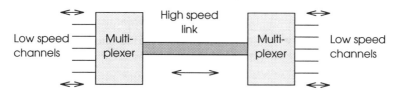

Figure 8.6 *Multiplexers operating over a high speed link*

It is unlikely that all channels will be operating at full speed at the same time. There will therefore be many NUL characters sent along the link, wasting available capacity. A more efficient use of the link is provided by a *statistical multiplexer,* which scans each register in turn as before, but skips over empty ones. Time slots are now not wasted. Each character is sent with a short identifying code which allows the receiving demultiplexer to route it to the corresponding device. This adds to the data transmission burden, but overall there is a net saving. This permits either a lower speed link to be used for the same number of channels, or for more channels to be available over the same speed link. It will still be possible for the link to become overloaded and data can be lost, but data link control procedures such as those discussed later in this chapter can overcome this potential problem.

More sophisticated techniques of multiplexing are discussed in the later sections on networks. In particular, data is usually grouped into units called *packets* which can contain variable numbers of bits – often many hundreds – and this saves on the overhead of the relative size of the identifying label and the actual data.

▶ 8.4 Transmission Media

Various physical media are in use for the task of transmitting data. The simplest is a single pair of wires, which are often twisted to reduce the effects of interference. These twisted pairs allow data rates up to about 10 Mbps. Coaxial cables permit higher data rates of several hundred Mbps but, if very high rates are required, these cables are more expensive. Still higher rates can be achieved using fibre optic cables. In addition to these physical connectors, radio and satellite technologies are employed. The drivers and receivers required to send data down all these media were described in Chapter 2.

The three physically connected media are described in the rest of this section. Following this is a description of some electromagnetic media that can be used to send data without requiring a physical connection. The characteristics of these media are then summarized (in Table 8.1). Finally a short description is given of the public switched telephone network which employs a combination of all these media.

8.4.1 Twisted pair

A pair of insulated copper wires twisted in a helical fashion provides the cheapest transmission medium – the twisted pair, which can be used for both digital and analogue signals. It is used in the telephone network between subscribers and the exchange and also in some local office networks. The wires are twisted in order to minimize electromagnetic interference. Typical installations have data rates of around 64 kbps, but high quality wires can reach rates of several million bits per second. The main drawback to the twisted pair is its limited distance. The signal degenerates relatively quickly over distances over about two kilometres, and it is also prone to noise from nearby electrical cables, although shielding the pair with a metal braid reduces this effect.

8.4.2 Coaxial cable

Coaxial cable (co-ax) consists of two electrical conductors but, unlike the twisted pair, one of the conductors is cylindrical and encloses the other conductor. Because of this construction, coaxial cable is less susceptible to noise than twisted pair and has a higher attainable data rate. It can carry either digital or analogue signals. 'Co-ax' is commonly used for television distribution, local area networks and long-distance telephone communications. It can be used over greater distances than twisted pair but still requires repeaters or amplifiers about every ten kilometres. Data rates of about a million bits per second can be achieved.

8.4.3 Optical fibre

Optical fibre is a very thin glass or plastic semi-flexible cylinder with an outer protective coating. The diameter of an optical fibre is of the order of one tenth of a millimetre. It transmits light waves by a process known as *total internal reflection* where the light is guided along the inside of the fibre even around sharp angles. Because the transmission medium employs light waves, only analogue signalling can be used and data are transmitted using amplitude modulation. When digital data are transmitted in this way, rather than employing amplifiers to boost the signal at regular intervals, the data are read in its digital form and used to modulate a new local light source for retransmission. This, strictly speaking, is a repeater rather than an amplifier. The light source is either a light emitting diode (LED) or a laser. The LED is cheaper but the laser is capable of much higher data rates and permits greater distances between repeaters. Optical fibres are unaffected by electrical interference and, when this is combined with their high capacities, explains why they are the preferred medium for medium to long distance high speed data transmission. Typical data rates are over a billion bits per second, with repeaters required about every 10 kilometres for LED sources, and at intervals of up to 100 kilometres for laser sources.

8.4.4 Radio

Radio transmission in the context of data communications includes the frequency bands used for FM radio and VHF television. The main advantage of radio over cable is that no physical link is required between the transmitter and receiver. The frequency range used – typically around 500 MHz – should in theory give a high data rate but, because the radio frequency range is heavily used, only small bandwidths are available and common data rates are of a few thousand bits per second. Radio waves propagate in all directions and thus afford a high degree of mobility and the opportunity of reaching many different receiving stations. They do, however, suffer from reflections from physical objects, which results in some interference.

8.4.5 Land based microwave

Land based microwave transmission employs the high frequency electromagnetic band of between 2 and 40 GHz. Because of this high frequency, extremely fast data rates are possible. Like radio, the frequency band is regulated and so limited bandwidths have to be used but data rates of the order of 100 million bits per second are typical. Unlike radio waves, microwaves are focused into a narrow beam, requiring dish or horn antennae for transmission and reception. The transmitter must have a clear line of sight to the receiving dish and, for this reason, the dishes are usually placed high above the ground. Assuming no intervening building or hills, the limiting factor is the curvature of the earth. A dish placed at 100 metres above the ground gives a range of about 80 kilometres. For transmission over greater distances repeater stations are used. The main use for land based microwave transmissions is as an alternative to laying coaxial or fibre optic cable. Common uses include telecommunications and short distance links between buildings where a cable is not practical.

8.4.6 Satellite microwave

Communication satellites act as relay stations. The principle is similar to the land based microwave system except that the satellite has both a receiver and a transmitter dish. The terrestrial transmitter sends its signal to the satellite which then amplifies or repeats the signal and re-transmits it to earth. Because the satellite has a view of almost half the earth's surface, transmission over great distances is easily achieved. The satellite must remain in line of sight of the terrestrial transmitter and receiver and so it needs to be placed into a geostationary orbit, which is achieved at a height above the earth of 35 784 km. In addition to this point-to-point use of the satellite, broadcast satellites transmit their signals in a conical pattern in order to reach receivers over a large area. The frequency band used is between 1 and 10 GHz. Above this range the signal cannot easily penetrate the atmosphere and, below this range, the signal suffers significantly from noise due to differing atmospheric conditions.

8.4.7 Public switched telephone network

For data transmissions over distances of a few kilometres and beyond, by far the most commonly used medium is the telephone circuit provided by the PTT. It can simply be because it would be uneconomic for the user to lay a private cable. Moreover, in many countries, only the PTT is authorized to provide cable transmission over or under public land. The network will often employ all six of the above transmission media. Twisted pair cables are the most common connection between a subscriber and the local exchange. Trunk lines between exchanges are commonly provided by fibre optic or coaxial cable or land based microwave. Intercontinental links are either by cable or satellite.

The conventional *dial-up* network or PSTN (public switched telephone network) is shown in schematic form in Figure 8.7. Each subscriber is connected to a local exchange or switching centre by, usually, a cheap two-wire circuit using twisted pairs. This local exchange makes connections between local subscribers connected directly to it. For calls to more distant subscribers, the local exchanges are linked by high capacity links to switching centres. In this way, a network hierarchy is established. This tree-structured hierarchy can be extended for very large PSTNs.

Table 8.1 *Summary of physical media characteristics*

Media	Speed (bps)	Digital signal	Analogue signal	Carrier
Twisted Pair	10M	●	●	Electrical
Coaxial Cable	1G	●	●	Electrical
Optical Fibre	2G		●	Light
Radio	30M-1G		●	Radio Electromagnetic
Land Microwave	2-40G		●	Microwave Electromagnetic
Satellite Microwave	1-10G		●	Microwave Electromagnetic

The PSTN has the advantage of flexibility, in that any destination is easily accessed by dialling the appropriate code. This type of connection is called *switched* or *dial-up*. Switching equipment can, however, be electrically noisy, and significant numbers of errors can be caused when transmitting data. This problem arises out of the fact that PSTNs were originally designed for the communication of speech and not data. Modern connectors and exchanges are designed with both speech and data in mind and this source of error should eventually be minimal. The introduction of *Integrated Services Digital Network (ISDN)* also improves the integrity of data transmissions. ISDN is described in a later section. The noise, and hence error rate, can be reduced by private dedicated lines provided by the PSTN which by-pass the switching centres. These private lines are unswitched and have a fixed route between subscribers using either two-wire or four-wire links. The four-wire line can readily permit full-duplex communication, which is also possible with a two-wire link, but with a consequent increase in complexity and, often, a decrease in speed. Switched connections are charged on a time-used basis and so costs increase with the use made. Private connections are usually leased at a fixed charge and costs are independent of usage. The choice between using switched or private links is therefore made largely on economic grounds, but other factors such as the flexibility of switched lines, and the low error-rate of private lines, will also be taken into account.

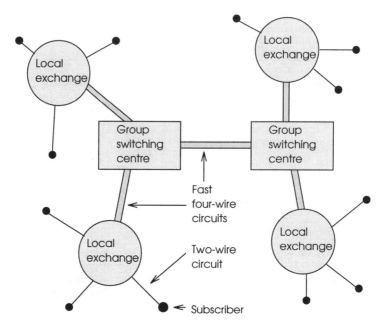

Figure 8.7 *The public switched telephone network*

▶ 8.5 Modems

Telephone circuits are intended to carry speech and therefore normally optimised for propagating signals in the frequency range of 300–3400 Hz, as shown in Figure 8.8. Data transmission is therefore not straightforward, because signal frequencies in the range 0–300 Hz are cut off. If a data sequence is applied directly to a telephone circuit then difficulties can arise, as illustrated in Figure 8.9. In this example, the data sequence changes from a few zeros to a sequence of ones. The sequence of ones is equivalent to a constant voltage, that is, it has zero frequency, and since this is outside the transmission band the output of the telephone circuit quickly dies away and the later bits of the sequence are lost. The upper limit of the telephone frequency range gives a usable baud rate of under 3000. A common rate used is 2400 baud.

In order to transmit digital data over an analogue telephone line, a frequency or set of frequencies lying in the permissible range is selected and modulated, using the techniques described earlier. The receiver then demodulates the incoming analogue signal to recreate the digital information. A device which performs this task is called a modem. The word

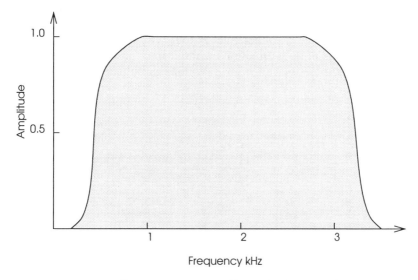

Figure 8.8 *Frequency range of the telephone system*

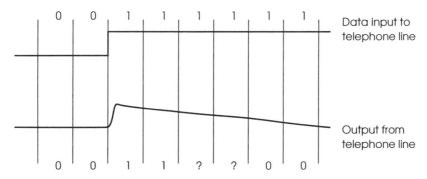

Figure 8.9 *Difficulty of transmitting data directly on telephone lines*

modem is a contraction of the two words *mod*ulation and *dem*odulation. Such a device can transmit and receive digital signals by modulating either the amplitude, frequency or phase of analogue carrier signals. A typical arrangement of the connection of modems to a telephone link is shown in Figure 8.10. The computer or peripheral (that is, the data terminal equipment, DTE), is coupled to the modem (that is, the data communication equipment, DCE) using an RS232C or V24 interface of the form that was described in Chapter 2.

Most modems operate over the two-wire PSTN link which is the usual subscriber circuit. The private dedicated leased two-wire and four-wire links referred to in the previous section are also used, and these generally provide a more efficient connection. A four-wire circuit allows simultaneous transmissions in both directions without interference. Techniques exist to allow communications in both directions simultaneously on two-wire circuits also.

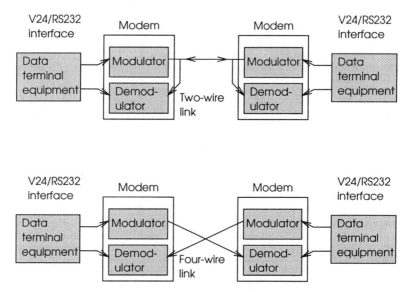

Figure 8.10 *General modem arrangements for 2-wire and 4-wire circuits*

One problem with the PSTN is that its attenuation and time-delay characteristics vary with frequency. This has the effect of distorting the shape of the signal and can cause errors. The receiver is often therefore compensated by a filter, called an *equalizer,* which has characteristics that are complementary to those of the telephone line and so restore the signal shape. This may not be a complete cure, as line characteristics change with time, and the exact route selected through the switching circuits in the exchanges will be different on different calls. More complex modems are used to answer this problem, which make use of *auto-equalizers* which automatically change the equalizing filter characteristics to match the telephone circuit.

Early modems utilized frequency modulation and a typical arrangement would use the frequencies 1300 Hz for a data one and 2100 Hz for a data zero. Transmission speed was limited to a little over 1200 baud by the available bandwidth of the telephone system. For full-duplex transmission the available bandwidth is halved and two pairs of frequencies are used. For example, a two-channel system might use the following frequencies: channel one – 1850 Hz and 1650 Hz; channel two – 1180 Hz and 980 Hz. This two-channel system often seeks to maximize the available bandwidth by supporting one fast channel and one slow one. Some modems offer speeds of 1200 bps and 75 bps for the two channels. This is usable if the slow channel is connected to the (human operated) keyboard of a terminal while the fast channel is used to receive information. It is also used when the communication involves essentially one-way traffic, and the slow channel in the reverse direction can be used to convey occasional acknowledgement of the transaction, as will be discussed later in the section on error detection.

Sophisticated circuitry can allow the full bandwidth of the telephone system to be exploited, allowing baud rates of up to 2400. Even higher data transfer rates can be provided by four further techniques: *bit grouping, combined modulation, echo cancellation* and *data compression*. Throughout the history of the modem, combinations of these techniques have been standardized by a series of CCITT modem recommendations starting with recommendation V21 which employs simple frequency modulation and a transmission rate of 300 bps full-duplex. At the time of writing, the recommendations have achieved data rates in excess of 14 400 bps using all of the above techniques in recommendations V32, V32bis and V42bis. The recommendation V34 has almost become universally accepted and extends speeds to 28 800 bps. Table 8.3 shows some of the CCITT recommendations. The qualifiers *bis* and *ter* refer to second and third extensions to an existing recommendation, where these are not considered to warrant a new number in their own right.

Table 8.2 *Dibit phase modulation using four phase shifts*

Dibit	00	01	10	11
Phase change	0°	90°	180°	270°

8.5.1 Bit grouping

The simplest forms of modulation make changes to either the amplitude, frequency or phase of the carrier signal between one of two values. More refined equipment can distinguish between more than two values and one refinement is to group the data bits into pairs. This gives four possible combinations – 00, 01, 10 and 11. These pairs are called *dibits* and each can be assigned one of four different amplitudes, frequencies or phases. Phase modulation is most commonly employed with bit grouping. At each baud time-slot, the phase of the carrier wave is shifted by one of four angles as shown in Table 8.2. The phase shift is often with respect to the previous phase of the carrier. Special methods are employed in order to keep track of these, making use of a reference phase value of 0°. The most common method is *differential phase-shift keying (DPSK)*.

8.5.2 Combined modulation

At each baud time interval a combination of amplitude, frequency and phase can be changed in order to provide more information. In practice, it is a combination of amplitude and phase change that is employed. The V32 standard uses combined modulation with a carrier wave of 1800 Hz whose phase and amplitude are altered between sixteen different combinations. These values are shown in Figure 8.11, and the standard is able to provide a data transfer rate of 9600 bps. Each circle in the figure represents a particular phase change and amplitude. The phase change is represented by the angle of the associated arrow. The amplitude is given by the length of the arrow. With sixteen different combinations, each baud change can encode four binary bits and, in this way, the data transfer rate in bits per second (9600) is four times the available baud rate (2400). The phase change associated with each of the sixteen groups of four bits shown in Figure 8.11 is relative to the previous phase received. This ensures some change of signal at each baud time interval, and so there is no problem of synchronisation. The four values highlighted are also used to transfer dibit coding when connected to simpler earlier modems. Later standards employ even more combinations of phase and amplitude and can achieve rates of 14 400 bps and more. With these transmission speeds, the individual signals are weaker and so more difficult to detect. V32 includes coding techniques called *trellis coding* which ensures that sequences of values can be examined, and that individual consecutive signals will differ from each other as much as possible.

8.5.3 Echo cancellation

Echo cancellation effectively doubles the capacity of a transmission line by allowing data transmissions in both directions simultaneously with each signal using the full available bandwidth. This means that each receiver is receiving both the intended signal and an echo of its own transmission. This echo is cancelled by an echo canceller, which is a circuit that filters out its own known transmitted signal from the incoming transmission. This technique is also used in the V32 standard to permit simultaneous two-way transmissions at 9600 bps.

8.5.4 Data compression

Data compression techniques similar to those described in Chapter 5 can be used in order to transmit more data in a given time. The techniques described in Chapter 5 utilized redundancies in the data to code it into a shorter form. A standard known as V42bis employs these techniques and compresses the data immediately prior to transmission. Depending upon

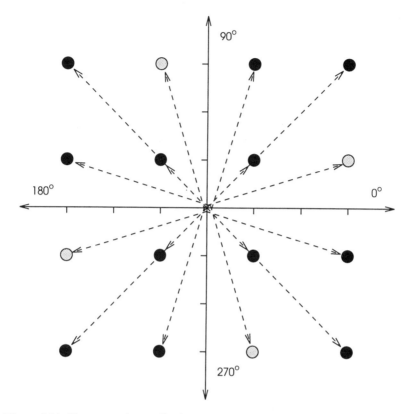

Figure 8.11 *Phase and amplitude combinations for 9600 bps transmission*

the type of data being transmitted, speed improvements of up to three-and-a-half times are achieved. V42bis is associated with the V42 standard which covers error correction. Error correction becomes increasingly necessary as the above techniques push the technology to its limits in order to squeeze higher data transmission rates, and is described in greater detail in a later section.

▶ 8.6 Fax – Facsimile Transmission

Facsimile transmission of images is commonly called fax, and involves sending graphical information along a transmission line, usually using a modem. A stand-alone fax system basically consists of a transmission and receiving device, an optical scanner and a graphics printer. These devices

Table 8.3 *CCITT recommendations concerned with modems*

CCITT Recommendation	Description	Rate (bps)	Line type	Modulation method
V21	First standard full-duplex modem	300	P/2	F
V22	Full-duplex modem	1200	P/2	P
V22bis	Full-duplex combined modulation	2400	P/2	A/P
V23	General for use on all lines	1200/600/75	P/2/4	F
V26	Leased line only	2400	4	P
V26bis/ter	All lines	2400	P/2/4	P
V27	Modem with manual equalizing circuitry	4800	2/4	P
V27bis	Automatic equalizing circuitry	4800/2400	2/4	P
V27ter	Extension to PSTN	4800/2400	P/2/4	P
V29	Point to point fast modem	9600	4	A/P
V32	General fast modems	9600	P/2	A/P
V32bis	Speed improvement	14 400	P/2	A/P
V33		14 400	4	A/P
V34	Very fast	up to 28 800	P/2	A/P
V35/V36		48 000	4	A/P
V37		72 000	4	A/P
V42	Error correction using LAPM			
V42bis	Data compression			

Line type			Modulation method		
P	-	PSTN	A	-	Amplitude
2	-	2-wire dedicated	F	-	Frequency
4	-	4-wire dedicated	P	-	Phase

have already been described earlier in this chapter and in Chapter 3 and Chapter 7. Fax cards are also available which make use of their host computer's modem, scanner and printer. They can also store received messages on the host computer's disks, display messages on the screen, and send text and graphical files without needing a scanner.

Fax machines view an image as a set of scan-lines in a similar fashion to television picture broadcast. A typical A4 image is made up of 1142 scan-lines each containing 1728 pixels. Early fax machines sent analogue data indicating the brightness of each scan-line as it was scanned. In the mid 1960s both the EIA and the CCITT produced recommendations for analogue fax. The EIA standard is RS328. The CCITT recommendations covered the Group 1 and Group 2 standards. These standards use analogue data and a typical time to transmit one page is three minutes. The most common standard in use now is the Group 3 digital fax standard. Group 3 codes each of the 1728 pixels on each of the 1142 scan-lines as black or white. Group 4 standard is a large extension to Group 3 offering grey scales and colour, but is primarily designed to work over dedicated lines or ISDN. The CCITT T30 standard divides a fax transmission into five phases, in order that the two fax machines can establish contact, and can determine whether the transmission is to conform to Group 1, Group 2 or Group 3 standard. The pixel information is coded under Group 3 in order to compress it and speed up the transfer. Both the T30 specification and the coding are described below.

8.6.1 T30 Fax procedure

A T30 fax transmission is divided into five phases named Phase A to Phase E. Phase A is concerned with recognizing that two fax machines are communicating over the line. The sending fax machine, upon answer of the call, sends a 1100 Hz tone for a brief time and then waits for three seconds. This can be used at the remote end to divert the call automatically to a fax machine instead of receiving it on the voice equipment. The remote fax machine then identifies itself as a fax machine by sending a 2100 Hz tone. The sender may abort the transmission if this signal is not received within a short time.

Phase B is now entered and involves a brief conversation between the two machines to determine whether Group 1, Group 2 or Group 3 capabilities are present and, if Group 3, the modem capabilities. Phase B for Group 3 transmission is performed under modem standard V21 at 300 bps. The remainder of this description assumes that the transmission will occur under Group 3 standard.

The two fax machines then select the fastest modem speed that is common between them and Phase C is entered. It is under Phase C that the actual fax is transmitted. Some fax machines are equipped with error detection circuitry and, if both machines are so equipped, corrupted sections of the data can be detected and requests for retransmission made.

When a page has been received, Phase D starts. If the fax message consists of more than one page, the sender sends a *multipage signal* and Phase C is restarted. Other messages can be sent during Phase D to indicate problems that may have occurred or to ask for operator intervention.

Finally Phase E is entered. It consists of one of the machines sending a *disconnect signal* and it then hangs up the line.

8.6.2 Fax Coding

An A4 Group 3 page has 1728 pixels across and 1142 pixels from top to bottom – 1 973 376 in total. Even at high modem rates this would take an unacceptably long time to transmit. The pixels are coded in order to compress the infornation and speed up the call. The coding used is called *modified Huffman coding*.

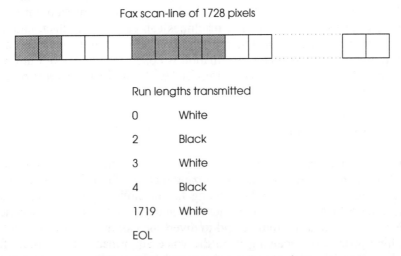

Fax scan-line of 1728 pixels

Run lengths transmitted

0	White
2	Black
3	White
4	Black
1719	White
EOL	

Figure 8.12 *Run length coding on fax*

Advantage is taken of the fact that, on each scan-line, large runs of white or black will usually be found. Instead of each of the 1728 pixels being described separately, the scan-line is transmitted as a sequence of black and white runs. Each run is just described by its length and each line is a sequence of such lengths alternating between white and black. Although the receiver can determine that a scan-line ends when the total lengths of the runs equal 1728, each scan-line is followed by a special *end of line* code. This is so that any error in transmission should affect only the current scan-line. The first run of each scan-line is assumed to be white. If the actual line starts black then a white run length of zero is sent first. To cater for the possibility of A3 fax, the maximum run length is almost 2600.

This would require sending 12 bits of information for each run length. An example of the coding for a scan-line is shown in Figure 8.12

This coding by itself will normally greatly speed up transmission as there will be many scan-lines which have long runs of white or black. The coding is further compressed using modified Huffman coding. Huffman coding is used when some codes to be sent are much more common than others. It is found experimentally, for example, that run lengths of between 2 and 7 white pixels are very common. Run lengths of between 1 and 4 black pixels are also very common. The common run lengths are assigned short codes of only 2, 3 or 4 bits while other lengths may require up to 13 bits. The coding is called *Modified* Huffman coding because two Huffman codes are used – one for black runs and the other for white runs. Some of the codes used are shown in Table 8.4.

Table 8.4 *Some modified Huffman codes used in fax transmission*

Run length	White run	Black run
0	00110101	0000110111
1	000111	010
2	0111	11
3	1000	10
4	1011	011
5	1100	0011
6	1110	0010
7	1111	00011
8	10011	000101
..	..	..
55	01011000	000000100111
56	01011001	000000101000
57	01011010	000001011000
58	01011011	000001011001
59	01001010	000000101011
60	01001011	000000101100
61	00110010	000001011010
62	00110011	000001100110
63	00110100	000001100111

The coding can be used to specify run lengths of between 0 and 63. The length of the codes varies between 4 and 8 bits for white runs and between 2 and 12 bits for black runs. Note that the coding is unique and so no code can start with a sequence that is itself an existing code. The code for end of line (EOL) is 00000000001 – eleven 0s followed by a 1. For run lengths greater than 63 there are thirty *make-up codewords* for specifying lengths in units of 64 from 64 up to 2560. For run lengths over 63, two codes are sent. First the make-up codeword corresponding to the multiples of 64 is sent, followed by the normal run length code to specify the remainder. The full codes sent to represent the scan-line in Figure 8.12 are shown in Table 8.5.

Table 8.5 *Modified Huffman codes for earlier scan-line*

Code sent	Meaning
00110101	white run of 0 length
11	black run of 2
1000	white run of 3
011	black run of 4
011000	white make-up code length 1664 (26×64)
01011000	white run of 55
000000000001	EOL – end of scan-line

This coding is called *one-dimensional coding* because it takes advantage of the fact that adjacent pixels in scan-lines are often the same or follow a particular and related pattern. A *two-dimensional coding* also exists which, additionally, takes advantage of the fact that adjacent pixels in successive scan-lines are often the same. This sends the scan-lines in groups of two or more. The first scan-line is coded as before. Successive scan-lines are coded in terms of differences and similarities between this scan-line and the previous one. The groups have to be kept small – no more than four scan-lines – because, if the first scan-line in the group has been corrupted, then this would also cause corruption of all the other scan-lines in that group. Whether one-dimensional or two-dimensional coding is to be used is part of the protocols agreed between the two fax machines during Phase B of the T30 standard. In the case of two-dimensional coding, the number of scan-lines in the groups is also decided at that stage. Two-dimensional coding is found on stand-alone fax machines but it is rare on PC fax-cards. The reason for this is that many computers for which the cards are designed cannot perform the computationally intensive work necessary at the high rate of a fax transmission.

▶ 8.7 Errors

Errors in the movement of data within a computer are rare. However, the situation is very different when computers and peripheral devices are linked over data communications circuits, where errors are regarded as a natural feature. The two principle causes of error are:

• *Distortion* As was mentioned earlier, distortion occurs because the characteristics of the circuit alter the transmitted signal. Errors caused by this can be minimized by using equalizers. On dedicated lines special conditioning can be obtained to further improve performance.

• *Noise* This can come from a variety of sources such as continuous background thermal noise, *cross-talk* from signals on adjacent lines, impulse noise from electrical cables, equipment and switches, and short breaks in the transmission path. Electrical storms and, in particular, lightning are catastrophic contributors to noise. Often errors are grouped together in bursts.

Average error rates depend on a number of factors, but on telephone lines these are typically of the order of one erroneous bit for each 10 000 bits transmitted. At higher data rates, there is also a tendency for the error rate to increase. Dedicated lines are not as subject to noise from switches as are dial-up connections, and so have lower error rates.

Even error rates as seemingly low as 1 in 10 000 can be significant. For example, to refresh a VDU screen in one operation may require, say, 1000 characters. Assuming each character is 8 bits long, the total message is 8000 bits long and there is therefore a significant chance of an error appearing.

8.7.1 Error detection and control

One of the simplest methods of detecting errors is to add odd or even parity bits to each character, as was described in Chapter 2. Any error in data transmission involving a single bit or, in general, an odd number of bits alters the parity condition and this is easily checked at the receiving end. Errors involving an even number of bits do not alter the parity condition and so go undetected. It is unfortunately a real possibility that more than one bit in a byte is altered because of the occurrence of error *bursts*. So simple parity checks are not sufficient for use in data communications.

One powerful technique which is used is called the *cyclic redundancy check (CRC)* method. The CRC is a *block check character (BCC)* added at the end of a data sequence. Here the data block is treated as a continuous sequence of bits and not as a group of bytes or characters. Suppose that these data bits are treated as one large binary number and that this is divided, using long division, by an agreed number. The quotient is discarded and the remainder is attached to the data as a block check character. At the receiver the remainder is again calculated and compared with that attached by the transmitter. Any errors in transmission are very likely to show up as some difference between the two numbers. For CRC, in practice, the long division is carried out using modulo-two arithmetic. The receiver includes the BCC at the end of the data in its division and so a remainder of zero should indicate error-free transmission.

The rules for modulo-two addition and multiplication are the same as in binary arithmetic except that 1+1 = 0 and not 10. That is, there is no carry bit. Under modulo-two arithmetic subtraction is the same as addition. The divisor is called a generating polynomial – a name that arises out of the algebraic theoretical background of this method. For example, the generating polynomial:

$$X^2 + 1 \qquad (8.1)$$

is equal to:

$$(1)X^2 + (0)X^1 + (1)X^0 \qquad (8.2)$$

and corresponds to the binary generator number 101.

A small example of the calculations of the CRC at the transmitter and the error check at the receiver is shown in Figure 8.13. In practice the data sequence and the generator number are longer than shown. The polynomial:

$$X^{16} + X^{12} + X^5 + 1 \qquad (8.3)$$

specified in CCITT recommendation V41 is often used. This polynomial has been found to allow, in a block size of 260 bits, the detection of every pattern of single and odd numbers of errors, any single error burst up to 16 bits in length, and a large percentage of other error patterns. A feature of CRC techniques is the high protection obtained with relatively few redundant check bits. Other polynomials are also used, such as CRC-16, which is:

$$X^{16} + X^{15} + X^2 + 1 \qquad (8.4)$$

Automatic repeat request (ARQ) methods are most commonly used for the control of errors. They are based on the straightforward idea that the receiver, on detection of an error, informs the transmitter and the block containing the error is retransmitted. Clearly this requires that a communications link is available in both directions.

A commonly used method is *stop and wait ARQ,* which is also called *idle* ARQ. This is illustrated in Figure 8.14. The transmitter sends a block and stops and waits for a positive acknowledgement (ACK) from the receiver, to confirm that this was received without errors being detected. The transmitter then sends the next block of data and so on. If a block is received with an error, a negative acknowledgement (NAK) is returned,

Source data

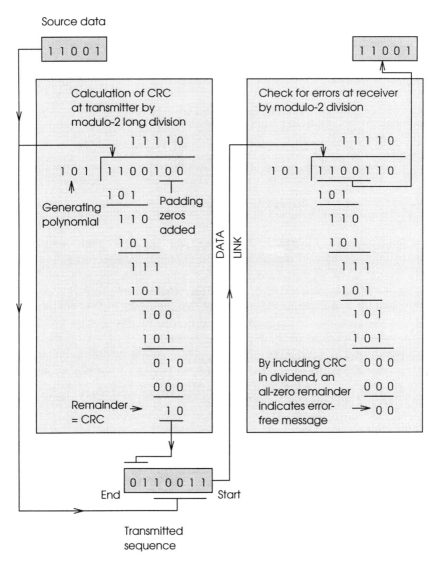

Figure 8.13 *Cyclic redundancy check calculations at transmitter and receiver*

and the block is retransmitted. This kind of ARQ is simple and is used in basic types of data-link protocols. It has the advantage that only a half-duplex channel is required. However, because the transmitter must wait for acknowledgements, the effective data rate is less than the maximum possible for the channel.

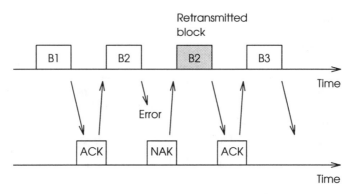

Figure 8.14 *Stop and wait ARQ*

Continuous ARQ methods are an improvement on stop and wait ARQ, in that data blocks are transmitted continuously without waiting for an acknowledgement. A full-duplex channel is now required. A *go back two* scheme is illustrated in Figure 8.15. Here the return channel replies of ACK or NAK refer to the previously transmitted block. When a NAK is returned the transmitter completes transmission of the present block and then repeats the message sequence starting two blocks back. If there is a large round trip delay, then a go back 3 or more system will be necessary. Such a system requires knowledge about the length of the blocks and the delay time in transmission, in order to calculate how many blocks back it needs to go.

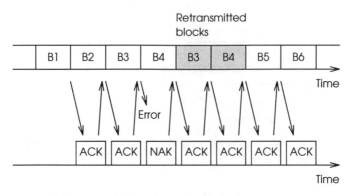

Figure 8.15 *Go back two ARQ*

A more satisfactory approach is to number each transmitted block. Each returned ACK and NAK can then include the block number, so that the transmitter can start retransmission at any named block when a NAK is received. With this numbering system the receiver does not need to return an ACK after each error-free block, but only has to send a NAK when necessary. It is however convenient to return the ACKs always, so that the transmitter can be confident that the receiver is listening and that the link has not been broken. The CCITT recommendation V42 uses CRC error detection and ARQ error correction.

While not strictly an ARQ technique, *echoplexing* is mentioned here. This technique is often used with keyboard devices. Here there is no direct connection between the keyboard and the associated display. Instead, the characters are sent to the remote computer which in turn echoes them back to the display. Erroneous characters can then be seen by the operator who must then manually correct them.

8.7.2 Forward error correction

Forward error correction is an approach which forwards extra information with its data in an attempt to allow the receiver to correct erroneous data. These methods are often simply described as *error correction*. Error detection and ARQ control, as described in the previous subsection, are examples of *backward error correction*, where the receiver sends information back to the transmitter which may then retransmit erroneous data. Forward error correction is not so common in data communications because retransmission schemes are usually more efficient. It is useful if there is no return path, or if the transmitter is broadcasting to several receivers. It is also useful in long-haul communications where the time taken to return the ACK or NAK makes ARQ impractical.

A commonly used method is the combined vertical redundancy check (VRC) and longitudinal redundancy check (LRC). This is illustrated in Figure 8.16. The message is assumed to be made up of characters and individual parity bits are assigned to each character (these are the VRC bits). The block check character comprises a set of parity bits each of which is a parity check on the corresponding bits in all characters in the block (these are the LRC bits). If a single bit in the block is received wrongly, then this will simultaneously cause a corresponding parity bit error in both the VRC and the LRC to be detected by the receiver. As shown in Figure 8.17, these two bits provide a pair of coordinates to locate the error, which is then corrected by reversing its binary state.

Hamming codes are also used for this purpose and extra check bits are attached to groups of data bits. Typically four data bits are protected by three check bits to make a unit of seven bits. If any one of these seven bits is received in error, not only is the error detected, but the erroneous bit can be determined by a straightforward table look-up. Other techniques exist which can be used to correct multiple errors. Because of the large number of redundant bits which must be transmitted when using forward error correction, the effective data rate is greatly diminished and so, whenever possible, backward error correction is employed in data communications.

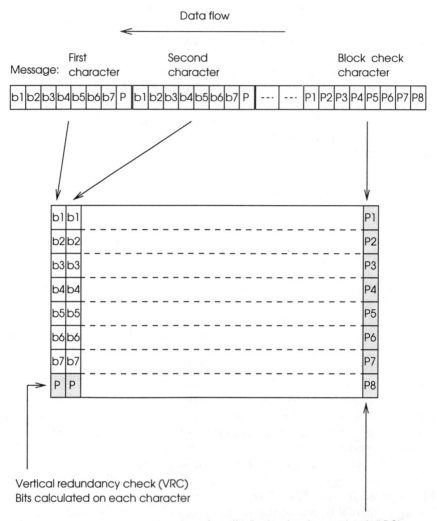

Figure 8.16 *Block-check character using LRC for error detection*

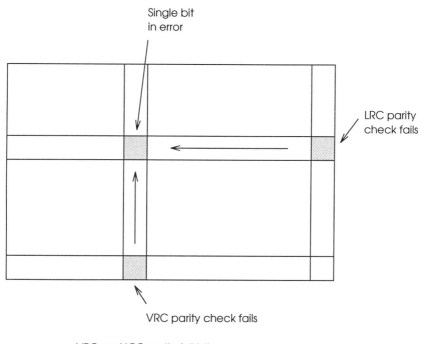

Single bit
in error

LRC parity
check fails

VRC parity check fails

VRC and LRC parity fail bits
point to location of error

Figure 8.17 *Error correction using VRC/LRC*

▶ 8.8 Data Network Configurations

There are various configurations, or *topologies,* of data network in use. Some of the common network configurations are shown in Figure 8.18. The lines in the figures represent physical circuits or *links* which join together geographically separated *nodes.* These nodes can be terminals, computers, etc.

The mesh topology of Figure 8.18(a) has more than the minimum number of links necessary to connect all nodes. As a result more than one path exists between many, or perhaps all, pairs of nodes. Paths may be direct across one link or may involve several links and other nodes. The advantage is that, if one path is out of service, then an alternative is available. If a link is placed between every pair of nodes then the mesh is *fully* connected, and this maximizes the protection against link breakdown. This protection is, naturally, obtained at the cost of providing the links.

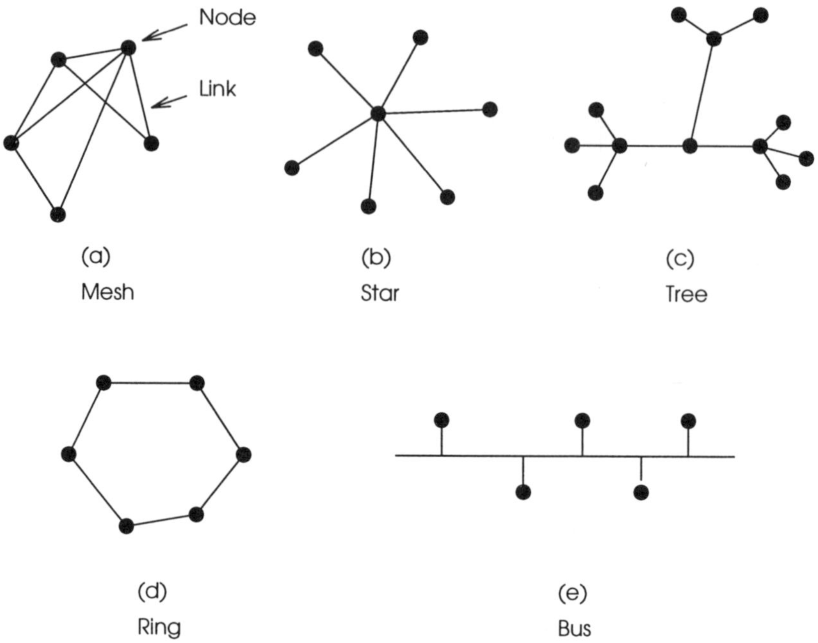

Figure 8.18 *Network topologies*

In the star topology, as shown in Figure 8.18(b), the central node performs the switching function. The outer nodes are therefore relieved of this task. In exchange this means that the network is very dependent on the reliability of the central node. If a single link becomes faulty then just one outer node is affected.

The tree topology, Figure 8.18(c), is a generalization of the star network. The central node, which is a switching node, is connected to nodes which are at the centre of a cluster of outer nodes. A node at the centre of a cluster must also perform switching operations. The main advantage of the tree topology compared with the star topology is that the number of links to the central node is reduced. In networks with widely dispersed nodes in which clustering can be identified, line costs can be reduced. An example is a branch office which is situated in another town from the main office.

The ring topology, Figure 8.18(d), and the bus topology, Figure 8.18(e), are popular in local area networks. The advantage of these topologies is that new nodes can be connected relatively easily at any point on a link without the need to lay new cables. Care has to be taken to preserve the reliability of these two topologies, because any break in a link can disable the whole, or a major part, of the network.

▶ 8.9 Terminal Networks

Terminal networks were the earliest type of data communications network. The 'terminals' can be VDUs, personal computers acting as a terminal emulator, or other character devices such as printers.

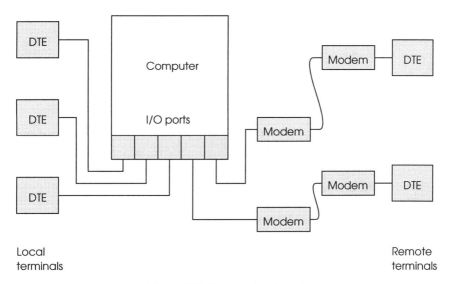

Figure 8.19 *Terminal network*

The basic form of the network is shown in Figure 8.19. Because it is a star network, the computer is in charge of the communications and the terminals are interfaced to it using ports as described in Chapter 2. Terminals can be local or remote to the computer: remote terminals normally communicate via telephone lines, using modems.

More efficient use of the I/O ports and the data links can be obtained using *multi-drop connections* (sometimes called *multi-point connections)* as shown in Figure 8.20. Modems can be inserted in the links if required. This arrangement allows several terminals to be connected to one port. Each terminal has a unique address to identify itself. Clearly the terminals cannot transmit or receive data simultaneously and so the computer controls the arrangement. When the computer transmits data this needs to include a terminal's address so that only the addressed terminal accepts the data, while the others ignore it. For a terminal to transmit data it must wait for the computer to request data from it. The computer will *poll* each terminal in turn requesting data, and the terminal addressed will send back either some data or a negative acknowledgement. Such terminals are called *intelligent terminals,* as they implement this protocol. Arrangements for controlling data flow are the subject of the next section.

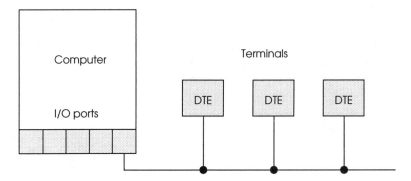

Figure 8.20 *Multi-point, multi-drop arrangement*

A more common approach to connecting many terminals to computers is to use a multiplexer, as described in an earlier section, but increasingly it is becoming common to use a *cluster controller.* The cluster controller is a small dedicated computer which communicates directly with the terminals. Each terminal has a dedicated line to the cluster controller and so the terminals do not need to be intelligent. The cluster controller communicates with the main computer through a single high speed link, as shown in Figure 8.21.

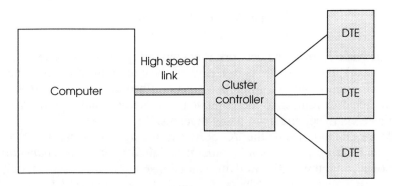

Figure 8.21 *Cluster controller*

The topology has now changed from that of a star to a tree, since several cluster controllers can be connected to the same computer. A cluster controller is often also called a *terminal concentrator* which is, perhaps, a more descriptive term, and originally these devices were called *front-end processors.* The data can be sent between the controller and computer in the same manner as in the multi-point system described above but it is more usual to use a multiplexing scheme whereby the controller and computer have multiplexing hardware built in internally or, more commonly, they simulate multiplexers in their software.

▶ 8.10 Data Link Control

To achieve data communication it is not sufficient merely to set up the links in accordance with the appropriate standard such as V24. Procedures are required to control the transfer of messages, for control of errors, to maintain character synchronisation and, should it be required, to regulate the flow of data. The procedures are referred to as *protocols* and are concerned with what is known as *data link control (DLC)*.

Two protocols are in widespread use: binary synchronous control (BSC), which is character orientated, and high-level data link control (HDLC), which is bit orientated.

8.10.1 Binary synchronous control (BSC)

The ISO standard covering this half-duplex protocol refers to it as *basic mode*. However, its implementation in IBM equipment is so widespread that it is usually referred to by using the name that has been given to it by that company: BSC or *bisync*.

Information is sent as blocks of characters. Certain control characters have special meanings under BSC and the most common ones are listed in Table 8.6

The master station will establish communication with one of the DTEs by sending it either a *poll request* or a *select request*. All messages start with two SYN characters in order that the receiving device can synchronize. Communication is sought by the master station by sending a message consisting of an ENQ followed by the DTE address. A poll request is used to receive information from a DTE and a select request is used to send information to a DTE. A poll request is distinguished from a select request only by the case of the (alphabetic) address: upper case for a poll request and lower case for a select request. The DTE whose address is quoted replies with an ACK if it is ready to send/receive. If it is not ready to receive it sends a NAK and if it is not ready to send it sends an EOT. These requests are shown in Figure 8.22.

Once communication is established, only the addressed DTE and the master station may use the link until the communication is terminated by the master station sending an EOT. If the request was a poll then the DTE sends information to the master station. If the request was a select then the master station sends information to the DTE. In both cases the information is sent as text messages packaged into blocks. The message starts with

Table 8.6 *BSC control codes*

Control character	Meaning	Description
SOH	Start of header	Announces start of (optional) header
STX	Start of text	Announces start of data text
ETX	End of text	Announces end of data text
ETB	End of block block	Announces end of data block
EOT	End of transmission	Ends connection between computer and DTE
ENQ	Enquiry	Enquire if DTE is ready
ACK	Acknowledge	Positive reply to block / enquiry
NAK	Negative acknowledgement	Negative reply to block / enquiry
DLE	Data link escape	Used to allow control codes to appear as data
SYN	Synchronize	Two SYNs are sent before each message to synchronize

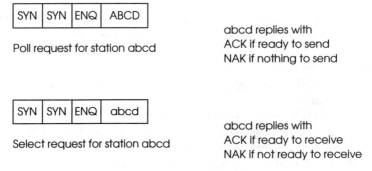

| SYN | SYN | ENQ | ABCD |

Poll request for station abcd

abcd replies with
ACK if ready to send
NAK if nothing to send

| SYN | SYN | ENQ | abcd |

Select request for station abcd

abcd replies with
ACK if ready to receive
NAK if not ready to receive

Figure 8.22 *BSC poll and select requests*

two SYNs. Following can be a header which, if present, starts with a SOH. The contents of the header are not specified by BSC and it contains user specific information such as timing details. Next comes the text itself preceded by a STX. The text is terminated with an ETX and a block check character (BCC). The block check character is either a CRC, or LRC, as described in the earlier section on errors. BSC uses a simple ARQ system.

If the message is received correctly the receiver sends an ACK. If it is not received correctly then a NAK is sent.

Long messages are divided up and sent as several blocks. The text of the last block of a sequence terminates with an ETX as before. The other blocks terminate with an ETB. The receiver sends an ACK or NAK for each of these blocks. Examples of these block formats are shown in Figure 8.23.

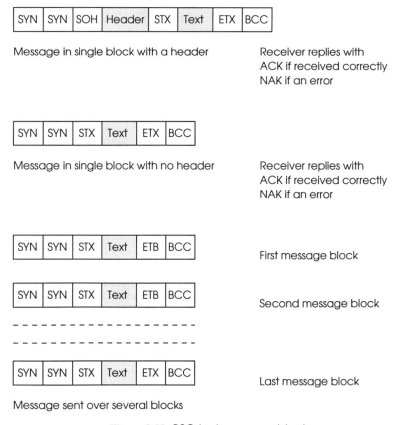

| SYN | SYN | SOH | Header | STX | Text | ETX | BCC |

Message in single block with a header

Receiver replies with
ACK if received correctly
NAK if an error

| SYN | SYN | STX | Text | ETX | BCC |

Message in single block with no header

Receiver replies with
ACK if received correctly
NAK if an error

| SYN | SYN | STX | Text | ETB | BCC |

First message block

| SYN | SYN | STX | Text | ETB | BCC |

Second message block

– – – – – – – – – – – – – – – – – –
– – – – – – – – – – – – – – – – – –

| SYN | SYN | STX | Text | ETX | BCC |

Last message block

Message sent over several blocks

Figure 8.23 *BSC text message blocks*

A problem arises if the text data contains either of the ETX or ETB characters. To allow for this, a second type of block is defined as a *transparent block*. The text of such a block is started by the pair DLE STX instead of just STX and the text terminates with DLE ETX (or DLE ETB). In the transparent text all characters are treated as data. This itself creates more problems. Firstly the pairs DLE ETX or DLE ETB may actually occur in the data. To allow this, any DLE in the data is replaced by the pair DLE DLE. On encountering this pair the receiver deletes the first DLE and treats the second one as data. Secondly the pair SYN SYN is periodically sent within the text to guarantee character synchronisation. In a normal block these pairs are not treated as data by the receiver. In a transparent block they would, and must be, as they could be real data. To overcome this, in a transparent block, the SYN SYN synchronisation pair is replaced by the DLE SYN pair. An example of a transparent block is given in Figure 8.24.

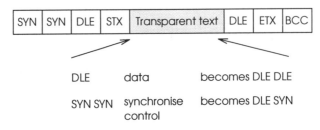

| | | DLE | data | becomes DLE DLE |
| | | SYN SYN | synchronise control | becomes DLE SYN |

Figure 8.24 *BSC transparent text block*

8.10.2 *High-level data link control (HDLC)*

BSC protocol is character orientated and half-duplex in operation. Even if a full-duplex link is available, BSC protocol cannot take advantage of this. High-level data link control (HDLC), on the other hand, is a full-duplex bit orientated protocol. It is more flexible than BSC and is in wide use in all forms of digital networks. HDLC is defined under two configurations. The *unbalanced configuration* is similar to BSC in that there is one master station and one or more slave stations. The second is the *balanced configuration* which operates between two nodes of equal status and is used widely in computer–computer communications. HDLC has three modes of operation. The first is called *normal response mode (NRM),* which is an unbalanced mode used on multi-point configurations with one master station. This is similar in concept to BSC in that only the master station may initiate communication. The second is *asynchronous response mode (ARM)* which is like NRM but allows slave stations to initiate communication, but with the master station still retaining control. The third is *asynchronous balanced mode (ABM)* which gives each station equal status.

Flag 01111110	Address 8 bits	Control 8/16 bits	Information variable length	FCS 16/32 bits	Flag 01111110

Figure 8.25 *HDLC frame format*

Like BSC, HDLC conveys information in blocks, which in HDLC are called *frames*. The standard frame is partitioned as shown in Figure 8.25. The flag at each end is a unique 8-bit sequence – 01111110 – which marks the frame boundaries. Again the problem with data transparency could arise if this flag should occur naturally elsewhere in the frame. It is dealt with by the use of simple hardware at both ends. The transmitting end inserts a zero after every sequence of five ones inside the frame. This prevents the formation of six ones, which is part of the flag, from occurring in the data. The receiver suppresses a zero following a sequence of five ones inside the frame. These processes are called *bit stuffing* and *bit stripping* respectively. Bit stuffing and bit stripping are actually slightly more complex, and also allow for the receiver to detect an abort frame request. Whenever the receiver finds a sequence of a zero followed by five ones it looks at the next bit. If that is a zero, then it is ignored, and reception continues as normal. If it is a one, then the next bit after that is examined. If that is a zero, then the frame flag has been received. If it is a one then this is taken as an abort signal, as it cannot occur as part of an HDLC frame. The transmitter can then signal an abort with a sequence of a zero and seven or more ones. This process is shown in Figure 8.26.

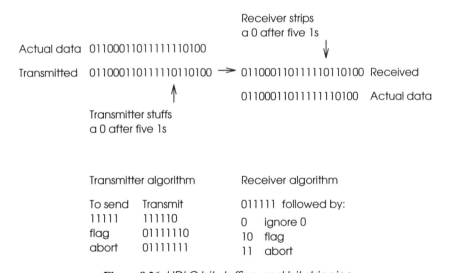

Figure 8.26 *HDLC bit stuffing and bit stripping*

The frame is made up of four fields. The *address field* is an 8-bit code unique to a station. This is the destination address for the frame and all other stations will ignore frames which are not addressed to them. The special address 11111111 is interpreted as a broadcast and all stations will read frames with that address. While the address is not needed when only two stations are linked (ABM) it is always included.

The *control field* can be either 8 or 16 bits long and indicates the presence of one of three types of frame, together with additional specific frame information. The three basic types of frame are *information frame, supervisory frame* and *unnumbered frame*. Information frames have a control field which starts with a 0. These frames contain data. The control field also carries frame sequence numbers, both of this frame and the last correctly received frame, so that a continuous ARQ error control can be used. Supervisory frames have a control field which starts with 10. These frames are used for flow and error control. Unnumbered frames have a control field which starts with 11. They have no sequence numbers and are used, amongst other things, to set operating modes and initiate transfers.

The *information field* is only present in information frames and contains the message itself. It can be any length, but in practice there is an upper limit imposed by the system.

The *frame check sequence* is a 16-bit cyclic redundancy check sequence, calculated using the CCITT V41 generating polynomial. It does not include the frame flags in the calculation. Some systems use a 32-bit CRC sequence for greater frame lengths, or if the link is known to be of a poor quality.

Frames are sent independently in both directions in full-duplex, and the frame sequence numbers in messages going in one direction allow control of errors occurring in the other direction. Faulty messages are repeated. If one end of the link has no data to send, error control is maintained by sending short supervisory frames containing the relevant frame sequence number.

▶ 8.11 Layered Model of Computer Network Architectures

Figure 8.27 represents two computers communicating via a data network. The data network can be a public or private network, and in practice many more than two computers can be connected. Computer-to-computer communication is unlike that in terminal networks, where a single processing device is linked to subservient terminals. Networked computers communicate more on the basis of equals and have a wider range of requirements. Necessarily, the protocols are more complicated and it is the usual practice to structure these into a hierarchy of layers called a network architecture. Each layer performs its own set of defined functions.

First developments of computer networks were proprietary products such as IBM's *system network architecture (SNA)* and DEC's *DECNET.* These architectures are closed in the sense that only products of the company can take part in the communication activity. An open architecture

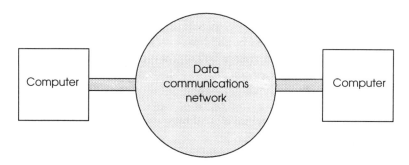

Figure 8.27 *Computer-computer data communications network*

allows computers of any manufacture to communicate, provided that they conform to the agreed network protocols. The progress of open architectures has been greatly influenced by the development of the ISO reference model of open system interconnections (OSI). The aim of this is to:

provide a common basis for the co-ordination of standards development for the purpose of system interconnection, while allowing existing standards to be placed into perspective within the overall reference model.

Thus the model is not a single real architecture itself but a framework for the development and harmonization of other standard network architectures.

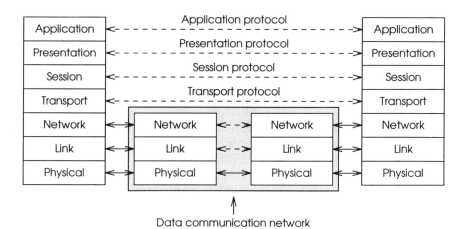

Figure 8.28

The ISO reference model OSI has seven layers, as shown in Figure 8.28. The protocols at any layer, called *peer processes,* are the same. That is, a process at a given level on one host thinks it is communicating with a similar process at the corresponding level in the other host. When a process communicates to its peer, it uses the services of all processes provided by the lower layers. Between any two layers an *interface* defines the services and operations provided by the lower one.

Information that host A wishes to communicate to host B passes down the layers, which modify or add to it. The information has a *frame* or *packet* format. In general a layer envelopes the frame with a header and trailer in accordance with the protocol at that level. The next layer does the same so that the structure of the architecture is mirrored in the encapsulation of the message within its envelopes. At the bottom layer the frame is physically transported across the network. At host B it passes up through the layers, where the envelopes are successively removed, and is delivered at the top.

The OSI reference model defines the services and functions of each layer. Layers 1–3 relate to protocols of the data communications network. Layers 5–7 allow the operating system in the hosts (which may well be of a different type) to communicate. Layer 4 shields the upper layers from the workings of the network.

The *physical layer* defines the electrical and mechanical interface to the network. It is the only layer with real communication. The protocols at higher levels then have *virtual communication*. Standards at the physical layer include V24, RS232C and some of X21.

The *data link layer* is responsible for ensuring reliable communication of each packet across a physical link. Its tasks include packet sequencing as well as error notification and correction. An example of a standard at this level is the HDLC protocol described earlier.

The *network layer* performs the necessary routing functions along what may be a number of physical links, using network addresses. Actual routing strategies are not defined in the model. This layer is responsible for the establishment and termination of network connections. A common example of a protocol at this level is the X25, which is described later in the context of *packet switching networks*.

The *transport layer* ensures efficient and reliable end-to-end services for messages across the data network. Data networks can take different forms, and the transport layer shields the upper layer by offering a network-independent service. Its complexity depends upon the standards used at level 3. If level 3 is minimal, then the transport layer might have to perform more error checking. If layer 3 is complex and reliable then the transport layer is usually small.

The *session layer* provides a service which is analogous to the login and logout procedures in a terminal network. This connection is called a *session*.

The *presentation layer* is concerned with data representation. For example, if necessary it will convert between ASCII and EBCDIC formats where these are used by the two application processes. Other functions include encryption and virtual terminal protocols. An example of a virtual terminal protocol is the *packet assembler-disassembler (PAD),* which is mentioned later in the description of packet switched networks.

The *application layer* is the highest layer in the OSI model. It is concerned with providing services which make use of the data communications networks. The range of services is wide and includes distributed data bases, file transfer and electronic mail.

▶ 8.12 Local Area Networks

A local area network (LAN) is normally installed at a single site comprising a building or group of buildings such as a factory, hospital, business or educational campus. Typically, a LAN is 1 km or less in total length of interconnections. A LAN normally uses a dedicated data link rather than one from the public telephone network, and so can provide data communications at higher rates. Devices that are networked include computers, office workstations, printers, plotters and file servers. This allows a wide range of services to be obtained across the network such as electronic mail, sharing of data bases, networked wordprocessing and communal access to high-quality printers. A typical system for an office is shown in Figure 8.29. It may have several personal computers with little or no disk space individually, connected to a large personal computer which itself controls a large capacity disk and other devices such as a printer. This larger computer is usually called a *file server,* even though it is also providing printing and, possibly, other services.

The main characteristics of any particular LAN technology concerns its topology, transmission media and the access control method to that medium. LANs have generated much interest and activity amongst manufacturers and there are many different architectures. The following subsections describe some of the more important of them.

8.12.1 CSMA/CD local area network – Ethernet

The media access method termed *carrier sense multiple access and collision detect (CSMA/CD)* is most commonly identified with the Ethernet system from the Xerox Corporation. This LAN architecture, as shown in Figure 8.30, is a bus topology based on a 50 ohm coaxial cable as the medium, although other transmission media can be used. The cable length has a maximum size of a few hundred metres, but this can be extended by using repeaters. Many DTEs can be connected to the cable, giving multiple access.

Such a connection is provided by a non-intrusive tap, which connects an adjacent transceiver unit (TU) to the cable. The transceiver unit is

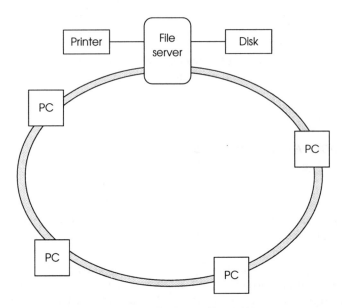

Figure 8.29 *Typical office LAN*

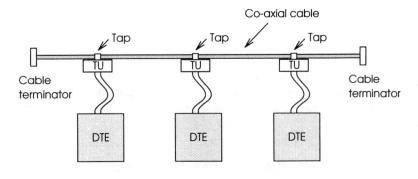

TU   Transceiver Unit
DTE   Data Terminal Equipment

Figure 8.30 *The CSMA/CD (Ethernet) bus*

powered by the DTE and is able to inject signals into, and sense signals on, the coaxial cable. The TU is connected to the host DTE either directly or by a twisted pair or coaxial cable and balanced drivers/differential receivers, as described in Chapter 2, can be used, so this connection can be up to fifty metres long. This gives freedom in siting a DTE computer within (say) an office area.

A DTE with data to send constructs a *frame,* including the data, source and destination addresses, a type and a 32-bit cyclic redundancy check sequence – the frame check sequence. The frame starts with a *preamble* to provide synchronisation. The format of an Ethernet frame is shown in Figure 8.31. Other CSMA/CD standards differ slightly from this format. The cable is then sensed to ensure that no other DTE is sending a frame and the frame is then launched on the cable by the TU. All DTEs will check the frame and it is then accepted by the one to which it is addressed.

Preamble 64 bits	Destination address 48 bits	Source address 48 bits	Type 16 bits	Data (variable)	FCS 32 bits

Figure 8.31 *The Ethernet frame format*

With this form of access, more than one DTE can attempt to send frames together, because of the finite length of time it takes the frame to pass down the cable, so that a *collision* can occur. Each source DTE involved in sending a frame senses the carrier – *carrier sense* – and is able to detect the collision – *collision detection* – because the signal on the cable differs from that which the source DTE intended. The source DTEs then inject a jam sequence of random bits to fully corrupt the data on the line so that it is not mistakenly received by any DTE as a good frame. The source DTEs causing the collision then delay resending for a short independently computed random period of time and then try again. Fortunately, collisions are normally quite rare, and they have negligible effect on actual data rates.

The DTEs contain a *medium access control (MAC)* unit to implement the CSMA/CD access method and also a separate microprocessor to handle the network functions. These, with the physical arrangement for the coaxial cable and TU, provide the lowers layers of the ISO reference model. A CSMA/CD LAN architecture is covered by the IEEE standard 802.2 and 802.3.

8.12.2 Token access local area networks

Local area networks using this method of communication pass a *token* among the DTEs in the network. Any DTE with data to send only has permission to do so when it possesses the token. The token consists of a special frame.

Token access can be readily implemented on a ring topology, as shown in Figure 8.32(a), and is referred to as *token ring.* Data frames and token frames are passed clockwise round the ring. Another topology is the *token bus* as shown in Figure 8.32(b). Because the addressing of adjacent DTEs is independent of their physical sequencing, the tokens need not follow the physical sequence of DTEs, as is shown.

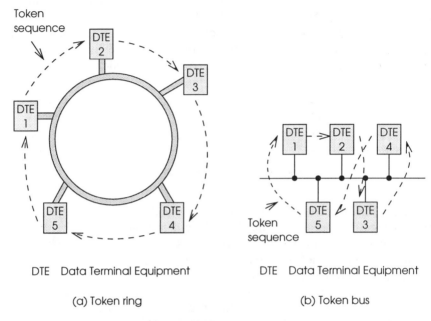

DTE   Data Terminal Equipment   DTE   Data Terminal Equipment

(a) Token ring   (b) Token bus

Figure 8.32 *Token local area networks – ring and bus*

Token access networks allow selective permission to transmit to be given to DTEs by attaching priority indicators to the token. Also, where appropriate, DTEs can have their ability to send frames removed, but still retain their ability to receive data. In some situations involving very high data rate transmissions, token LANs may also have an advantage over CSMA/CD LANs, where multiple collisions might occur. Balanced with this is the fact that token LANs require supervision of the token and one station is required to be a *monitor* which, amongst other things, regenerates the token should it get lost.

Examples of token access LANs include the IBM token ring. Both token bus and token ring topologies are covered by IEEE standard 802.4 and 802.5 respectively, together with IEEE standard 802.2. The latter standard also applies to CSMA/CD networks and provides a common interface of the ISO reference model link layer to the network layer.

8.12.3 The PABX approach

Most organizations which have local area network requirements also have a local private automatic branch telephone exchange (PABX). PABXs are usually implemented digitally and so can be used to provide an alternative form of data network to those of the true LANs described above. Some PABXs will also include the ISDN system described in the next section, which greatly enhances their capabilities in digital data communications. A PABX network has a star topology, with the exchange as the central node. Although the data rates are slower than on LANs, the PABX can be attractive for some applications, because of the relatively low extra cost of providing the data-networking facilities as an addition to the telephone switching facilities.

▶ 8.13 Wide Area Networks

8.13.1 Private wide area networks

A wide area network is taken to be one where at least some of its nodes is widely dispersed, so that use need to be made of links supplied by a PTT.

Some large organizations, such as banks, where the speed and volume of data that is moved is high, need wide area networking of computers. In such cases, the public switched telephone network (PSTN) is not adequate because of the relatively low data rates available. This requirement arose before the inception of public data networks, and so private networks were assembled from private lines leased from the PTT. The communications protocol functions were provided by network architecture software products supplied by computer manufacturers. Prominent among these are the IBM's system network architecture (SNA), DEC's DECNET and the earlier ARPANET. These are layered architectures but, because they predate the ISO reference model for OSI, they do not correspond exactly to the latter. The approximate equivalences of SNA and DECNET to the ISO reference model is shown in Figure 8.33. The nodes in the SNA network are of four types:

• terminals
• controllers of terminals and peripherals
• front-end processors
• host processors.

Each node has an item of software called a *network addressable unit (NAU)*. Each NAU has an address that is used by the communicating process to connect itself to the network. Information is sent in bit-oriented frames and it is governed by a data link control protocol called *synchronous data link control (SDLC)*. This protocol was later taken over, with small modifications, to become the high-level data link control (HDLC) described in Section 8.10.2. Information is passed down the SNA protocol layers in a similar manner to that described for the ISO reference model, and a sequence of headers and tails is attached. The frame then

Layer	ISO	SNA	DECNET
7	Application	End user	Application
6	Presentation	NAU services	Application
5	Session	Data flow control	(No layer)
4	Transport	Transmission control	Network services
3	Network	Path control	Transport
2	Link	Data link control	Data link control
1	Physical	Physical	Physical

Figure 8.33 *Approximate equivalences of SNA and DECNET to ISO reference model*

passes across the physical network and up through the protocol layers at the recipient host.

DECNET has similar goals to SNA, that is, to allow the user to set up a private network for distributed processing and networking. The frames or packets in DECNET are not bit-oriented, but are assembled from characters. Like the SNA frame, DECNET frames can be of any length but, in DECNET, the length is denoted by a character count in the header rather than by unique header/tail flags.

8.13.2 Public data networks (PDN)

A *public data network (PDN)* is one set up and administered by a PTT or equivalent body. Because of economies of scale and the use of modern purpose-built networking equipment other than leased lines, a PDN can be expected to provide data networking at lower cost than private networks. A wider base of users can be served who may not need to convey large volumes of high-speed data. Moreover, users may communicate using equipment from different manufacturers.

After some experimental investigations, the CCITT issued the X-series of recommendations. These are the digital counterparts to the V-series for analogue telephone links and cover data rates and interfacing. In general the X-series recommendations cover the lower layers of the ISO reference model. Two types of PDN are covered: the *packet-switched data network (PSDN)* and the *circuit-switched data network (CSDN)*. These are described in the following two subsections.

8.13.3 Packet-switched data network

In a packet-switched data network information is assembled into packets containing the source and destination addresses and entered into the network, where they go to a local packet switching exchange (PSE). The network consists of PSE nodes connected by data links as shown in Figure 8.34. The PSE looks at the addresses, and by consulting a routing directory, it determines the output link on which to forward the packet. In this way the packet journeys from PSE to PSE. The final PSE passes it to the destination data terminal equipment (DTE).

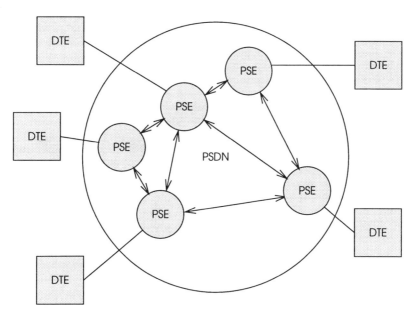

DTE	Data terminal equipment
PSE	Packet switching exchange
PSDN	Packet switching data network

Figure 8.34 *Packet-switching data network (PSDN)*

Any one link contains interspersed packets from several sources going to various destinations. To avoid any very long packet causing undue delays to other packets at a PSE, a maximum length for packets is set. Because of this, one of the tasks in the ISO reference model transport layer is to split a long packet into a number of short packets.

Two types of service are offered called *datagram* and *virtual call* (or *virtual circuit*). In the datagram service each packet is treated as a short self-contained packet and is entered and delivered to the destination without reference to other packets. In the virtual call service, a message is made up of a sequence of packets which contain a reference number called the *logical channel number.* This allows the destination DTE to identify from which of several sources the packet was sent. This in effect sets up an end-to-end circuit. Because it is not a physical circuit, but consists of packets moving through possibly differing routes through the network, it is called a *virtual circuit.*

The user's DTE is interfaced to the PSDN by *data circuit terminating equipment (DCTE),* which plays a similar role to the modem in analogue links, and this is illustrated by Figure 8.35. This interface is covered by the X25 network access control which, in fact, is a set of protocols covering the lower layers of the ISO reference model.

The physical layer is defined in recommendation X21, which was described in Chapter 2. The link layer protocol is based on HDLC and called link access procedure version B (LAPB). The packet layer is also defined and corresponds to the network layer in the ISO reference model.

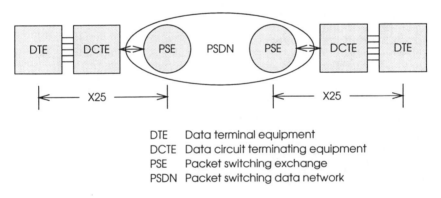

DTE   Data terminal equipment
DCTE   Data circuit terminating equipment
PSE   Packet switching exchange
PSDN   Packet switching data network

Figure 8.35 *The X25 protocol*

With X25 the user DTE needs to be intelligent enough to handle packets. A particular problem that must be addressed is that, because different packets can take different routes, the packets might arrive at their destination in a different sequence from that order in which they were sent. Where the DTE is a computer this need not be a problem. In many cases the user's equipment is a simple character device and in those cases a special piece of equipment is needed called a packet assembler-disassembler (PAD). The operation of the PAD is defined by the X3, X25 and X28 standards.

8.13.4 *Circuit-switched data network and ISDN*

A conventional analogue public switched telephone network is an example of a circuit-switched data network. These networks have largely been replaced by computer controlled digitally switched networks in many countries. This, with the conversion to all-digital transmission, means that data can be networked at higher speeds and without the need for modems. This type of network is referred to as an *integrated services digital network (ISDN)* since it can carry voice, picture and other forms of data. It is illustrated in Figure 8.36. A standard single customer ISDN connection consists of a two-wire 192 kbps digital link. Information is transmitted in units of 48-bit frames. With the overhead of synchronizing and control bits, 144 kbps are available for data, and this is divided into three channels by multiplexing.

Two of the channels are known as B-channels and they are intended to carry user data at 64 kbps. The third channel is known as a D-channel and is used for control signalling at 16 kbps. There also exist other channels on more sophisticated ISDN connections, called H-channels, and E-channelss which are, effectively, faster versions of the B and D channels respectively. Two other connections exist which are intended for larger customers and operate at 2.048 Mbps and 1.544 Mbps. The first is common in Europe while the second is more common in the U.S.A. They are multiplexed into one D-channel and either 30 B-channels (in the 2.048 Mbps link) or 23 B-channels (in the 1.544 Mbps link). The B-channels act as two independent digital telephone connections. The choice of 64 kbps was made because this was the most effective rate for digitized speech transmission at that time. Now, with more advanced technology, speech can be transmitted at lower rates at the same quality. The B-channels may be connected to DTE equipment. Further, they may themselves be split into sub-channels to allow many items of equipment to use the connection simultaneously. Finally, the two B-channels may be linked together to provide one fast (128 kbps) data channel.

The control of user equipment and the use of the B-channels is maintained over the D-channel. The D-channel may also, exceptionally, be used as a data channel. ISDN allows three kinds of connection over a B-channel: a normal circuit-switched link, a packet-switched link, or a *semipermanent* link to another user, set up by prior arrangement. This third form is therefore similar to a private leased line.

A circuit-switched data network effectively sets up a direct path between the two ends, which is permanent for the duration of the call. Unlike packet-switched data networks, a call once set up must be paid for on a time basis, and does not depend on the quantity and rate of data that is conveyed. Unlike packet-switching on circuit-switched data networks, no error detection and control is provided. The physical interface of the user DTE to the CSDN is covered by X21, the same as for PSDN. As an

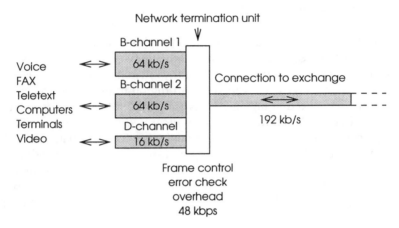

Figure 8.36 *Integrated services digital network (ISDN)*

interim measure, while analogue telephone systems are still in use, an alternative, X21bis, is provided. The link layer protocol can also be the same as the LAPB protocol used in packet switching.

▶ 8.14 Further Reading

Black U., *Computer networks – protocols, standards and interfaces,* Prentice-Hall, 1987.

Brownlie J.D. and Cusack E.L., *Duplex transmission at 4800 and 9600 bit/s on the PSTN and the use of channel coding with a partitioned signal constellation,* British Telecom Technology Journal, Vol. 2, No. 4, 1984.

Da Silva E., *Introduction to data communications and LAN technology,* Collins, 1986.

Flint D.C., *The data ring main,* Wiley, 1983.

Halsall F., *Introduction to data communications and computer networks,* Addison Wesley, 1985.

Hopper A., Temple S., and Williamson R., *Local area network design,* Addison Wesley, 1986.

Hunter R. and Robinson A.H., *International digital facsimile coding standards,* Proceedings of the IEEE, Vol. 68, No. 7, 1980

Scott P.R.D., *Modems in data communications,* NCC Publications, 1980.

Stallings S., *Data and computer communications,* Macmillan, 1988.

Index